·四川大学精品立项教材·

美国重要历史文献选读（修订版）

Selected Readings of American History

主编　叶英

编者（按姓氏拼音排序）

邓晓熹　税　红　王玉兰　王　乜

游　航　邹　青

四川大学出版社

SICHUAN UNIVERSITY PRESS

图书在版编目（CIP）数据

美国重要历史文献选读 = Selected Readings of American History : 汉文、英文 / 叶英主编. — 2版（修订版）. — 成都 : 四川大学出版社，2022.6
四川大学精品立项教材
ISBN 978-7-5690-4884-1

Ⅰ. ①美… Ⅱ. ①叶… Ⅲ. ①英语—阅读教学—高等学校—教材—汉文、英文②历史—文献—美国—汉文、英文 Ⅳ. ①H319.37 ②K712.06

中国版本图书馆CIP数据核字（2021）第158272号

书　　名：美国重要历史文献选读（修订版）
　　　　　Meiguo Zhongyao Lishi Wenxian Xuandu（Xiuding Ban）
主　　编：叶　英
丛 书 名：四川大学精品立项教材

选题策划：张　晶
责任编辑：张　晶　敬铃凌
责任校对：于　俊
装帧设计：墨创文化
责任印制：王　炜

出版发行：四川大学出版社有限责任公司
　　　　　地址：成都市一环路南一段24号（610065）
　　　　　电话：（028）85408311（发行部）、85400276（总编室）
　　　　　电子邮箱：scupress@vip.163.com
　　　　　网址：https://press.scu.edu.cn
印前制作：成都跨克创意文化传播有限公司
印刷装订：成都市新都华兴印务有限公司

成品尺寸：185mm×260mm
印　　张：17.5
字　　数：471千字

版　　次：2013年12月 第1版
　　　　　2022年 6 月 第2版
印　　次：2022年 6 月 第1次印刷
定　　价：68.00元

本社图书如有印装质量问题，请联系发行部调换

四川大学出版社
微信公众号

修订版序

编写本书的初衷是配合四川大学外国语学院硕士研究生课程“美国重要历史文献选读”的课程建设和课程教学。自2013年初版以来，本书一直是该课程的主教材，在教学中达到了预期的目的，即“让学生通过阅读原汁原味的美国重要历史文献，了解美国的政治思想、外交理念、价值准则，以及种族、性别、阶级等观念的发展脉络和历史演变”。与此同时，本书也被其他一些高校用作英语专业英美文化方面课程教学的辅助教材和本科高年级学生考研的参考书。

在编写初期，我们就力图将其打造成优秀的教材，从文献的选择、编辑，到章节内容的设计和撰写，都花了大量的心思。而且，在出版之后，我就跟几位参编人员说，希望大家在阅读和使用该书的过程中，仔细留意有没有需要改进的地方，虚心听取他人的意见和建议，以待将来再版时纠正错误，弥补不足，进一步提升质量，将其打造成精品。

因此，在过去9年的使用过程中，我们一直以挑剔的目光来看待此书，而且也的确发现了本书第一版中的一些错误和不足。归纳起来，主要有以下几类：（1）个别地方有打印错误，如“1835”错成了“1935”，“idea”错成了“ideal”。（2）个别人名、地名的翻译不统一，没有严格遵照商务印书馆出版的《英语姓名译名手册》和《外国地名译名手册》的标准来翻译。如“Jefferson”多处被译成“杰斐逊”，但在某些地方被译成了“杰弗逊”；“Livingston”有一处被译为“利文斯顿”，在另一处又被译成了“李维顿”。（3）某些地方的语言不够严谨、准确、精炼或流畅。（4）在涉及相同的人物或事件时，某些介绍性的信息在不同篇章的“导读”或“注释”中存在前后重复的现象。（5）“美国重要历史文献选读”这门课程设置的教学时长是32学时，即一个学期。然而，在过去几年的教学实践中，我们发现，对于一个学期的教学内容来说，本书第一版编选的篇目稍微多了一些。

针对上述前四类问题，我们在此次修订的过程中逐一进行了认真的校对、纠正和修改。针对第五类问题，我们在综合考虑各方面因素（比如文献的重要性、影响力、历史的连贯性等）的情况下，尤其是在尽量不影响编写此教材初衷的基础上，删掉了8个篇章，保留了34个篇章。

此外，为了响应教育部《高等学校课程思政建设指导纲要》，修订版对某些篇章“导读”和“思考题”的内容也进行了一些细微的调整和修改。2020年5月28日，教育部印发了《高等学校课程思政建设指导纲要》，明确指出：“培养什么人、怎样培养人、为谁培养人是教育的根本问题，立德树人成效是检验高校一切工作的根本标准。落实立德树人根本任务，必须将价值塑造、知识传授和能力培养三者融为一体，不可割裂。全面推进课程思政建设，就是要寓价值观引导于知识传授和能力培养之中，帮助学生塑造正确的世界观、人生观、价值观，这是人才培养的应有之义，更是必备内容。”四川大学外国语学院设置的“美国重要历史文献选读”这门课程既是专业知识课，也是思政课，虽然介绍的是美国历史文化中的各种观念和思潮，但是培养的目标却是“爱党、爱国、爱社会主义、爱人民、爱集体”的英语高级人才。我们了解美国历史文化的目的是知己知彼，是取其精华去其糟粕，而不是崇洋媚外。所以，在编写之初，我们就充分考虑到要让读者在了解美国政治思想、外交理念、价值准则，以及种族、性别、阶级等观念的同时，清楚地认识到美国民主的虚伪和矛盾之处。从所选文献中，读者可以看到，在美国主流社会高谈平等、自由、民主的同时，美国黑人正发出反奴役、反压迫的愤怒呐喊，美国原住民正被迫踏上西迁的“血泪之路”，美国妇女正为争取平等的权利而斗争；从所选文献中，读者还可以看到，当今美国的一些做法和观念并非无源之水、无本之木，而是有着深厚的历史和文化根源。比如美国第四十五任总统唐纳德·特朗普成天挂在嘴上的“美国优先”论就并非他的发明。在美国政治思想中，私利（Self Interest）从来就是考虑美国内政外交等诸多问题的出发点。特朗普不过将这一惯性思维赤裸裸、不加掩饰地表达了出来，而其他人在谈到这个话题时，讲得遮遮掩掩。在认真学习了《高等学校课程思政建设指导纲要》之后，我们认为，在某些篇章的“导读”和“思考题”中，还可以进一步强化批判意识，引导读者正确认识这些历史文献所蕴含的各种思想观念。因此，在修订“导读”和“思考题”的过程中，我们增加了一些更具批判性的内容，删掉了一些不必要的评价，力图寓价值观引导于知识传授和能力培养之中，使学生在增加美国历史和文化知识的同时，强化爱国精神，提升人文素养，建立起正确的价值观、世界观和人生观。

需要申明的是，我们虽然做了认真、细致的修订，但并不认为这个修订版就已经完美无缺。所以，对于任何建设性的意见和建议，我们都非常欢迎，万分感激。

叶　英

2022年5月于成都市华西坝

初版前言

2007年5月19日，我从美国圣路易斯大学美国研究系毕业，获得美国研究（American Studies）专业博士学位（Ph. D.）。13天之后（当年6月3日），我已踏上了中国的土地。在我留学之初，我的导师（也是该系的系主任）马修·曼西尼（Matthew Mancini）教授曾问我毕业后的打算，我答道："回中国，为中国的教育和科研事业做点贡献。"我至今还清楚地记得曼西尼当时脸上不相信的神情，估计他见多了一到美国就不想归国的留学生，知道很多人的留学目的其实就是移民美国。我也清楚地记得在毕业典礼后的第二天曼西尼在图书馆碰到我时的情景。当时，我正头也不抬、全神贯注地忙着用图书馆的设备，把我留学五年来在美国积累下来的所有复印资料打孔、装订并装箱。曼西尼走过来叫住我，问我在干什么。我说我在准备把这些资料运回中国。曼西尼这下才明白我五年前的回答并非戏言，而是肺腑之言。他走过来拍拍我的肩膀，给了我一个大大的拥抱。

回到中国，我也选择回到我原来的工作单位——四川大学。在学术研究的同时，我给我校英语语言文学专业美国研究方向的研究生开设了"美国研究入门""托克维尔与美国"和"美国重要历史文献选读"三门课程。"托克维尔与美国"这门课程以托克维尔（Alexis de Tocqueville, 1805—1859）的鸿篇巨制《民主在美国》（*Democracy in America*）为主要教学内容，辅以相关的史料和学术论著；"美国研究入门"的教学内容是美国研究学科发展过程中一些具有里程碑意义或指导性价值的论文和专著；本书选编的文献则是"美国重要历史文献选读"这门课的教学内容。我一直打算把后者编写成课本，一来方便自己教学，二来也为那些对美国历史文化感兴趣的读者提供一个读本。但由于每年的教学和科研任务繁重，我一直挤不出时间来将这个想法付诸行动。最近我有幸参加国家"985"工程"四川大学南亚及当代国际问题研究创新基地"项目，正好有机会实现我长久以来的这个愿望。鉴于完成该项目的时间限制，原拟由我个人完成的编写工作只好由我和我原来的几位学生共同完成。

如上所述，编写本书的初衷是为了配合"美国重要历史文献选读"这门研究生课程，让学生通过阅读原汁原味的美国重要历史文献，了解美国政治体制、政治思想、外交理念、价值准则，以及种族、性别、阶级等观念的发展脉络和历史演变。在美国两百多年的历史中，产生过的重要文献不可悉数，非一书一卷所能囊括。本书所选篇目虽不可能涉及美国历史上的每一个重要事件、每一种重要思潮或每一次重要的社会运动，但都是特别具有代表性，对美国历史与文化产生过重大影响的文献。

本书遴选篇目共42篇，时间跨度从殖民地时期到21世纪，文献类型包括著名的演说词、政论、宣言、司法判决、文学作品或其他形式的文献等，内容涵盖美国的政治思想、价值观念、种族问题、妇女运动、外交理念等。全书共42章，为了凸显美国历史与文化的演变和发展，让读者对其不仅有一个纵向的认识，也有一个横向的了解，本书编排以文献产生的历史时间为顺序，而不是以主题思想为板块。这样，读者更容易观察到在同一历史时期，美国不同社会群体不同的关注点和生存状态。比如读者可以看到，在美国主流社会高谈平等、自由、民主的同时，美国黑人正在发出反奴役、反压迫的愤怒呐喊（如大卫·沃克的《呼吁》），美国原住民正被迫踏上西迁的"血泪之路"（如安德鲁·杰克逊总统倡议和签署的《印第安人迁移法》）。

本书每章由"导读""英文文献""注释"和"思考题"四个部分构成。

"导读"包括对该文献之作者、历史文化背景以及该文献本身的介绍。"导读"中的注释采用脚注形式。

"英文文献"有的独立成篇，有的因原著篇幅过长，只节选其核心或具有代表性的一部分，删节之处用省略号替代。独立成篇的文献都保留了原来的篇名，节选的文献有的在篇名上有所变化。比如第10章所选文献来自门罗（James Monroe）总统1823年向国会提出的一篇国情咨文，该咨文内容丰富，本书只节选了涉及门罗宣言的那一部分，因而该章就以选文所表达的核心思想"门罗主义"（The Monroe Doctrine）为标题。

"注释"是对该文献中一些需要解释说明之处加以解释说明，有助于读者更好地理解该文献。

"思考题"是一些与该文献相关的、引发读者思考和讨论的话题。我们在拟定这些问题时，考虑的读者群是选修"美国重要历史文献选读"这门课程的研究生以及对美国历史文化感兴趣的本科生和普通读者。

除主编之外，本书的编者大都是刚刚涉足学术界的青年学者。王也是我教过的本科生，今年5月刚从美国圣路易斯大学获得美国研究专业硕士学位；邓晓熹、税红、王玉兰、游航、邹青是我近些年指导过的四川大学美国文化方向的硕士研究生，他们现在都已是高校教师。虽然他们初涉学界，但都功底扎实，治学严谨，工作认真。

作为主编，我负责本书的主体框架设计、文献的选择、每章每稿的审阅、修改和校订以及全书的统稿。六位青年学者负责编写，具体分工如下：邓晓熹负责1～8

章，游航负责9～15章，王玉兰负责16～22章，邹青负责23、27、39～42章，税红负责24～26、28～31章，王乜负责32～38章。

本书可用作高等院校英语专业美国研究方向研究生的专业教材，亦可用作本科高年级英美文化课程的教学用书或辅助教材。对英语专业其他研究方向的学生以及对美国历史文化感兴趣的普通读者，本书也具有一定的参考价值。

叶　英

2013年秋于四川大学

目录 Contents

1. The Mayflower Compact (1620)[①]

The Pilgrim Separatists[②]

导读：

古希腊哲学家亚里士多德在其《政治学》一书中谈道："我们如果对任何事物，对政治或其他各问题，追溯其原始而明白其发生的端绪，我们就可获得最明朗的认识。"[③]如果说美国精神是清教、契约、民主、平等、自由，那么其原始和端绪正是《五月花公约》。

《五月花公约》的由来可以溯源至16至17世纪欧洲的宗教改革。这场变革给英王詹姆士一世统治下的宗教格局带来了一些不同的声音：新教徒开始倡导一系列宗教改革，同时期的天主教徒在索求权利未果后，企图策划火药阴谋[④]（Gunpowder Plot）谋杀英王。这些行动直接威胁着统治的稳定。在经历了一系列残酷的镇压后，一部分清教徒开始选择客居荷兰避难，但步步紧跟的肃清脚步并没有因此停止。最终，搭载着清教徒的"五月花号"轮船于1620年8月从荷兰出发，绕行英国后，开始驶往美洲新大陆，出航66天后，最终停靠在今天的马萨诸塞海岸以北的普利茅斯。

"五月花号"抛锚后，全体乘客并没有立即登陆，他们面临三大迫

---

① "The Mayflower Compact", http://www.ushistory.org/documents/mayflower.htm (accessed Oct. 1, 2021).《五月花公约》原件目前已经遗失，现在通行的有两个版本：其一是1622年面世的威廉·布拉德福德（William Bradford）手抄本，另一个出现在纳撒尼尔·默顿（Nathaniel Morton）的《新英格兰回忆录》（*New England Memorial*, 1669）中。为方便读者阅读，本书选择的是更接近现代英语的1669年版。

② 关于《五月花公约》的作者目前有三大主流观点：（1）由全体清教徒共同起草；（2）威廉·布拉德福德主笔；（3）威廉·布鲁斯特（William Brewster）主笔，威廉·布拉德福德和约翰·卡弗（John Carver）给予了一定辅助。

③ 亚里士多德：《政治学》，吴寿彭译，北京：商务印书馆，1965年，第2–3页。

④ 16至17世纪的欧洲宗教改革打破了中世纪天主教一统天下的局面。伊丽莎白一世当政的英国在保证政局稳定的同时，一方面削弱了天主教的权威，另一方面对各类宗教采取了相对宽容的政策。到了詹姆士一世时期，英国的天主教徒在寻求复辟天主教一统失败后，其中的一些极端分子于1605年11月5日策划了火药阴谋，企图谋杀英王全家。阴谋败露后，詹姆士一世一改早期包容的宗教政策，对各类宗教相应实施了严格的监管。

在眉睫的难题：一，按照清教徒们在远赴北美前与伦敦的弗吉尼亚公司（Virginia Company）①签订的合同，哈德逊河口区为合法停靠区；但因天气偏航的轮船，最终在不隶属于任何管辖范围的普利茅斯抛锚。全体乘客亟待解决土地使用的合法性问题。二，“五月花号”上的102名乘客并不完全由清教徒组成，其中还包括在南开普敦登船的商人、冒险家和仆人。轮船偏航的消息传开后，这些乘客主张登陆后各奔东西，各行其是。三，普利茅斯地广人稀，一片荒凉；清教徒孤立无援，举步维艰。无政府状态、乘客间的纠纷、最残酷的生存危机都迫使全体乘客展开紧急磋商。共同协商的结果便是《五月花公约》这份临时起草的公共社会契约。

《五月花公约》共两句话196词，文字简练而不失法律语言的严谨。第一句话是全文的重点：开篇致敬英王之后，《五月花公约》开始阐述清教徒先祖（Pilgrim Fathers）移居的原因、目的，以及缔约的形式和原则。在美国后来两百余年中形成的诸如清教精神、宪政精神、民主精神、个人主义精神在《五月花公约》中都可以找到雏形。

最终，41名成年男性乘客在船上签署了这份公约。这41名签署人包括“五月花号”上每个家庭的一家之主、每个成年单身男子以及大多数雇佣的男仆。当时，妇女没有政治权利，被排除在公约签署人之外。从这一点来看，美国民主在其肇始之际，就不是所有人的民主，而只是部分人的特权。也正因如此，美国两百多年的历史充满了不同社会群体为争取民主、自由和平等而发起的斗争。

In the name of God, Amen. We, whose names are underwritten, the loyal subjects of our dread Sovereigne Lord, King James, by the grace of God, of Great Britaine, France, and Ireland, King, defender of the faith, etc.[1] having undertaken, for the glory of God, and advancement of the Christian faith, and honor of our king and country, a voyage to plant the first colony in the Northerne parts of Virginia, doe by these presents solemnly and mutually in the presence of God and one another, covenant and combine ourselves together into a civill body politick,[2] for our better ordering, and preservation and furtherance of the ends aforesaid; and by virtue hereof to enact, constitute, and

① 弗吉尼亚公司包括两个重要的子公司：伦敦公司（London Company，又称Virginia Company of London）和普利茅斯公司（Plymouth Company，又称Virginia Company of Plymouth）。

frame such just and equall laws, ordinances, acts, constitutions and offices, from time to time, as shall be thought most meete and convenient for the generall good of the colonie unto which we promise all due submission and obedience. In witness whereof we have hereunder subscribed our names at Cape-Cod the 11. of November, in the year of the raigne of our sovereign lord, King James, of England, France, and Ireland, the eighteenth, and of Scotland the fiftie-fourth. Anno Dom. 1620.[3]

注释：

1. etc.：当时的英国国王詹姆士二世也是爱尔兰国王，还继承了金雀花王朝留下的法兰西国王名号。
2. civill body politick：公民的政治团体，又译公民共同体。“civill body politick”后面的文字解释了该团体成立所需的三个基本条件：一，公民自愿；二，公平、正义的法制；三，团体中的全体公民必须遵守相关条例。
3. 1669年版的《五月花公约》最后还包括41名签约乘客的名字，详细名单参考“Mayflower Compact”，http://www.ushistory.org/documents/mayflower.htm (accessed Oct. 1, 2021)。

思考题：

1. How are the key words in America like Puritanism, republicanism, legal awareness, democracy, and individualism reflected in “Mayflower Compact”?
2. According to the spirit of “Mayflower Compact,” why and how do citizens combine to establish a “civill body politick” ? Do you think it is rational?

2. The Declaration of Independence (1776)[①]

Thomas Jefferson

导读：

如果说1620年的《五月花公约》是英籍清教徒开拓北美殖民地伊始的摸索，那么1776年同样出现在这片大陆的《独立宣言》则标志着美利坚合众国的诞生。

从殖民地到独立的国家，北美殖民地走过了一个半世纪。历史在这一段变迁中一直围绕两条线索：殖民地的本地经验以及殖民地与宗主国的关系。早期北美的移居者笃信清教，相信勤劳致富是他们的天职；在开拓殖民地的过程中，他们自立、自治；伴随经济的发展和人口的增长，一套独立于英国的本地社会规约渐渐形成。七年战争（Seven Years' War, 1756—1763）结束后，英国为转嫁战时的高额债务，在殖民地颁布了一系列新税法[②]。在北美殖民者看来，新税法并不合理，因为没有议会代表权的课税等同于剥夺殖民地居民的财产和自由。随后，“课税—抗议—更多课税—更多抗议”的恶性循环在双方的紧张关系中不停轮转，每一次轮转后，双方的敌对情绪和矛盾冲突都愈演愈烈：波士顿事件[③]中五名波士顿人丧命；议会单方面继续实施《茶税法》（“Tea Act”），意图在殖民地倾销积压的茶叶；波士顿倾茶事件后，殖民地遭受经济制裁；第一届大陆会议递交的有限请愿被英王视为叛乱；在1775年列克星敦的冲突中，双方短兵相接，各有死伤。最终，为

① “The Declaration of Independence”, http://www.ushistory.org/declaration/document/index.htm (accessed Oct. 1, 2021). 在大陆会议最后的定稿中，《独立宣言》的全名是“A Declaration by the Representatives of the United States of America, in General Congress Assembled”，后来简称为“The Declaration of Independence”。

② 如英国议会分别于1764年和1765年制定的《糖税法》（“Sugar Act”）和《印花税法》（“Stamp Act”）。

③ 1770年3月5日，为保障税法执行而驻扎波士顿的英军遭到民众的激烈抗议。部分民众不停辱骂驻扎士兵，并砸投石块。在没有任何上级批示的情况下，部分英军士兵被激怒后开枪射杀了五名波士顿人。美国历史称这次事件为“Boston Massacre”（波士顿大屠杀）。鉴于史学界一直对这次事件的归责问题争论不休，本书选择了较为中性的提法“波士顿事件”。

维护殖民地利益，第二届大陆会议于1776年7月4日正式通过《独立宣言》，宣告殖民地独立。

第二届大陆会议于1776年6月11日组成五人《独立宣言》编写委员会，其中约翰·亚当斯、本杰明·富兰克林、罗伯特·利文斯顿和罗杰·谢尔曼负责拟订大纲及修订，托马斯·杰斐逊主笔①。《独立宣言》行文简明、庄重，节奏鲜明。排比、连词并列、首语重复、掉尾句等修辞手法的运用恰到好处，读来朗朗上口，令人过目难忘。全文三部分逻辑缜密，层次分明：第一部分阐明对公民与政府关系的理解，第二部分逐一列举英国政府对殖民地的伤害，最后一部分宣布独立。《独立宣言》的政治思想架构以启蒙思想家约翰·洛克（John Locke, 1632—1704）的政治思想为主。读者不难发现，《独立宣言》第一部分提到的“... that among these are Life, Liberty and the pursuit of Happiness. —That to secure these rights, Governments are instituted among Men”与洛克在其《政府论》中论及的自然权利（natural rights）、民众的同意（consent）、社会契约（social contract）等概念异曲同工。

独立战争伊始问世的《独立宣言》是美国历史的一个拐点。从此，北美大陆由英属殖民地变成了美利坚合众国。《独立宣言》中“人人生而平等”这一立国原则，也成了美国两百多年历史中被奴役、被压迫、被歧视的人们反奴役、反压迫、反歧视的有力武器。

In Congress, July 4, 1776

The unanimous Declaration of the thirteen United States of America.

When in the Course[1] of human events it becomes necessary for one people[2] to dissolve the political bands which have connected them with another and to assume among the powers of the earth, the separate and equal station to which the Laws of Nature and of Nature's God entitle them, a decent respect to the opinions of mankind requires that they should declare the causes which impel them to the separation.

We hold these truths to be self-evident, that all men are created equal, that they are endowed by their Creator with certain unalienable Rights, that among these are Life, Liberty and the pursuit of Happiness. —That to secure these rights, Governments

① 《独立宣言》最后的成型经历了三个版本：杰斐逊的初稿、五人编委会修改的二稿，以及经大陆会议修改后的定稿。三稿间的异同请参见http://www.ushistory.org/declaration/document/compare.htm (accessed Oct. 1, 2021)。本文选自大陆会议的定稿。

are instituted among Men, deriving their just powers from the consent of the governed, —That whenever any Form of Government becomes destructive of these ends, it is the Right of the People to alter or to abolish it, and to institute new Government, laying its foundation on such principles and organizing its powers in such form, as to them shall seem most likely to effect their Safety and Happiness. Prudence, indeed, will dictate that Governments long established should not be changed for light and transient causes; and accordingly all experience hath shewn[3] that mankind are more disposed to suffer, while evils are sufferable than to right themselves by abolishing the forms to which they are accustomed. But when a long train of abuses and usurpations, pursuing invariably the same Object evinces a design to reduce them under absolute Despotism, it is their right, it is their duty, to throw off such Government, and to provide new Guards for their future security. —Such has been the patient sufferance of these Colonies; and such is now the necessity which constrains them to alter their former Systems of Government. The history of the present King of Great Britain[4] is a history of repeated injuries and usurpations, all having in direct object the establishment of an absolute Tyranny over these States. To prove this, let Facts be submitted to a candid world.

He has refused his Assent to Laws, the most wholesome and necessary for the public good.

He has forbidden his Governors to pass Laws of immediate and pressing importance, unless suspended in their operation till his Assent should be obtained; and when so suspended, he has utterly neglected to attend to them.

He has refused to pass other Laws for the accommodation of large districts of people, unless those people would relinquish the right of Representation in the Legislature, a right inestimable to them and formidable to tyrants only.

He has called together legislative bodies at places unusual, uncomfortable, and distant from the depository of their Public Records, for the sole purpose of fatiguing them into compliance with his measures.

He has dissolved Representative Houses repeatedly, for opposing with manly firmness his invasions on the rights of the people.

He has refused for a long time, after such dissolutions, to cause others to be elected, whereby the Legislative Powers, incapable of Annihilation, have returned to the People at large for their exercise; the State remaining in the mean time exposed to all the dangers of invasion from without, and convulsions within.

He has endeavoured to prevent the population of these States; for that purpose obstructing the Laws for Naturalization of Foreigners; refusing to pass others to encourage their migrations hither, and raising the conditions of new Appropriations of Lands.

He has obstructed the Administration of Justice by refusing his Assent to Laws for establishing Judiciary Powers.

He has made Judges dependent on his Will alone for the tenure of their offices, and the amount and payment of their salaries.

He has erected a multitude of New Offices, and sent hither swarms of Officers to harass our people and eat out their substance.

He has kept among us, in times of peace, Standing Armies without the Consent of our legislatures.

He has affected to render the Military independent of and superior to the Civil Power.

He has combined with others to subject us to a jurisdiction foreign to our constitution, and unacknowledged by our laws; giving his Assent to their Acts of pretended Legislation:

For quartering large bodies of armed troops among us:

For protecting them, by a mock Trial from punishment for any Murders which they should commit on the Inhabitants of these States:

For cutting off our Trade with all parts of the world:

For imposing Taxes on us without our Consent:

For depriving us in many cases, of the benefit of Trial by Jury:

For transporting us beyond Seas to be tried for pretended offences:

For abolishing the free System of English Laws in a neighbouring Province, establishing therein an Arbitrary government, and enlarging its Boundaries so as to render it at once an example and fit instrument for introducing the same absolute rule into these Colonies.

For taking away our Charters, abolishing our most valuable Laws and altering fundamentally the Forms of our Governments:

For suspending our own Legislatures, and declaring themselves invested with power to legislate for us in all cases whatsoever.

He has abdicated Government here, by declaring us out of his Protection and waging War against us.

He has plundered our seas, ravaged our coasts, burnt our towns, and destroyed the lives of our people.

He is at this time transporting large Armies of foreign Mercenaries to compleat[5] the works of death, desolation, and tyranny, already begun with circumstances of Cruelty & Perfidy scarcely paralleled in the most barbarous ages, and totally unworthy the Head of a civilized nation.

He has constrained our fellow Citizens taken Captive on the high Seas to bear Arms against their Country, to become the executioners of their friends and Brethren, or to fall themselves by their Hands.

He has excited domestic insurrections amongst us, and has endeavoured to bring on the inhabitants of our frontiers, the merciless Indian Savages whose known rule of warfare, is an undistinguished destruction of all ages, sexes and conditions.

In every stage of these Oppressions We have Petitioned for Redress in the most humble terms: Our repeated Petitions have been answered only by repeated injury. A Prince, whose character is thus marked by every act which may define a Tyrant, is unfit to be the ruler of a free people.

Nor have We been wanting in attentions to our British brethren. We have warned them from time to time of attempts by their legislature to extend an unwarrantable jurisdiction over us. We have reminded them of the circumstances of our emigration and settlement here. We have appealed to their native justice and magnanimity, and we have conjured them by the ties of our common kindred to disavow these usurpations, which would inevitably interrupt our connections and correspondence. They too have been deaf to the voice of justice and of consanguinity. We must, therefore, acquiesce in the necessity, which denounces our Separation, and hold them, as we hold the rest of mankind, Enemies in War, in Peace Friends.

We, therefore, the Representatives of the united States of America, in General Congress,[6] Assembled, appealing to the Supreme Judge of the world for the rectitude of our intentions, do, in the Name, and by Authority of the good People of these Colonies, solemnly publish and declare, That these United Colonies are, and of Right ought to be Free and Independent States, that they are Absolved from all Allegiance to the British Crown, and that all political connection between them and the State of Great Britain, is and ought to be totally dissolved; and that as Free and Independent States, they have full Power to levy War, conclude Peace, contract Alliances, establish Commerce, and to do all other Acts and Things which Independent States may of right do. —And for the support of this Declaration, with a firm reliance on the protection of Divine Providence, we mutually pledge to each other our Lives, our Fortunes, and our sacred Honor.

注释：

1. 根据英文文法，专有名词需要大写。大写的Course被赋予了专有名词的色彩，以此强调美国独立的性质在人类历史的进程中是普遍的、正当的。后文中有很多类似的大写表达，如第二段的Rights，Government，Men等。
2. one people：这里的one people既不指北美殖民地居民，也不指代美国人，而是用one people这样一个泛指，将反对暴政、追求平等推到全人类历史的高度，从而使美国革命正当化。
3. hath shewn：同has shown。
4. the present King of Great Britain：英王乔治三世（1738—1820）。《独立宣言》矛头直指乔治三世。但实际情况是，1688年光荣革命（Glorious Revolution）后，王权受限，议会权力扩大。在整个殖民地与英国的矛盾中，议会同样扮演着重要的角色。
5. compleat：同complete。
6. General Congress：第二届大陆会议，也称为Second Continental Congress。

思考题：

1. Of the two factors preparing the War of Independence, one being local experience and the other British influence, which do you think played a greater part in shaping the national identity for Americans?
2. Do you think the ideal that "all men are created equal, that they are endowed by their Creator with certain unalienable rights, that among these are Life, Liberty and the pursuit of Happiness" still reads rational and consistent, in an era when widening gap between the rich and the poor, gun abuse and police violence are rampant in the United States?

3. What Is an American? (1782)[①]

J. Hector St. John de Crèvecoeur

导读：

赫克托·圣约翰·德·克雷沃克尔（J. Hector St. John de Crèvecoeur, 1735—1813）[②]是18世纪著名的博物学家和文学家。他生于法国，父亲是诺曼底贵族，母亲是位成功的银行家。七年战争期间，他负责法军的地图测绘工作，从中获得不少北美大陆的一手资料。法国落败后，他移居北美殖民地继续从事测绘工作，1764年以纽约公民的身份加入英国国籍。殖民地的新生活让他着迷，但亲英的立场同时也让他在独立战争中的处境颇为尴尬。1779年他回法国处理继承事宜的途中被英军逮捕，后几经周折返回法国。1783年《巴黎和约》签署后，他又以法国领事的身份回到纽约。重返北美后，战争的暴行让他震惊：独立战争中印第安人烧掉了他的庄园，妻子被杀，子女流离失所。从此，他不再耕作。后来他和托马斯·杰斐逊交往密切，在美法关系以及美国的农耕事业上建树颇多。1790年返法后，其贵族身份将他卷入了法国大革命的漩涡。他向美国驻法领事馆申请重返美国失败，1813年在法国病故。克雷沃克尔的一生都处在时代变革的激流当中。各种社会力量之间的张力牵引着他一生的起起伏伏，这些也被他写进了《一位美国农夫的来信》（*Letters from an American Farmer*, 1782）中。

《一位美国农夫的来信》撰写时正值美国独立战争（1775—1783）爆发前夕[③]，各殖民地在反抗英国中走到了一起，美利坚民族逐渐觉醒。与同时期的政治思想家托马斯·潘恩（Thomas Paine, 1737—

① J. Hector St. John Crevecoeur, *Letters from an American Farmer*, http://xroads.virginia.edu/~hyper/crev/letter03.html (accessed Oct. 1, 2021).

② 原名米歇尔·纪尧姆·让·德·克雷沃克尔（Michel Guillaume Jean de Crèvecoeur），1764年加入英国国籍后更名。

③《一位美国农夫的来信》成书于1774至1776年间。1779年独立战争期间克雷沃克尔因继承问题准备返法，途经纽约时因间谍嫌疑被英军拘留三个月；被释放后，1782年游历至英国时出版了《一位美国农夫的来信》。

1809）的《常识》（*Common Sense*, 1776）[1]不同，《一位美国农夫的来信》没有义愤填膺、独立自主、奋起革命的激进论调。作为观察者的克雷沃克尔，将各种社会力量的冲撞带进他的创作：美国梦的民主平等、奴隶制的实行、农业经济下的田园牧歌[2]、商业经济中的尔虞我诈、新民族的赞歌、效忠英王的誓言——所有这些在当时社会转型中的种种冲突，不仅让克雷沃克尔难以保持观察者的冷静，同时也让《一位美国农夫的来信》充斥着乐观—悲观、希望—失望的矛盾笔调。

《一位美国农夫的来信》集18世纪典型的书信体和散文体于一身，由一位美国农夫写给一位英国绅士的12封信件组成，每封信都是对北美社会的一个独立观察点。本文为第三封《何为美国人？》。克雷沃克尔在此提出的"美国人究竟是什么样的人？"这一经典设问，在美国研究这一领域"成了美国知识界不断叩问和探究的问题，成了美国的美国研究之初因和源泉"[3]。在对新世界和旧世界的反复比较中，这封信洋溢着对殖民地人民民主、平等、自由、独立、勤劳的赞誉。在美国，本文是探索美国民族意识的早期代表之作。

…It is not composed, as in Europe, of great lords who possess every thing and of a herd of people who have nothing. Here are no aristocratical families, no courts, no kings, no bishops, no ecclesiastical dominion, no invisible power giving to a few a very visible one; no great manufacturers employing thousands, no great refinements of luxury. The rich and the poor are not so far removed from each other as they are in Europe. Some few towns excepted, we are all tillers of the earth….

---

① 《常识》是一部激进的民主主义经典论著。列克星敦事件后，国父们虽然紧急召开了第二届大陆会议，组建了陆军，但他们在是否独立的问题上依然摇摆不定。《常识》理性地分析了各方面的形势，并大胆喊出了"独立"一词。该书问世后非常畅销，在一定程度上推动了美国革命的进程。

② 对于克雷沃克尔早期在《一位美国农夫的来信》中描写的田园生活，目前的主流评论一般认为带有"理想主义""乌托邦"色彩。但是，一方面，田园生活中潜藏的美国梦构成了美国性的主题，在整个美国经验中贯穿始终；另一方面，仅仅是在几年后的1789年，重农主义还是重商主义的争论就被提到了立国之本的高度，在第一届政府内部引起争议，成为后世美国经济发展模式的一个主要议题，也为随后的南北冲突埋下了伏笔。

③ 叶英：《中美两国的美国研究及美国学在中国的学科建设》，载《西南民族大学学报》2010年第5期，第204-210页。

...What then is the American, this new man? He is either an European, or the descendant of an European,[1] hence that strange mixture of blood, which you will find in no other country. I could point out to you a family whose grandfather was an Englishman, whose wife was Dutch, whose son married a French woman, and whose present four sons have now four wives of different nations. He is an American, who leaving behind him all his ancient prejudices and manners, receives new ones from the new mode of life he has embraced, the new government he obeys, and the new rank he holds. He becomes an American by being received in the broad lap of our great Alma Mater.[2] Here individuals of all nations are melted into a new race of men, whose labours and posterity will one day cause great changes in the world. Americans are the western pilgrims, who are carrying along with them that great mass of arts, sciences, vigour, and industry which began long since in the east; they will finish the great circle.[3] The Americans were once scattered all over Europe; here they are incorporated into one of the finest systems of population which has ever appeared, and which will hereafter become distinct by the power of the different climates they inhabit. The American ought therefore to love this country much better than that wherein either he or his forefathers were born. Here the rewards of his industry follow with equal steps the progress of his labour; his labour is founded on the basis of nature, self-interest; can it want a stronger allurement? Wives and children, who before in vain demanded of him a morsel of bread, now, fat and frolicsome, gladly help their father to clear those fields whence[4] exuberant crops are to arise to feed and to clothe them all; without any part being claimed, either by a despotic prince, a rich abbot, or a mighty lord. I lord religion demands but little of him;[5] a small voluntary salary to the minister, and gratitude to God; can he refuse these? The American is a new man, who acts upon new principles; he must therefore entertain new ideas, and form new opinions. From involuntary idleness, servile dependence, penury, and useless labour, he has passed to toils of a very different nature, rewarded by ample subsistence. —This is an American.

注释：

1. He is either an European, or the descendant of an European ...：本句出处参见Michel Guillaume Jean De Crevecoeur, "Letter Ⅲ What Is an American", in *Letters from an American Farmer* (New York: Fox, Duffield, 1904)。本句的另一个版本是"He is neither an European, nor the descendant of an European ...", 出处参见J. Hector St. John de

Crevecoeur, *Letters from an American Farmer and Sketches of Eighteenth-Century America* (Harmondsworth: Penguin, 1981), 46–47。

2. Alma Mater：现代英语中指母校；其词源为拉丁语*Alma Māter*，意指母亲。联系上下文，这里指后者。
3. they will finish the great circle："they"在这里指美国人。前句中的"east"和现代意义上的东方有所出入，克雷沃克尔的东方概念既包括亚洲又包括当时的北美殖民地；所以他提到兴于东方的"great mass of arts，sciences，vigour，and industry"传到西方后，随着欧洲人移民至北美殖民地而完成了一个伟大的循环。
4. whence：同from where。
5. I lord religion demands but little of him：本句的出处参见Michel Guillaume Jean De Crevecoeur, "Letter Ⅲ What Is an American", in *Letters from an American Farmer* (New York: Fox, Duffield, 1904)。本句的另一个版本是"Here religion demands but little of him", 出处参见J. Hector St. John de Crevecoeur, *Letters from an American Farmer and Sketches of Eighteenth-Century America* (Harmondsworth: Penguin, 1981), 46–47。

思考题：

1. What historical and cultural elements together help to shape the American identity?
2. Some people describe American society as a "melting pot" while others see it as a "salad bowl." What is your opinion of the two metaphors?

4. The Federalist No. 10 (1787)[1]

James Madison

导读：

詹姆斯·麦迪逊（James Madison, 1751—1836）是美国第四任总统，也是美国最后一位辞世的国父（Founding Fathers）[2]。他出生在弗吉尼亚的一个大种植园家庭。在普林斯顿大学[3]求学期间，他涉猎诸多学科，尤以演说见长。毕业后，他放弃家族经营的种植园事业，开始满怀热情地投入反英革命。1787年代表弗吉尼亚参加制宪会议（Constitutional Convention）期间，他拟定《弗吉尼亚方案》（“Virginia Plan”）[4]，随后在批准宪法运动中起草《权利法案》（“Bill of Rights”）并递交国会。在关于美国应该以工商立国还是以农业立国的建国之争中，托马斯·杰斐逊（Thomas Jefferson）联合麦迪逊共同创建了民主共和党（Democratic-Republican Party），开创了美国两党政治的先河。杰斐逊政府时期（1801—1809），麦迪逊司职国务卿，积极促成路易斯安那购地（Louisiana Purchase, 1803）。他出任美国第四任总统（1809—1817）期间领导的第二次英美战争（War of 1812）巩固了国家的统一，维护了民族的团结。

麦迪逊叱咤美国政坛，其政治声誉的鹊起与“宪法之父”的美誉密不可分。作为《宪法》的雏形，《弗吉尼亚方案》在艰难的三个月中历经多次协商、反对、妥协、修订、增补和表决，最后勉强得到了多数州代表的签字。批准宪法运动随即在全国展开。这一年，麦迪逊年仅36

---

① James Madison, “The Federalist No. 10”, http://www.constitution.org/1-Constitution/fed/federa10.htm (accessed Oct. 2, 2021).

② 国父（Founding Fathers），又译建国元勋或开国元勋。指投身独立革命，签署《独立宣言》，参与制定《宪法》的美国政治家。国父的详细名录请参见http://commons.m.wikimedia.org/wiki/Founding_Fathers_of_the_United_States (accessed Oct. 10, 2021)。

③ 普林斯顿大学在当时称为新泽西学院（College of New Jersey）。

④《弗吉尼亚方案》由詹姆斯·麦迪逊起草，弗吉尼亚代表埃德蒙·伦道夫（Edmund Randolph）在制宪会议伊始宣读。方案中论及的三权分立、两院制立法机构、制衡原则、人口议员制等基本议题，后来演变成了整个制宪会议的坐标，引领着讨论的始终。

岁。后来，为争取民众的支持，制宪会议中逐渐分离的两大阵营开始在本地报刊撰文①，围绕国家主义、州权主义、公民权利等焦点问题展开辩论。在这场论辩中，麦迪逊联合亚历山大·汉密尔顿（Alexander Hamilton, 1755—1804）、约翰·杰伊（John Jay, 1745—1829）②于1787年10月21日到次年的8月6日先后发表文章，捍卫《宪法》，敦促各州尽快加入联邦。1787年，这些文章以《联邦党人文集》（*The Federalist Papers*）的题名结集出版。时至今日，《联邦党人文集》依然被视作解释《宪法》的最高权威参考，时常被美国最高法院引用。

演变为《宪法》脚注的《联邦党人文集》共由85篇论文组成，其中26篇出自麦迪逊之手。在第九篇中，汉密尔顿着重回应了州权主义者援引的理论：共和国在国土相对较小、人口相对较少的共同体内才有可能建立③；继而针锋相对地论述了联邦政府的必要性。麦迪逊的第十篇承接前一篇的议题，以自由主义和共和主义为框架，反复比较和论证统一（union）和分裂（faction）的优劣。全文文字通俗易懂，逻辑严密，层次清晰，是《联邦党人文集》中最广为人知的一篇。

To the People of the State of New York:

AMONG the numerous advantages promised by a well constructed Union, none deserves to be more accurately developed than its tendency to break and control the violence of faction. The friend of popular governments[1] never finds himself so much alarmed for their character and fate, as when he contemplates their propensity to this dangerous vice. He will not fail, therefore, to set a due value on any plan which, without violating the principles to which he is attached, provides a proper cure for it. The instability, injustice, and confusion introduced into the public councils, have, in truth, been the mortal diseases under which popular governments have everywhere perished; as they continue to be the favorite and fruitful topics from which the adversaries to liberty derive their most specious declamations. The valuable improvements made by the American constitutions on the popular models,

① 如制宪会议结束仅17天，弗吉尼亚代表乔治·梅森（George Mason, 1725—1792）就率先在费城的报刊上公开撰文拥护州权，宣扬个体权利。

② 约翰·杰伊，时任外交国务秘书（Secretary of Foreign Affairs），相当于今天美国政府中的国务卿一职；1789至1795年任美国首席大法官，1795至1801年任纽约州州长。

③ 反联邦党人的理论支撑主要来自法国启蒙思想家孟德斯鸠（Montesquieu, 1689—1755）的《论法的精神》（*The Spirit of Laws*, 1750）一书。

both ancient and modern, cannot certainly be too much admired; but it would be an unwarrantable partiality, to contend that they have as effectually obviated the danger on this side, as was wished and expected. Complaints are everywhere heard from our most considerate and virtuous citizens, equally the friends of public and private faith, and of public and personal liberty, that our governments are too unstable, that the public good is disregarded in the conflicts of rival parties, and that measures are too often decided, not according to the rules of justice and the rights of the minor party, but by the superior force of an interested and overbearing majority. However anxiously we may wish that these complaints had no foundation, the evidence, of known facts will not permit us to deny that they are in some degree true. It will be found, indeed, on a candid review of our situation, that some of the distresses under which we labor have been erroneously charged on the operation of our governments; but it will be found, at the same time, that other causes will not alone account for many of our heaviest misfortunes; and, particularly, for that prevailing and increasing distrust of public engagements, and alarm for private rights, which are echoed from one end of the continent to the other. These must be chiefly, if not wholly, effects of the unsteadiness and injustice with which a factious spirit has tainted our public administrations.

By a faction, I understand a number of citizens, whether amounting to a majority or a minority of the whole, who are united and actuated by some common impulse of passion, or of interest, adversed to the rights of other citizens, or to the permanent and aggregate interests of the community.

There are two methods of curing the mischiefs of faction: the one, by removing its causes; the other, by controlling its effects.

There are again two methods of removing the causes of faction: the one, by destroying the liberty which is essential to its existence; the other, by giving to every citizen the same opinions, the same passions, and the same interests.

It could never be more truly said than of the first remedy, that it was worse than the disease. Liberty is to faction what air is to fire, an aliment without which it instantly expires. But it could not be less folly to abolish liberty, which is essential to political life, because it nourishes faction, than it would be to wish the annihilation of air, which is essential to animal life, because it imparts to fire its destructive agency.

The second expedient is as impracticable as the first would be unwise. As long as the reason of man continues fallible, and he is at liberty to exercise it, different opinions will be formed. As long as the connection subsists between his reason and his self-love, his opinions and his passions will have a reciprocal influence on each other; and the former will be objects to which the latter will attach themselves. The diversity in the faculties of men, from which the rights of property originate, is not less an insuperable obstacle to a uniformity of interests. The protection of these faculties is the first object of government. From the protection of different and unequal faculties of acquiring property, the possession of different degrees and kinds of property immediately results; and from the influence of these on the sentiments and views of the respective proprietors, ensues a division of the society into different interests and parties.

The latent causes of faction are thus sown in the nature of man; and we see them everywhere brought into different degrees of activity, according to the different circumstances of civil society. A zeal for different opinions concerning religion, concerning government, and many other points, as well of speculation as of practice; an attachment to different leaders ambitiously contending for pre-eminence and power; or to persons of other descriptions whose fortunes have been interesting to the human passions, have, in turn, divided mankind into parties, inflamed them with mutual animosity, and rendered them much more disposed to vex and oppress each other than to co-operate for their common good. So strong is this propensity of mankind to fall into mutual animosities, that where no substantial occasion presents itself, the most frivolous and fanciful distinctions have been sufficient to kindle their unfriendly passions and excite their most violent conflicts. But the most common and durable source of factions has been the various and unequal distribution of property.[2] Those who hold and those who are without property have ever formed distinct interests in society. Those who are creditors, and those who are debtors, fall under a like discrimination. A landed interest, a manufacturing interest, a mercantile interest, a moneyed interest, with many lesser interests, grow up of necessity in civilized nations, and divide them into different classes, actuated by different sentiments and views. The regulation of these various and interfering interests forms the principal task of modern legislation, and involves the spirit of party and faction in the necessary and ordinary operations of the government.

No man is allowed to be a judge in his own cause, because his interest would certainly bias his judgment, and, not improbably, corrupt his integrity. With equal, nay with greater reason, a body of men are unfit to be both judges and parties at the same time; yet what are many of the most important acts of legislation, but so many judicial determinations, not indeed concerning the rights of single persons, but concerning the rights of large bodies of citizens? And what are the different classes of legislators but advocates and parties to the causes which they determine? Is a law proposed concerning private debts? It is a question to which the creditors are parties on one side and the debtors on the other. Justice ought to hold the balance between them. Yet the parties are, and must be, themselves the judges; and the most numerous party, or, in other words, the most powerful faction must be expected to prevail. Shall domestic manufactures be encouraged, and in what degree, by restrictions on foreign manufactures? are questions which would be differently decided by the landed and the manufacturing classes, and probably by neither with a sole regard to justice and the public good. The apportionment of taxes on the various descriptions of property is an act which seems to require the most exact impartiality; yet there is, perhaps, no legislative act in which greater opportunity and temptation are given to a predominant party to trample on the rules of justice. Every shilling with which they overburden the inferior number, is a shilling saved to their own pockets.

It is in vain to say that enlightened statesmen will be able to adjust these clashing interests, and render them all subservient to the public good. Enlightened statesmen will not always be at the helm. Nor, in many cases, can such an adjustment be made at all without taking into view indirect and remote considerations, which will rarely prevail over the immediate interest which one party may find in disregarding the rights of another or the good of the whole.

The inference to which we are brought is, that the causes of faction cannot be removed, and that relief is only to be sought in the means of controlling its effects.

If a faction consists of less than a majority, relief is supplied by the republican principle, which enables the majority to defeat its sinister views by regular vote. It may clog the administration, it may convulse the society; but it will be unable to execute and mask its violence under the forms of the Constitution. When a majority is included in a faction, the form of popular government, on the other hand, enables it to sacrifice to its ruling passion or interest both the public good and the rights of other citizens. To secure the public good and private rights against the danger of such a faction, and at the same time to preserve the spirit and the form of popular government, is then the great object to which our inquiries are directed. Let me add that it is the great desideratum by which this form of government can be rescued from the opprobrium under which it has so long labored, and be recommended to the esteem and adoption of mankind.

By what means is this object attainable? Evidently by one of two only. Either the existence of the same passion or interest in a majority at the same time must be prevented, or the majority, having such coexistent passion or interest, must be rendered, by their number and local situation, unable to concert and carry into effect schemes of oppression. If the impulse and the opportunity be suffered to coincide, we well know that neither moral nor religious motives can be relied on as an adequate control. They are not found to be such on the injustice and violence of individuals, and lose their efficacy in proportion to the number combined together, that is, in proportion as their efficacy becomes needful.

From this view of the subject it may be concluded that a pure democracy,[3] by which I mean a society consisting of a small number of citizens, who assemble and administer the government in person, can admit of no cure for the mischiefs of faction. A common passion or interest will, in almost every case, be felt by a majority of the whole; a communication and concert result from the form of government itself; and there is nothing to check the inducements to sacrifice the weaker party or an obnoxious individual. Hence it is that such democracies have ever been spectacles of turbulence and contention; have ever been found incompatible with personal security or the rights of property; and have in general been as short in their lives as they have been violent in their deaths. Theoretic politicians, who have patronized this species of government, have erroneously supposed that by reducing mankind to a perfect equality in their political rights, they would, at the same time, be perfectly equalized and assimilated in their possessions, their opinions, and their passions.

A republic, by which I mean a government in which the scheme of representation takes place, opens a different prospect, and promises the cure for which we are seeking. Let us examine the points in which it varies from pure democracy, and we shall comprehend both the nature of the cure and the efficacy which it must derive from the Union.

The two great points of difference between a democracy and a republic are: first, the delegation of the government, in the latter, to a small number of citizens elected by the rest; secondly, the greater number of citizens, and greater sphere of country, over which the latter may be extended.

The effect of the first difference is, on the one hand, to refine and enlarge the public views, by passing them through the medium of a chosen body of citizens, whose wisdom may best discern the true interest of their country, and whose patriotism and love of justice will be least likely to sacrifice it to temporary or partial considerations. Under such a regulation, it may well happen that the public voice, pronounced by the representatives of the people, will be more consonant to the public good than if pronounced by the people themselves, convened for the purpose. On the other hand, the effect may be inverted. Men of factious tempers, of local prejudices, or of sinister designs, may, by intrigue, by corruption, or by other means, first obtain the suffrages, and then betray the interests, of the people. The question resulting is, whether small or extensive republics are more favorable to the election of proper guardians of the public weal; and it is clearly decided in favor of the latter by two obvious considerations:

In the first place, it is to be remarked that, however small the republic may be, the representatives must be raised to a certain number, in order to guard against the cabals of a few; and that, however large it may be, they must be limited to a certain number, in order to guard against the confusion of a multitude. Hence, the number of representatives in the two cases not being in proportion to that of the two constituents, and being proportionally greater in the small republic, it follows that, if the proportion of fit characters be not less in the large than in the small republic, the former will present a greater option, and consequently a greater probability of a fit choice.

In the next place, as each representative will be chosen by a greater number of citizens in the large than in the small republic, it will be more difficult for unworthy candidates to practice with success the vicious arts by which elections are too often carried; and the suffrages of the people being more free, will be more likely to centre in men who possess the most attractive merit and the most diffusive and established characters.

It must be confessed that in this, as in most other cases, there is a mean, on both sides of which inconveniences will be found to lie. By enlarging too much the number of electors, you render the representatives too little acquainted with all their local circumstances and lesser interests; as by reducing it too much, you render him unduly attached to these, and too little fit to comprehend and pursue great and national objects. The federal Constitution forms a happy combination in this respect; the great and aggregate interests being referred to the national, the local and particular to the State legislatures.

The other point of difference is, the greater number of citizens and extent of territory which may be brought within the compass of republican than of democratic government; and it is this circumstance principally which renders factious combinations less to be dreaded in the former than in the latter. The smaller the society, the fewer probably will be the distinct parties and interests composing it; the fewer the distinct parties and interests, the more frequently will a majority be found of the same party; and the smaller the number of individuals composing a majority, and the smaller the compass within which they are placed, the more easily will they concert and execute their plans of oppression. Extend the sphere, and you take in a greater variety of parties and interests; you make it less probable that a majority of the whole will have a common motive to invade the rights of other citizens; or if such a common motive exists, it will be more difficult for all who feel it to discover their own strength, and to act in unison with each other. Besides other impediments, it may be remarked that, where there is a consciousness of unjust or dishonorable purposes, communication is always checked by distrust in proportion to the number whose concurrence is necessary.

Hence, it clearly appears, that the same advantage which a republic has over a democracy, in controlling the effects of faction, is enjoyed by a large over a small republic, —is enjoyed by the Union over the States composing it. Does the advantage consist in the substitution of representatives whose enlightened views and virtuous sentiments render them superior to local prejudices and schemes of injustice? It will not be denied that the representation of the Union will be most likely to possess these requisite endowments. Does it consist in the greater security afforded by a greater variety of parties, against the event of any one party being able to outnumber and oppress the rest? In an equal degree does the increased variety of parties comprised within the Union, increase this security. Does it, in fine, consist in the greater obstacles opposed to the concert and accomplishment of the secret wishes of an unjust and interested majority? Here, again, the extent of the Union gives it the most palpable advantage.

The influence of factious leaders may kindle a flame within their particular States, but will be unable to spread a general conflagration through the other States. A religious sect may degenerate into a political faction in a part of the Confederacy; but the variety of sects dispersed over the entire face of it must secure the national councils against any danger from that source. A rage for paper money, for an abolition of debts, for an equal division of property, or for any other improper or wicked project, will be less apt to pervade the whole body of the Union than a particular member of it; in the same proportion as such a malady is more likely to taint a particular county or district, than an entire State.

In the extent and proper structure of the Union, therefore, we behold a republican remedy for the diseases most incident to republican government. And according to the degree of pleasure and pride we feel in being republicans, ought to be our zeal in cherishing the spirit and supporting the character of Federalists.

Publius[4]

注释：

1. popular governments：平民政府。这里指由公民投票选举产生的共和政府。
2. 在约翰·洛克的理论框架中，个体持有的私有财产是个体自由的基本前提，是建立富裕社会的根本保障。
3. a pure democracy：一种纯粹的民主政体。在这里指古典共和主义——政府在追求公共性政府权力的同时实行直接民主，全体公民直接参与政府决策。古典共和主义的政治思想代表有古罗马帝国时期的西塞罗（Cicero，公元前106—公元前43）和普鲁塔克（Plutarch, 46—120）。后文中麦迪逊着重对比了两种政府形态：democracy（民主政体）和republic（共和政体）。democracy一词是前面a pure democracy的同义反复，republic意指实行间接民主的自由共和主义。
4. Publius：普布利乌斯。《联邦党人文集》在纽约报刊登载期间的署名，以此致敬建立罗马共和国的人民之友普布利乌斯·瓦雷列乌斯·普布利库拉（Publius Valerius Publicola）。

思考题：

1. Which one played a major role in ratifying the Constitution of America, *The Federalist Papers* or the natural historical progression?
2. Do you agree with Madison's stance on direct democracy and indirect democracy? And why?
3. Throughout American history, do you think the role of federal government stays consistent with Madison's description here?

5. The Constitution of the United States of America (1787)[①]

导读：

有别于多数国家先立国后制宪的做法，立国和立宪在美国经验中既共生又平行。宣告殖民地独立的《独立宣言》标志着美国跨出立国的第一步，其后的《邦联条例》（“Articles of Confederation”，1781—1789）将各自为政的邦[②]联系到了一起，而最终确立一个完整意义上的主权国家[③]则主要归功于立宪。

1776年7月4日大陆会议发表《独立宣言》，宣布“联合殖民地”[④]独立。次年11月15日，《邦联条例》应运而生；大陆会议相继转型为邦联国会（Congress of Confederation, 1781—1789），行使国家的立法职能。邦之联盟虽然在通往主权国家的道路上已迈出第二步，但作为国家其羽翼并不丰满[⑤]。对内，各邦基本保留财政权，邦联无权征税，难以应对通货膨胀，无法偿还独立战争期间欠下的高额债务[⑥]；同时各邦又大多拥有自己的成文宪法，邦联名义上可以制定法律，但往往形同虚

① “The United States Constitution”, http://constitutionus.com/ (accessed Oct. 2, 2021).

② 从《独立宣言》到《邦联条例》再到《宪法》，殖民地（colonies）从邦（State）演变成了联邦下的州（state）。由于《邦联条例》下的State拥有自己的独立立法权，具有半国家的性质，因此国内学界目前普遍选择“邦”一词与之对应。

③ 一般认为，主权国家应具备固定的领土、一定的居民、一定的政权组织形式以及建立外交关系的能力。

④《独立宣言》最后一段的功能是宣布独立，行文中对独立主体的描述选择了“United States of America”“United Colonies”“Independent States”。

⑤ 邦联政府在美国历史上虽然饱受诟病，但并非毫无建树。如邦联政府期间，各邦在西部土地开发的归属、权限和利益等问题上争执不休，1787年出台的《西北条例》（“Northwest Ordinance”）通过西部土地的国有化，统一了西部土地的开发程序，规避了各州在西部土地问题上的冲突，由此在一定程度上将后世的美国西进运动合法化了。

⑥ 独立战争期间欠下的债务可分为四类：拖欠法国的债款、以国家名义向殖民地居民征取的债款、各州向殖民地居民征取的债款和拖欠士兵的军饷。

设①。对外，面对外围的英军要塞、印第安人的袭击、西班牙的贸易封锁、海盗的勒索，邦联回应乏力；同时，半国家性质的邦联也在国际政治舞台上处境尴尬，难以行使完整主权国家的职能。1786年，独立战争的退伍军人谢斯（Daniel Shays, 1747—1825）以极端的武装暴动形式放大了邦联政府中的所有隐患。修订《邦联条例》势在必行。

1787年5月至9月，制宪会议在费城举行，整个过程非常困难。美国文化中根深蒂固的多元性决定了邦际利益的错综复杂。多数邦代表一方面在很多问题上存在颇多分歧，另一方面又迫于形势无奈出席。会议以辩论和民主表决的形式展开，整个过程中的分析、说服、权衡、讨价还价和妥协，理性而务实。不久，以修订《邦联条例》为初衷的费城会议转向开始制定新宪法。各邦间利益的多元性最终由纠葛和冲突演变成《宪法》中的求同存异、相互妥协，以及相互实现。

1787年《宪法》由序言和七条正文组成。序言以简短的一句话52词说明了制宪的原因和目的。宪法的前三条分别界定了联邦政府的三权分立。第四条规定了联邦和州的相互关系和权限，以及西部疆土的开拓程序。第五条重点阐释修宪。第六条的着眼点是合众国的法律体系以及国债的问题。第七条规定了《宪法》生效的程序。

值得一提的是，1787年《宪法》虽然没有直接提及奴隶或奴隶制，但却默认了奴隶制的合法性，如《宪法》第一条第二款中提到“所有其他人口之五分之三”（three fifths of all other Persons），这“所有其他人口”指的就是奴隶。

Preamble to the US Constitution

We the People of the United States, in Order to form a more perfect Union, establish Justice, insure domestic Tranquility, provide for the common defence, promote the general Welfare, and secure the Blessings of Liberty to ourselves and our Posterity, do ordain and establish this Constitution for the United States of America.

① 根据《邦联条例》，全国立法需要得到13个邦中至少9个邦的同意，这往往非常困难。

Article I

Section 1

All legislative Powers herein granted shall be vested in a Congress of the United States, which shall consist of a Senate and House of Representatives.

Section 2

1. The House of Representatives shall be composed of Members chosen every second Year by the People of the several States, and the Electors in each State shall have the Qualifications requisite for Electors of the most numerous Branch of the State Legislature.

2. No Person shall be a Representative who shall not have attained to the Age of twenty five Years, and been seven Years a Citizen of the United States, and who shall not, when elected, be an Inhabitant of that State in which he shall be chosen.

3. Representatives and direct Taxes shall be apportioned among the several States which may be included within this Union, according to their respective Numbers, which shall be determined by adding to the whole Number of free Persons, including those bound to Service for a Term of Years, and excluding Indians not taxed, three fifths of all other Persons.[1] The actual Enumeration shall be made within three Years after the first Meeting of the Congress of the United States, and within every subsequent Term of ten Years, in such Manner as they shall by Law direct. The Number of Representatives shall not exceed one for every thirty Thousand, but each State shall have at Least one Representative; and until such enumeration shall be made, the State of New Hampshire shall be entitled to chuse[2] three, Massachusetts eight, Rhode-Island and Providence Plantations one, Connecticut five, New-York six, New Jersey four, Pennsylvania eight, Delaware one, Maryland six, Virginia ten, North Carolina five, South Carolina five, and Georgia three.

4. When vacancies happen in the Representation from any State, the Executive Authority thereof shall issue Writs of Election to fill such Vacancies.

5. The House of Representatives shall chuse their Speaker and other Officers; and shall have the sole Power of Impeachment.

Section 3

1. The Senate of the United States shall be composed of two Senators from each State, chosen by the Legislature thereof, for six Years; and each Senator shall have one Vote.

2. Immediately after they shall be assembled in Consequence of the first Election, they shall be divided as equally as may be into three Classes. The Seats of the Senators of the first Class shall be vacated at the Expiration of the second Year, of the second Class at the Expiration of the fourth Year, and of the third Class at the Expiration of the sixth Year, so that one third may be chosen every second Year; and if Vacancies happen by Resignation, or otherwise, during the Recess of the Legislature of any State, the Executive thereof may make temporary Appointments until the next Meeting of the Legislature, which shall then fill such Vacancies.

3. No Person shall be a Senator who shall not have attained to the Age of thirty Years, and been nine Years a Citizen of the United States, and who shall not, when elected, be an Inhabitant of that State for which he shall be chosen.

4. The Vice President of the United States shall be President of the Senate, but shall have no Vote, unless they be equally divided.

5. The Senate shall chuse their other Officers, and also a President pro tempore, in the Absence of the Vice President, or when he shall exercise the Office of President of the United States.

6. The Senate shall have the sole Power to try all Impeachments. When sitting for that Purpose, they shall be on Oath or Affirmation. When the President of the United States is tried, the Chief Justice shall preside: And no Person shall be convicted without the Concurrence of two thirds of the Members present.

7. Judgment in Cases of impeachment shall not extend further than to removal from Office, and disqualification to hold and enjoy any Office of honor, Trust or Profit under the United States: but the Party convicted shall nevertheless be liable and subject to Indictment, Trial, Judgment and Punishment, according to Law.

Section 4

1. The Times, Places and Manner of holding Elections for Senators and Representatives, shall be prescribed in each State by the Legislature thereof; but the Congress may at any time by Law make or alter such Regulations, except as to the Places of chusing Senators.

2. The Congress shall assemble at least once in every Year, and such Meeting shall be on the first Monday in December, unless they shall by Law appoint a different Day.[3]

Section 5

1. Each House shall be the Judge of the Elections, Returns and Qualifications of its own Members, and a Majority of each shall constitute a Quorum to do Business; but a smaller Number may adjourn from day to day, and may be authorized to compel the Attendance of absent Members, in such Manner, and under such Penalties as each House may provide.

2. Each House may determine the Rules of its Proceedings, punish its Members for disorderly Behaviour, and, with the Concurrence of two thirds, expel a Member.

3. Each House shall keep a Journal of its Proceedings, and from time to time publish the same, excepting such Parts as may in their Judgment require Secrecy; and the Yeas and Nays[4] of the Members of either House on any question shall, at the Desire of one fifth of those Present, be entered on the Journal.

4. Neither House, during the Session of Congress, shall, without the Consent of the other, adjourn for more than three days, nor to any other Place than that in which the two Houses shall be sitting.

Section 6

1. The Senators and Representatives shall receive a Compensation for their Services, to be ascertained by Law, and paid out of the Treasury of the United States. They shall in all Cases, except Treason, Felony and Breach of the Peace, be privileged from Arrest during their Attendance at the Session of their respective Houses, and in going to and returning from the same; and for any Speech or Debate in either House, they shall not be questioned in any other Place.

2. No Senator or Representative shall, during the Time for which he was elected, be appointed to any civil Office under the Authority of the United States, which shall have been created, or the Emoluments whereof shall have been encreased[5] during such time; and no Person holding any Office under the United States, shall be a Member of either House during his Continuance in Office.

Section 7

1. All Bills for raising Revenue shall originate in the House of Representatives;

but the Senate may propose or concur with Amendments as on other Bills.

2. Every Bill which shall have passed the House of Representatives and the Senate, shall, before it become a Law, be presented to the President of the United States; If he approve he shall sign it, but if not he shall return it, with his Objections to that House in which it shall have originated, who shall enter the Objections at large on their Journal, and proceed to reconsider it. If after such Reconsideration two thirds of that House shall agree to pass the Bill, it shall be sent, together with the Objections, to the other House, by which it shall likewise be reconsidered, and if approved by two thirds of that House, it shall become a Law. But in all such Cases the Votes of both Houses shall be determined by yeas and Nays, and the Names of the Persons voting for and against the Bill shall be entered on the Journal of each House respectively. If any Bill shall not be returned by the President within ten Days (Sundays excepted) after it shall have been presented to him, the Same shall be a Law, in like Manner as if he had signed it, unless the Congress by their Adjournment prevent its Return, in which Case it shall not be a Law.

3. Every Order, Resolution, or Vote to which the Concurrence of the Senate and House of Representatives may be necessary (except on a question of Adjournment) shall be presented to the President of the United States; and before the Same shall take Effect, shall be approved by him, or being disapproved by him, shall be repassed by two thirds of the Senate and House of Representatives, according to the Rules and Limitations prescribed in the Case of a Bill.

Section 8

1. The Congress shall have Power To lay and collect Taxes, Duties, Imposts and Excises, to pay the Debts and provide for the common Defence and general Welfare of the United States; but all Duties, Imposts and Excises shall be uniform throughout the United States;

2. To borrow Money on the credit of the United States;

3. To regulate Commerce with foreign Nations, and among the several States, and with the Indian Tribes;

4. To establish an uniform Rule of Naturalization, and uniform Laws on the subject of Bankruptcies throughout the United States;

5. To coin Money, regulate the Value thereof, and of foreign Coin, and fix the Standard of Weights and Measures;

6. To provide for the Punishment of counterfeiting the Securities and current Coin of the United States;

7. To establish Post Offices and Post Roads;

8. To promote the Progress of Science and useful Arts, by securing for limited Times to Authors and Inventors the exclusive Right to their respective Writings and Discoveries;

9. To constitute Tribunals inferior to the supreme Court;

10. To define and punish Piracies and Felonies committed on the high Seas, and Offences against the Law of Nations;

11. To declare War, grant Letters of Marque and Reprisal, and make Rules concerning Captures on Land and Water;

12. To raise and support Armies, but no Appropriation of Money to that Use shall be for a longer Term than two Years;

13. To provide and maintain a Navy;

14. To make Rules for the Government and Regulation of the land and naval Forces;

15. To provide for calling forth the Militia to execute the Laws of the Union, suppress Insurrections and repel Invasions;

16. To provide for organizing, arming, and disciplining, the Militia, and for governing such Part of them as may be employed in the Service of the United States, reserving to the States respectively, the Appointment of the Officers, and the Authority of training the Militia according to the discipline prescribed by Congress;

17. To exercise exclusive Legislation in all Cases whatsoever, over such District (not exceeding ten Miles square) as may, by Cession of particular States, and the Acceptance of Congress, become the Seat of the Government of the United States, and to exercise like Authority over all Places purchased by the Consent of the Legislature of the State in which the Same shall be, for the Erection of Forts, Magazines, Arsenals, dock-Yards, and other needful Buildings;—And

18. To make all Laws which shall be necessary and proper for carrying into Execution the foregoing Powers, and all other Powers vested by this Constitution in the Government of the United States, or in any Department or Officer thereof.

Section 9

1. The Migration or Importation of such Persons as any of the States now existing shall think proper to admit, shall not be prohibited by the Congress prior to the Year

one thousand eight hundred and eight, but a Tax or duty may be imposed on such Importation, not exceeding ten dollars for each Person.

2. The Privilege of the Writ of Habeas Corpus[6] shall not be suspended, unless when in Cases of Rebellion or Invasion the public Safety may require it.

3. No Bill of Attainder or ex post facto Law shall be passed.

4. No Capitation, or other direct, Tax shall be laid, unless in Proportion to the Census or Enumeration herein before directed to be taken.

5. No Tax or Duty shall be laid on Articles exported from any State.

6. No Preference shall be given by any Regulation of Commerce or Revenue to the Ports of one State over those of another: nor shall Vessels bound to, or from, one State, be obliged to enter, clear, or pay Duties in another.

7. No Money shall be drawn from the Treasury, but in Consequence of Appropriations made by Law; and a regular Statement and Account of the Receipts and Expenditures of all public Money shall be published from time to time.

8. No Title of Nobility shall be granted by the United States: And no Person holding any Office of Profit or Trust under them, shall, without the Consent of the Congress, accept of any Present, Emolument, Office, or Title, of any kind whatever, from any King, Prince, or foreign State.

Section 10

1. No State shall enter into any Treaty, Alliance, or Confederation; grant Letters of Marque and Reprisal; coin Money; emit Bills of Credit; make any Thing but gold and silver Coin a Tender in Payment of Debts; pass any Bill of Attainder, ex post facto Law, or Law impairing the Obligation of Contracts, or grant any Title of Nobility.

2. No State shall, without the Consent of the Congress, lay any Imposts or Duties on Imports or Exports, except what may be absolutely necessary for executing it's inspection Laws: and the net Produce of all Duties and Imposts, laid by any State on Imports or Exports, shall be for the Use of the Treasury of the United States; and all such Laws shall be subject to the Revision and Controul[7] of the Congress.

3. No State shall, without the Consent of Congress, lay any Duty of Tonnage, keep Troops, or Ships of War in time of Peace, enter into any Agreement or Compact with another State, or with a foreign Power, or engage in War, unless actually invaded, or in such imminent Danger as will not admit of delay.

Article Ⅱ

Section 1

1. The executive Power shall be vested in a President of the United States of America. He shall hold his Office during the Term of four Years, and, together with the Vice President, chosen for the same Term, be elected, as follows.

2. Each State shall appoint, in such Manner as the Legislature thereof may direct, a Number of Electors, equal to the whole Number of Senators and Representatives to which the State may be entitled in the Congress: but no Senator or Representative, or Person holding an Office of Trust or Profit under the United States, shall be appointed an Elector.

3. The Electors shall meet in their respective States, and vote by Ballot for two Persons, of whom one at least shall not be an Inhabitant of the same State with themselves. And they shall make a List of all the Persons voted for, and of the Number of Votes for each; which List they shall sign and certify, and transmit sealed to the Seat of the Government of the United States, directed to the President of the Senate. The President of the Senate shall, in the Presence of the Senate and House of Representatives, open all the Certificates, and the Votes shall then be counted. The Person having the greatest Number of Votes shall be the President, if such Number be a Majority of the whole Number of Electors appointed; and if there be more than one who have such Majority, and have an equal Number of Votes, then the House of Representatives shall immediately chuse by Ballot one of them for President; and if no Person have a Majority, then from the five highest on the List the said House shall in like Manner chuse the President. But in chusing the President, the Votes shall be taken by States, the Representation from each State having one Vote; A quorum for this Purpose shall consist of a Member or Members from two thirds of the States, and a Majority of all the States shall be necessary to a Choice. In every Case, after the Choice of the President, the Person having the greatest Number of Votes of the Electors shall be the Vice President. But if there should remain two or more who have equal Votes, the Senate shall chuse from them by Ballot the Vice President.

4. The Congress may determine the Time of chusing the Electors, and the Day on which they shall give their Votes; which Day shall be the same throughout the United States.

5. No Person except a natural born Citizen, or a Citizen of the United States, at the time of the Adoption of this Constitution, shall be eligible to the Office of President; neither shall any Person be eligible to that Office who shall not have attained to the Age of thirty five Years, and been fourteen Years a Resident within the United States.

6. In Case of the Removal of the President from Office, or of his Death, Resignation, or Inability to discharge the Powers and Duties of the said Office, the Same shall devolve on the Vice President, and the Congress may by Law provide for the Case of Removal, Death, Resignation or Inability, both of the President and Vice President, declaring what Officer shall then act as President, and such Officer shall act accordingly, until the Disability be removed, or a President shall be elected.[8]

7. The President shall, at stated Times, receive for his Services, a Compensation, which shall neither be encreased nor diminished during the Period for which he shall have been elected, and he shall not receive within that Period any other Emolument from the United States, or any of them.

8. Before he enter on the Execution of his Office, he shall take the following Oath or Affirmation:—"I do solemnly swear (or affirm) that I will faithfully execute the Office of President of the United States, and will to the best of my Ability, preserve, protect and defend the Constitution of the United States."

Section 2

1. The President shall be Commander in Chief of the Army and Navy of the United States, and of the Militia of the several States, when called into the actual Service of the United States; he may require the Opinion, in writing, of the principal Officer in each of the executive Departments, upon any Subject relating to the Duties of their respective Offices, and he shall have Power to grant Reprieves and Pardons for Offences against the United States, except in Cases of Impeachment.

2. He shall have Power, by and with the Advice and Consent of the Senate, to make Treaties, provided two thirds of the Senators present concur; and he shall nominate, and by and with the Advice and Consent of the Senate, shall appoint Ambassadors, other public Ministers and Consuls, Judges of the supreme Court, and all other Officers of the United States, whose Appointments are not herein otherwise provided for, and which shall be established by Law: but the Congress may by Law vest the Appointment of such inferior Officers, as they think proper, in the President alone, in the Courts of Law, or in the Heads of Departments.

3. The President shall have Power to fill up all Vacancies that may happen during the Recess of the Senate, by granting Commissions which shall expire at the End of their next Session.

Section 3

He shall from time to time give to the Congress Information of the State of the Union, and recommend to their Consideration such Measures as he shall judge necessary and expedient; he may, on extraordinary Occasions, convene both Houses, or either of them, and in Case of Disagreement between them, with Respect to the Time of Adjournment, he may adjourn them to such Time as he shall think proper; he shall receive Ambassadors and other public Ministers; he shall take Care that the Laws be faithfully executed, and shall Commission all the Officers of the United States.

Section 4

The President, Vice President and all civil Officers of the United States, shall be removed from Office on Impeachment for, and Conviction of, Treason, Bribery, or other high Crimes and Misdemeanors.

Article Ⅲ

Section 1

The judicial Power of the United States, shall be vested in one supreme Court, and in such inferior Courts as the Congress may from time to time ordain and establish. The Judges, both of the supreme and inferior Courts, shall hold their Offices during good Behaviour, and shall, at stated Times, receive for their Services, a Compensation, which shall not be diminished during their Continuance in Office.

Section 2

1. The judicial Power shall extend to all Cases, in Law and Equity, arising under this Constitution, the Laws of the United States, and Treaties made, or which shall be made, under their Authority; —to all Cases affecting Ambassadors, other public Ministers and Consuls; —to all Cases of admiralty and maritime Jurisdiction; —to

Controversies to which the United States shall be a Party; —to Controversies between two or more States; —between a State and Citizens of another State; —between Citizens of different States, —between Citizens of the same State claiming Lands under Grants of different States, and between a State, or the Citizens thereof, and foreign States, Citizens or Subjects.

2. In all Cases affecting Ambassadors, other public Ministers and Consuls, and those in which a State shall be Party, the supreme Court shall have original Jurisdiction. In all the other Cases before mentioned, the supreme Court shall have appellate Jurisdiction, both as to Law and Fact, with such Exceptions, and under such Regulations as the Congress shall make.

3. The Trial of all Crimes, except in Cases of Impeachment, shall be by Jury; and such Trial shall be held in the State where the said Crimes shall have been committed; but when not committed within any State, the Trial shall be at such Place or Places as the Congress may by Law have directed.

Section 3

1. Treason against the United States, shall consist only in levying War against them, or in adhering to their Enemies, giving them Aid and Comfort. No Person shall be convicted of Treason unless on the Testimony of two Witnesses to the same overt Act, or on Confession in open Court.

2. The Congress shall have Power to declare the Punishment of Treason, but no Attainder of Treason shall work Corruption of Blood,[9] or Forfeiture except during the Life of the Person attainted.

Article Ⅳ

Section 1

Full Faith and Credit shall be given in each State to the public Acts, Records, and judicial Proceedings of every other State. And the Congress may by general Laws prescribe the Manner in which such Acts, Records and Proceedings shall be proved, and the Effect thereof.

Section 2

1. The Citizens of each State shall be entitled to all Privileges and Immunities of Citizens in the several States.

2. A Person charged in any State with Treason, Felony, or other Crime, who shall flee from Justice, and be found in another State, shall on Demand of the executive Authority of the State from which he fled, be delivered up, to be removed to the State having Jurisdiction of the Crime.

3. No Person held to Service or Labour in one State, under the Laws thereof, escaping into another, shall, in Consequence of any Law or Regulation therein, be discharged from such Service or Labour, but shall be delivered up on Claim of the Party to whom such Service or Labour may be due.

Section 3

1. New States may be admitted by the Congress into this Union; but no new State shall be formed or erected within the Jurisdiction of any other State; nor any State be formed by the Junction of two or more States, or Parts of States, without the Consent of the Legislatures of the States concerned as well as of the Congress.

2. The Congress shall have Power to dispose of and make all needful Rules and Regulations respecting the Territory or other Property belonging to the United States; and nothing in this Constitution shall be so construed as to Prejudice any Claims of the United States, or of any particular State.

Section 4

The United States shall guarantee to every State in this Union a Republican Form of Government, and shall protect each of them against Invasion; and on Application of the Legislature, or of the Executive (when the Legislature cannot be convened) against domestic Violence.

Article V

The Congress, whenever two thirds of both Houses shall deem it necessary, shall propose Amendments to this Constitution, or, on the Application of the Legislatures of two thirds of the several States, shall call a Convention for proposing Amendments, which, in either Case, shall be valid to all Intents and Purposes, as Part of this

Constitution, when ratified by the Legislatures of three fourths of the several States, or by Conventions in three fourths thereof, as the one or the other Mode of Ratification may be proposed by the Congress; Provided that no Amendment which may be made prior to the Year One thousand eight hundred and eight shall in any Manner affect the first and fourth Clauses in the Ninth Section of the first Article; and that no State, without its Consent, shall be deprived of its equal Suffrage in the Senate.

Article VI

1. All Debts contracted and Engagements entered into, before the Adoption of this Constitution, shall be as valid against the United States under this Constitution, as under the Confederation.

2. This Constitution, and the Laws of the United States which shall be made in Pursuance thereof; and all Treaties made, or which shall be made, under the Authority of the United States, shall be the supreme Law of the Land; and the Judges in every State shall be bound thereby, any Thing in the Constitution or Laws of any State to the Contrary notwithstanding.

3. The Senators and Representatives before mentioned, and the Members of the several State Legislatures, and all executive and judicial Officers, both of the United States and of the several States, shall be bound by Oath or Affirmation, to support this Constitution; but no religious Test shall ever be required as a Qualification to any Office or public Trust under the United States.

Article VII

The Ratification of the Conventions of nine States, shall be sufficient for the Establishment of this Constitution between the States so ratifying the Same.

Done in Convention by the Unanimous Consent of the States present the Seventeenth Day of September in the Year of our Lord one thousand seven hundred and Eighty seven and of the Independence of the United States of America the Twelfth In witness whereof We have hereunto subscribed our Names,

Go: Washington-Presidt. and deputy from Virginia

①Delaware: Geo: Read, Gunning Bedford jun, John Dickinson, Richard Bassett,

Jaco: Broom

②Virginia: John Blair-, James Madison Jr.

③South Carolina: J. Rutledge, Charles Cotesworth Pinckney, Charles Pinckney, Pierce Butler

④New Hampshire: John Langdon, Nicholas Gilman

⑤Connecticut: Wm. Saml. Johnson, Roger Sherman

⑥New Jersey: Wil. Livingston, David Brearly, Wm. Paterson, Jona: Dayton

⑦Maryland: James McHenry, Dan of St. Thos. Jenifer, Danl Carroll

⑧North Carolina: Wm Blount, Richd. Dobbs Spaight, Hu Williamson

⑨Georgia: William Few, Abr Baldwin

⑩Massachusetts: Nathaniel Gorham, Rufus King

⑪New York: Alexander Hamilton

⑫Pennsylvania: B. Franklin, Thomas Mifflin, Robt Morris, Geo. Clymer, Thos. Fitzsimons, Jared Ingersoll, James Wilson, Gouv Morris

注释：

1. 本条内容涉及各州在国会中的人数分配，该问题已由宪法第14条修正案修订。
2. chuse：同choose。
3. 本条涉及国会集会的规定，已由宪法第20条修正案修订。
4. Yeas and Nays：赞成票和反对票。
5. encrease：同increase。
6. Writ of Habeas Corpus：人身保护令。该法令规定被当局拘留的公民必须送往法院进行判决，旨在保护公民免于遭受政府实施的非法监督。
7. controul：同control。
8. 本条涉及总统卸任的细节，已由宪法第25条修正案修订。
9. Corruption of Blood：血统玷污。古代英国对于叛国罪的一种惩戒。这种惩戒除包含死刑外，还涉及剥夺被告家属的财产继承权的内容。

思考题：

1. What are the principles in Philadelphia Convention in 1787, in addition to its compromises?
2. How did the Americans stabilize their Constitution, and how did the Constitution stabilize American society in the early years of the United States?
3. What are the flexibility and the stability in American Constitution?

6. The Bill of Rights (1791) and Other Amendments to the Constitution (1798—1992)[①]

导读：

美国宪法是原则与妥协、稳固与机动的统一体。《宪法》诞生至今已有两百多年，但正文却从未有过修改，截至2021年共通过了27条修正案[②]。这些修正案在推动宪政与时俱进的同时，并未动摇《宪法》的基本精神。《宪法》和修正案就是在共和、法制、分权、制衡、统一、稳定等原则的框架下，尽可能地容纳、妥协、消解各利益群体之间的矛盾。

前十条修正案又称《权利法案》（“Bill of Rights”），是对《宪法》公民权部分的重要补充。1787年9月17日，在制宪会议通过后，《宪法》开始由邦联国会转交各邦进行投票表决。由此，制宪会议中那些未完的争论开始在广大民众中展开。论辩中，争论双方虽然在国家权力、邦权、公民权等问题上分歧大，然而却并没有输赢成败。以公民权为例，辩论伊始本来是一家之言，但随着剖析问题的步步深入，双方均越来越清楚地认识到缺乏人权保障的政府与权利滥用之间的天然联系[③]。于是，1789年4月的第一届国会便将制定《权利法案》提上日程，法案最终于1791年12月批准生效。

《权利法案》是美国宪政史上最快通过的修正案，在后来两百多年间成功通过的修正案总共不过17条。从《宪法》正文第五条可以看到，

---

① “The United States Constitution”, http://constitutionus.com/ (accessed Oct. 3, 2021).

② 美国历史上，国会讨论过的修正案已有一万余条。其中有六条修正案在参众两院的投票中以多数票通过，但未在规定时间内获得多数州的认可。最后正式生效的修正案仅27条。

③《宪法》正文实际存在一些关于人权的零散规定，如第一条第九节第二款的“The Privilege of the Writ of Habeas Corpus shall not be suspended, unless when in Cases of Rebellion or Invasion the public Safety may require it”，第八款的“No Title of Nobility shall be granted by the United States”等。但对于当时的广大美国民众来说，不久前英王的暴政仍然让他们心有余悸。这些松散而不成体系的条款远远不足以保障《独立宣言》中宣扬的生命权、自由权以及追求幸福的权利。

修正案生效的过程复杂而漫长，从国会提议到最终通过大多需要一至两年的时间①。修正案的内容自第11条往后开始延伸到美国政治、经济、文化的方方面面。如涉及联邦政府的第11、16条，关于政府官员选举的第12、17、20、22、25条，与公民的投票权相关的第15、19、24、26条等。每条修正案虽然言简意赅，但其历史文化底蕴深厚。

读一部美国《宪法》史就是在读一部美国社会史。笼统而抽象的《宪法》为美国的宪政带来稳定性和开放性。国父们将《宪法》的权威置于任何权力或个体之上，同时又将国家运行的具体细则留给了各州，留给了后世。在两百多年中，一代代的美国人正是在《宪法》精神的指引下，有选择地将社会文化环境过滤到修正案中，适应社会变迁，巩固宪政的稳定。

Amendments to the Constitution

Amendment Ⅰ（1791）

Congress shall make no law respecting an establishment of religion, or prohibiting the free exercise thereof; or abridging the freedom of speech, or of the press; or the right of the people peaceably to assemble, and to petition the Government for a redress of grievances.

Amendment Ⅱ（1791）

A well regulated Militia, being necessary to the security of a free State, the right of the people to keep and bear Arms, shall not be infringed.

Amendment Ⅲ（1791）

No Soldier shall, in time of peace be quartered in any house, without the consent of the Owner, nor in time of war, but in a manner to be prescribed by law.

① 美国历史上耗时最长的是第27条修正案，从1789年提案到1992年通过用时两百余年。

Amendment Ⅳ（1791）

The right of the people to be secure in their persons, houses, papers, and effects, against unreasonable searches and seizures, shall not be violated, and no Warrants shall issue, but upon probable cause, supported by Oath or affirmation, and particularly describing the place to be searched, and the persons or things to be seized.

Amendment Ⅴ（1791）

No person shall be held to answer for a capital, or otherwise infamous crime, unless on a presentment or indictment of a Grand Jury, except in cases arising in the land or naval forces, or in the Militia, when in actual service in time of War or public danger; nor shall any person be subject for the same offence to be twice put in jeopardy of life or limb; nor shall be compelled in any criminal case to be a witness against himself, nor be deprived of life, liberty, or property, without due process of law; nor shall private property be taken for public use, without just compensation.

Amendment Ⅵ（1791）

In all criminal prosecutions, the accused shall enjoy the right to a speedy and public trial, by an impartial jury of the State and district wherein the crime shall have been committed, which district shall have been previously ascertained by law, and to be informed of the nature and cause of the accusation; to be confronted with the witnesses against him; to have compulsory process for obtaining witnesses in his favor, and to have the Assistance of Counsel for his defence.

Amendment Ⅶ（1791）

In Suits at common law, where the value in controversy shall exceed twenty dollars, the right of trial by jury shall be preserved, and no fact tried by a jury, shall be otherwise re-examined in any Court of the United States, than according to the rules of the common law.

Amendment Ⅷ（1791）

Excessive bail shall not be required, nor excessive fines imposed, nor cruel and unusual punishments inflicted.

Amendment IX (1791)

The enumeration in the Constitution, of certain rights, shall not be construed to deny or disparage others retained by the people.

Amendment X (1791)

The powers not delegated to the United States by the Constitution, nor prohibited by it to the States, are reserved to the States respectively, or to the people.

Amendment XI (1798)

The Judicial power of the United States shall not be construed to extend to any suit in law or equity, commenced or prosecuted against one of the United States by Citizens of another State, or by Citizens or Subjects of any Foreign State.

Amendment XII (1804)

The Electors shall meet in their respective states, and vote by ballot for President and Vice-President, one of whom, at least, shall not be an inhabitant of the same state with themselves; they shall name in their ballots the person voted for as President, and in distinct ballots the person voted for as Vice-President, and they shall make distinct lists of all persons voted for as President, and of all persons voted for as Vice-President, and of the number of votes for each, which lists they shall sign and certify, and transmit sealed to the seat of the government of the United States, directed to the President of the Senate;

—The President of the Senate shall, in the presence of the Senate and House of Representatives, open all the certificates and the votes shall then be counted;

—The person having the greatest number of votes for President, shall be the President, if such number be a majority of the whole number of Electors appointed; and if no person have such majority, then from the persons having the highest numbers not exceeding three on the list of those voted for as President, the House of Representatives shall choose immediately, by ballot, the President. But in choosing the President, the votes shall be taken by states, the representation from each state having one vote; a quorum for this purpose shall consist of a member or members from two-thirds of the states, and a majority of all the states shall be necessary to a choice. And if the House of Representatives shall not choose a President whenever the right of choice shall devolve upon them, before the fourth day of March next following, then the

Vice-President shall act as President, as in the case of the death or other constitutional disability of the President.

—The person having the greatest number of votes as Vice-President, shall be the Vice-President, if such number be a majority of the whole number of Electors appointed, and if no person have a majority, then from the two highest numbers on the list, the Senate shall choose the Vice-President; a quorum for the purpose shall consist of two-thirds of the whole number of Senators, and a majority of the whole number shall be necessary to a choice. But no person constitutionally ineligible to the office of President shall be eligible to that of Vice-President of the United States.

Amendment XIII (1865) [1]

Neither slavery nor involuntary servitude, except as a punishment for crime whereof the party shall have been duly convicted, shall exist within the United States, or any place subject to their jurisdiction.

Congress shall have power to enforce this article by appropriate legislation.

Amendment XIV (1868)

1: All persons born or naturalized in the United States, and subject to the jurisdiction thereof, are citizens of the United States and of the State wherein they reside. No State shall make or enforce any law which shall abridge the privileges or immunities of citizens of the United States; nor shall any State deprive any person of life, liberty, or property, without due process of law; nor deny to any person within its jurisdiction the equal protection of the laws.

2: Representatives shall be apportioned among the several States according to their respective numbers, counting the whole number of persons in each State, excluding Indians not taxed. But when the right to vote at any election for the choice of electors for President and Vice President of the United States, Representatives in Congress, the Executive and Judicial officers of a State, or the members of the Legislature thereof, is denied to any of the male inhabitants of such State, being twenty-one years of age, and citizens of the United States, or in any way abridged, except for participation in rebellion, or other crime, the basis of representation therein shall be reduced in the proportion which the number of such male citizens shall bear to the whole number of male citizens twenty-one years of age in such State.

3: No person shall be a Senator or Representative in Congress, or elector of

President and Vice President, or hold any office, civil or military, under the United States, or under any State, who, having previously taken an oath, as a member of Congress, or as an officer of the United States, or as a member of any State legislature, or as an executive or judicial officer of any State, to support the Constitution of the United States, shall have engaged in insurrection or rebellion against the same, or given aid or comfort to the enemies thereof. But Congress may by a vote of two-thirds of each House, remove such disability.

4: The validity of the public debt of the United States, authorized by law, including debts incurred for payment of pensions and bounties for services in suppressing insurrection or rebellion, shall not be questioned. But neither the United States nor any State shall assume or pay any debt or obligation incurred in aid of insurrection or rebellion against the United States, or any claim for the loss or emancipation of any slave; but all such debts, obligations and claims shall be held illegal and void.

5: The Congress shall have power to enforce, by appropriate legislation, the provisions of this article.

Amendment XV（1870）

The right of citizens of the United States to vote shall not be denied or abridged by the United States or by any State on account of race, color, or previous condition of servitude.

The Congress shall have power to enforce this article by appropriate legislation.

Amendment XVI（1913）

The Congress shall have power to lay and collect taxes on incomes, from whatever source derived, without apportionment among the several States, and without regard to any census or enumeration.

Amendment XVII（1916）

1: The Senate of the United States shall be composed of two Senators from each State, elected by the people thereof, for six years; and each Senator shall have one vote. The electors in each State shall have the qualifications requisite for electors of the most numerous branch of the State legislatures.

2: When vacancies happen in the representation of any State in the Senate, the executive authority of such State shall issue writs of election to fill such vacancies: Provided, That the legislature of any State may empower the executive thereof to make temporary appointments until the people fill the vacancies by election as the legislature may direct.

3: This amendment shall not be so construed as to affect the election or term of any Senator chosen before it becomes valid as part of the Constitution.

Amendment XVIII (1919)

1: After one year from the ratification of this article the manufacture, sale, or transportation of intoxicating liquors within, the importation thereof into, or the exportation thereof from the United States and all territory subject to the jurisdiction thereof for beverage purposes is hereby prohibited.

2: The Congress and the several States shall have concurrent power[2] to enforce this article by appropriate legislation.

3: This article shall be inoperative unless it shall have been ratified as an amendment to the Constitution by the legislatures of the several States, as provided in the Constitution, within seven years from the date of the submission hereof to the States by the Congress.

Amendment XIX (1920) [3]

The right of citizens of the United States to vote shall not be denied or abridged by the United States or by any State on account of sex.

Congress shall have power to enforce this article by appropriate legislation.

Amendment XX (1933)

1: The terms of the President and Vice President shall end at noon on the 20th day of January, and the terms of Senators and Representatives at noon on the 3rd day of January, of the years in which such terms would have ended if this article had not been ratified; and the terms of their successors shall then begin.

2: The Congress shall assemble at least once in every year, and such meeting shall begin at noon on the 3rd day of January, unless they shall by law appoint a different day.

3: If, at the time fixed for the beginning of the term of the President, the President elect shall have died, the Vice President elect shall become President. If a President shall not have been chosen before the time fixed for the beginning of his term, or if the President elect shall have failed to qualify, then the Vice President elect shall act as President until a President shall have qualified; and the Congress may by law provide for the case wherein neither a President elect nor a Vice President elect shall have qualified, declaring who shall then act as President, or the manner in which one who is to act shall be selected, and such person shall act accordingly until a President or Vice President shall have qualified.

4: The Congress may by law provide for the case of the death of any of the persons from whom the House of Representatives may choose a President whenever the right of choice shall have devolved upon them, and for the case of the death of any of the persons from whom the Senate may choose a Vice President whenever the right of choice shall have devolved upon them.

5: Sections 1 and 2 shall take effect on the 15th day of October following the ratification of this article.

6: This article shall be inoperative unless it shall have been ratified as an amendment to the Constitution by the legislatures of three-fourths of the several States within seven years from the date of its submission.

Amendment XXI (1933)

1: The eighteenth article of amendment to the Constitution of the United States is hereby repealed.

2: The transportation or importation into any State, Territory, or possession of the United States for delivery or use therein of intoxicating liquors, in violation of the laws thereof, is hereby prohibited.

3: This article shall be inoperative unless it shall have been ratified as an amendment to the Constitution by conventions in the several States, as provided in the Constitution, within seven years from the date of the submission hereof to the States by the Congress.

Amendment XXII (1951)

1: No person shall be elected to the office of the President more than twice, and no person who has held the office of President, or acted as President, for more than two years of a term to which some other person was elected President shall be elected to the office of the President more than once. But this article shall not apply to any person holding the office of President when this article was proposed by the Congress, and shall not prevent any person who may be holding the office of President, or acting as President, during the term within which this article becomes operative from holding the office of President or acting as President during the remainder of such term.

2: This article shall be inoperative unless it shall have been ratified as an amendment to the Constitution by the legislatures of three-fourths of the several states within seven years from the date of its submission to the states by the Congress.

Amendment XXIII（1961）

1: The District constituting the seat of government of the United States shall appoint in such manner as the Congress may direct: A number of electors of President and Vice President equal to the whole number of Senators and Representatives in Congress to which the District would be entitled if it were a state, but in no event more than the least populous state; they shall be in addition to those appointed by the states, but they shall be considered, for the purposes of the election of President and Vice President, to be electors appointed by a state; and they shall meet in the District and perform such duties as provided by the twelfth article of amendment.

2: The Congress shall have power to enforce this article by appropriate legislation.

Amendment XXIV（1964）

1: The right of citizens of the United States to vote in any primary or other election for President or Vice President, for electors for President or Vice President, or for Senator or Representative in Congress, shall not be denied or abridged by the United States or any state by reason of failure to pay any poll tax[4] or other tax.

2: The Congress shall have power to enforce this article by appropriate legislation.

Amendment XXV（1967）

1: In case of the removal of the President from office or of his death or resignation, the Vice President shall become President.

2: Whenever there is a vacancy in the office of the Vice President, the President shall nominate a Vice President who shall take office upon confirmation by a majority vote of both Houses of Congress.

3: Whenever the President transmits to the President pro tempore[5] of the Senate and the Speaker of the House of Representatives his written declaration that he is unable to discharge the powers and duties of his office, and until he transmits to them a written declaration to the contrary, such powers and duties shall be discharged by the Vice President as Acting President.

4: Whenever the Vice President and a majority of either the principal officers of the executive departments or of such other body as Congress may by law provide, transmit to the President pro tempore of the Senate and the Speaker of the House of Representatives their written declaration that the President is unable to discharge the powers and duties of his office, the Vice President shall immediately assume the powers and duties of the office as Acting President.

Thereafter, when the President transmits to the President pro tempore of the Senate and the Speaker of the House of Representatives his written declaration that no inability exists, he shall resume the powers and duties of his office unless the Vice President and a majority of either the principal officers of the executive department or of such other body as Congress may by law provide, transmit within four days to the President pro tempore of the Senate and the Speaker of the House of Representatives their written declaration that the President is unable to discharge the powers and duties of his office. Thereupon Congress shall decide the issue, assembling within forty-eight hours for that purpose if not in session. If the Congress, within twenty-one days after receipt of the latter written declaration, or, if Congress is not in session, within twenty-one days after Congress is required to assemble, determines by two-thirds vote of both Houses that the President is unable to discharge the powers and duties of his office, the Vice President shall continue to discharge the same as Acting President; otherwise, the President shall resume the powers and duties of his office.

Amendment XXVI（1971）

1: The right of citizens of the United States, who are 18 years of age or older, to vote, shall not be denied or abridged by the United States or any state on account of age.

2: The Congress shall have the power to enforce this article by appropriate legislation.

Amendment XXVII（1992）

No law varying the compensation for the services of the Senators and Representatives shall take effect until an election of Representatives shall have intervened.

注释:

1. 对蓄奴问题，制宪会议的国父们出于政治需要采取了妥协的态度。对奴隶的描述，《宪法》正文选择了“other persons”，“a person held to Service or Labor”等隐晦的字眼，“奴隶制”（slavery）一词仅出现在后来的第13条修正案。为了解决1787年《宪法》中的这一历史遗留问题，林肯于1862年发表《解放奴隶宣言》（“The Emancipation Proclamation”）；国会又于1865年通过第13条修正案正式将废奴写进了《宪法》；1868年和1870年相继通过的第14和15条修正案，又为黑人的自由权、公民权和选举权提供了保障。
2. concurrent power：共同权利或并存权利，指联邦政府和州政府共同行使的权利。
3. 妇女选举权运动（Women's Suffrage Movement）的由来与1787年《宪法》相关。一方面，《宪法》正文在选举权的界定上模棱两可；另一方面又将具体的权利留给了各州，而各州在很长一段时间内均没有承认妇女的选举权。后来经过女权运动者的长期努力，1920年通过的第19条修正案正式赋予妇女选举权。
4. poll tax：人头税，同《宪法》正文第一条第九款的“capitation”，指向投票的选民征收的一类赋税。这一税种虽然额度不高，但通常会使穷人失去投票权，而第24条修正案意味着取缔了这一税种。
5. President pro tempore：参议院临时议长。在美国政体中，当兼任参议院议长的副总统因故无法组织参议院工作时，由参议院临时议长代替行使议长职权。

思考题:

1. Do you think “Bill of Rights” effectively protects people's civil rights? How do you comment on the content of the second Amendament?
2. Historically, how did different minority groups refer back to the Constitution and its amendments in their fighting for freedom and equality?
3. What is your understanding as to the interplay between the national power and civil rights?

7. First Inaugural Address (1789)[①]

George Washington

导读：

乔治·华盛顿（George Washington, 1723—1799）是独立战争时期的大陆军总司令，制宪会议主席，美国首任总统。他出生在弗吉尼亚的一个中层种植园家庭，七年战争期间为英军效力，积累了丰富的军事经验。27岁时他同当地一位富孀联姻，从而一跃成为北美殖民地最富有的种植园主之一。凭借战时的英勇事迹以及其名下的种植园产业，华盛顿开始在殖民地政坛崭露头角。在众多国父中，华盛顿的才能不在于拥有富兰克林（Benjamin Franklin, 1706—1790）般的博学，也不在于拥有麦迪逊（James Madison, 1751—1836）那样深厚的司法功底，他一生赢得的名誉和威望主要来自他的人格魅力、政治智慧和领导才能。

独立战争期间，华盛顿手握军事大权，在大小战役中展现了卓越的军事才能和领导艺术。殖民地独立后，处在权力巅峰的他虽然主张建立一个强大的中央政府，但主动解甲归田，返回家乡重新开始经营维农山庄园（Mount Vernon）[②]，以身作则，维护共和精神。

邦联政府期间，华盛顿受邀重返政坛，凭借自身的威望和领导力，将13个多元利益集团聚集到制宪会议，同时又以超越本邦利益的姿态主持、协调整个会议进程。会议期间他虽然力推《弗吉尼亚方案》，但作为会议主席并无实质性发言，仅以邦代表的身份投票附议。

制宪会议后华盛顿虽然重返家乡经营庄园，但在第一届大选上他众望所归，于1789年4月以全票当选第一任总统。

华盛顿第一届任期的就职演说共分六段：第一段表达了他就任总统职位时诚惶诚恐的心情；第二段着重论述美国革命是天命所归；

① George Washington, “First Inaugural Address of George Washington”, http://avalon.law.yale.edu/18th_century/wash1.asp (accessed Oct. 3, 2021).

② Mount Vernon又译“芒特弗农”或“弗农山庄”，位于美国弗吉尼亚州北部的费尔法克斯县（Fairfax County），是华盛顿的故居。华盛顿夫妇曾在此经营庄园，兴办小型织布厂，酿造威士忌。

其后三段援引了《宪法》第二条第三款中提及的“将他认为必要而适宜的措施提请国会审议”①，分别讨论了政府部门的权限、修宪和总统薪酬等问题；最后一段做出总结。字里行间，华盛顿理性而谦逊，对合众国的热爱之情和尽忠之心一览无遗。1787年《宪法》中并无对就职演说的规定，首任就职演说开创了先河，后世的美国总统纷纷效仿。

Fellow-Citizens of the Senate and of the House of Representatives:

Among the vicissitudes incident to life no event could have filled me with greater anxieties than that of which the notification was transmitted by your order,[1] and received on the 14th day of the present month. On the one hand, I was summoned by my Country, whose voice I can never hear but with veneration and love, from a retreat which I had chosen with the fondest predilection, and, in my flattering hopes, with an immutable decision, as the asylum of my declining years—a retreat which was rendered every day more necessary as well as more dear to me by the addition of habit to inclination, and of frequent interruptions in my health to the gradual waste committed on it by time. On the other hand, the magnitude and difficulty of the trust to which the voice of my country called me, being sufficient to awaken in the wisest and most experienced of her citizens a distrustful scrutiny into his qualifications, could not but overwhelm with despondence one who (inheriting inferior endowments from nature and unpracticed in the duties of civil administration) ought to be peculiarly conscious of his own deficiencies. In this conflict of emotions all I dare aver is that it has been my faithful study to collect my duty from a just appreciation of every circumstance by which it might be affected. All I dare hope is that if, in executing this task, I have been too much swayed by a grateful remembrance of former instances, or by an affectionate sensibility to this transcendent proof of the confidence of my fellow-citizens, and have thence too little consulted my incapacity as well as disinclination for the weighty and untried cares before me, my error will be palliated by the motives which mislead me, and its consequences be judged by my country with some share of the partiality in which they originated.

Such being the impressions under which I have, in obedience to the public

① 这里的原文是“He shall [...] recommend to their Consideration such Measures as he shall judge necessary and expedient; [...]”。“He”在这里指总统。

summons, repaired to the present station, it would be peculiarly improper to omit in this first official act my fervent supplications to that Almighty Being who rules over the universe, who presides in the councils of nations, and whose providential aids can supply every human defect, that His benediction may consecrate to the liberties and happiness of the people of the United States a Government instituted by themselves for these essential purposes, and may enable every instrument employed in its administration to execute with success the functions allotted to his charge. In tendering this homage to the Great Author[2] of every public and private good, I assure myself that it expresses your sentiments not less than my own, nor those of my fellow-citizens at large less than either.[3] No people can be bound to acknowledge and adore the Invisible Hand which conducts the affairs of men more than those of the United States. Every step by which they have advanced to the character of an independent nation seems to have been distinguished by some token of providential agency; and in the important revolution just accomplished in the system of their united government the tranquil deliberations and voluntary consent of so many distinct communities from which the event has resulted can not be compared with the means by which most governments have been established without some return of pious gratitude, along with an humble anticipation of the future blessings which the past seem to presage. These reflections, arising out of the present crisis, have forced themselves too strongly on my mind to be suppressed. You will join with me, I trust, in thinking that there are none under the influence of which the proceedings of a new and free government can more auspiciously commence.

By the article establishing the executive department it is made the duty of the President "to recommend to your consideration such Measures as he shall judge necessary and expedient. "[4] The circumstances under which I now meet you will acquit me from entering into that subject further than to refer to the great constitutional charter under which you are assembled, and which, in defining your powers, designates the objects to which your attention is to be given. It will be more consistent with those circumstances, and far more congenial with the feelings which actuate me, to substitute, in place of a recommendation of particular measures, the tribute that is due to the talents, the rectitude, and the patriotism which adorn the characters selected to devise and adopt them. In these honorable qualifications I behold the surest pledges that as on one side no local prejudices or attachments, no separate views nor party animosities, will misdirect the comprehensive and equal eye which ought to watch over this great assemblage of communities and interests, so, on another, that the foundation of our national policy will be laid in the pure and immutable principles of private morality, and the preeminence of free government be exemplified by all the attributes which can win the affections of its citizens and command the respect of the world. I dwell on this prospect with every satisfaction which an ardent love for my country can inspire, since there is no truth more thoroughly established than that there exists in the economy and course of nature an indissoluble union between virtue and happiness; between duty and advantage; between the genuine maxims of an honest and magnanimous policy and the solid rewards of public prosperity and felicity; since we ought to be no less persuaded that the propitious smiles of Heaven can never be expected on a nation that disregards the eternal rules of order and right which Heaven itself has ordained; and since the preservation of the sacred fire of liberty and the destiny of the republican model of government are justly considered, perhaps, as deeply, as finally, staked on the experiment entrusted to the hands of the American people.

Besides the ordinary objects submitted to your care, it will remain with your judgment to decide how far an exercise of the occasional power delegated by the fifth article of the Constitution is rendered expedient at the present juncture by the nature of objections which have been urged against the system, or by the degree of inquietude which has given birth to them. Instead of undertaking particular recommendations on this subject, in which I could be guided by no lights derived from official opportunities, I shall again give way to my entire confidence in your discernment and pursuit of the public good; for I assure myself that whilst you carefully avoid every alteration which might endanger the benefits of an united and effective government, or which ought to await the future lessons of experience, a reverence for the characteristic rights of freemen and a regard for the public harmony will sufficiently influence your deliberations on the question how far the former can be impregnably fortified or the latter be safely and advantageously promoted.

To the foregoing observations I have one to add, which will be most properly addressed to the House of Representatives. It concerns myself, and will therefore be as brief as possible. When I was first honored with a call into the service of my country, then on the eve of an arduous struggle for its liberties, the light in which I contemplated my duty required that I should renounce every pecuniary compensation. From this resolution I have in no instance departed; and being still under the impressions which produced it, I must decline as inapplicable to myself any share in the personal emoluments which may be indispensably included in a permanent provision for the executive department, and must accordingly pray that the pecuniary estimates for the station in which I am placed may during my continuance in it be limited to such actual expenditures as the public good may be thought to require.

Having thus imparted to you my sentiments as they have been awakened by the occasion which brings us together, I shall take my present leave; but not without resorting once more to the benign Parent of the Human Race in humble supplication that, since He has been pleased to favor the American people with opportunities for deliberating in perfect tranquillity, and dispositions for deciding with unparalleled unanimity on a form of government for the security of their union and the advancement of their happiness, so His divine blessing may be equally conspicuous in the enlarged views, the temperate consultations, and the wise measures on which the success of this Government must depend.

注释：

1. the notification was transmitted by your order：奉广大人民之命。同第二段中的public summon。
2. Great Author：在此指上帝。
3. nor those of my fellow-citizens at large less than either：either在此指华盛顿以及现场出席的官员。
4. By the article establishing the executive department it is made the duty of the President "to recommend to your consideration such measures as he shall judge necessary and expedient." 出自《宪法》第二条第三款。

思考题：

1. George Washington was one of the few wealthiest planters in Virginia. How did he stand on slavery?
2. How does George Washington's first inaugural speech refer back to the Article II and Article V of the Constitution?
3. What are the major "sentiments" that George Washington expresses in this speech? Please comment on each of them.

8. Farewell Address (1796)[①]

George Washington

导读：

1789年，乔治·华盛顿在举国一致拥戴中当选首任总统。历经八年对外战争和八年内政的紊乱，美国国力贫弱，国库空虚，对外贸易举步维艰。华盛顿出任总统一职从精神上维护了建国初期的稳定。面对复杂多变的国内外形势，两届任期内他谨言慎行，励精图治，时刻以维系国家统一为己任。在华盛顿政府的努力下国家运行逐渐走上正轨。

内政方面，华盛顿政府依据《宪法》的分权精神，着手搭建了联邦的司法和行政体系。通过设立内阁[②]、最高法院、财政部、战争部（Department of War）[③]等部门，国家政权的组织架构逐步完善。同时，华盛顿公开支持《权利法案》，上任11个月后该法案生效。在杰斐逊和汉密尔顿的分歧上，为维护新生联邦的统一和稳定，华盛顿着力规避派系之争，一生都未加入任何政党。虽然他尽力调停派系之争，但因支持联邦党人关于工商立国[④]的主张，第一届任期后他与来自民主共和党（Democratic-Republican Party）的杰斐逊分道扬镳。

对外事务上，18世纪后半叶美国人与印第安人在西北边疆冲突频仍。1790年华盛顿出兵平定战乱，成功地将俄亥俄州和部分印第安那州纳入美国版图。在同一时期的英法冲突中，出于对新生国家国力的考虑，华盛顿两届任期内尽量保持中立，避免为任何一方提供援助。然而

① George Washington, "Washington's Farewell Address 1796", http://avalon.law.yale.edu/18th_century/washing.asp (accessed Oct. 3, 2021).

② 首任内阁的成员包括副总统约翰·亚当斯（John Adams, 1735—1826）、国务卿托马斯·杰斐逊、财政部长亚历山大·汉密尔顿、战争部长亨利·诺克斯（Henry Knox, 1750—1806）、司法部长埃德蒙·伦道夫（Edmund Randolph, 1753—1813）、邮政部长塞缪尔·奥斯古德（Samuel Osgood, 1747—1813）。

③ 战争部于1947年改组为现在的美国国防部（Department of Defense）。

④ 独立战争期间北美殖民地外债高筑，邦联政府时期国库空虚，危机四伏。第一届政府上任后需要优先解决的问题就是国债。在此问题上，汉密尔顿主张工商立国，提出发行国债，建立国家税收体系；成立联邦银行，统一全国的金融体系。而杰斐逊则主张农业立国，倾向于保护南部农场主的利益。

1795年英美签订《杰依条约》（“Jay Treaty”）后，美国在贸易上逐渐偏向英国①，独立战争以来的美法联盟自此终结。此外，联邦政府还通过筹建海军部队，解决了常年困扰美国商船的海盗问题。

1796年9月两届任期届满后，华盛顿公开发表了美国历史上第一份总统《告别辞》②。《告别辞》首先陈述了主动卸任的缘由。而后集中就国内外相关问题进行了分析和建议，其中包括民族团结、党派政治和国家统一，三权分立和独裁政治，宗教信仰、道德操守和国家兴衰，孤立主义和对外贸易等。华盛顿的主动卸任保护了政权的和平移交，捍卫了共和传统。

Friends and Citizens:

The period for a new election of a citizen, to administer the executive government of the United States, being not far distant, and the time actually arrived, when your thoughts must be employed designating the person, who is to be clothed with that important trust, it appears to me proper, especially as it may conduce to a more distinct expression of the public voice, that I should now apprize you of the resolution I have formed, to decline being considered among the number of those out of whom a choice is to be made.

I beg you, at the same time, to do me the justice to be assured that this resolution has not been taken without a strict regard to all the considerations appertaining to the relation which binds a dutiful citizen to his country; and that in withdrawing the tender of service, which silence in my situation might imply, I am influenced by no diminution of zeal for your future interest, no deficiency of grateful respect for your past kindness, but am supported by a full conviction that the step is compatible with both.

The acceptance of, and continuance hitherto in, the office to which your suffrages

① 《杰依条约》的签订承认了英国在军事和贸易上的国际主导地位；美国的国际贸易开始偏向英国，空虚的国库迅速得到了补充；英军同时允诺撤出西北边疆；双方由此实现了一定时期内的和平共处。然而，该条约在国内并未得到普遍拥护，反对的声音主要集中在：（1）独立战争期间美法结成的友好同盟应该受到保护，而不应该被该条约打破；（2）部分美国人担心同君主制的英国开展贸易会在国内滋生君主制萌芽；（3）杰斐逊支持农业立国，怀疑过分扩展贸易会对国家发展产生危害。

② 18世纪末的科技不允许华盛顿的告别演说像今天一样通过电视在全国传播。告别演说最终以书面形式在各州报纸上刊登。因此，告别演说严格意义上讲并不是演说，而是告别辞。

have twice called me have been a uniform sacrifice of inclination to the opinion of duty, and to a deference for what appeared to be your desire. I constantly hoped, that it would have been much earlier in my power, consistently with motives, which I was not at liberty to disregard, to return to that retirement, from which I had been reluctantly drawn. The strength of my inclination to do this, previous to the last election, had even led to the preparation of an address to declare it to you; but mature reflection on the then perplexed and critical posture of our affairs with foreign nations, and the unanimous advice of persons entitled to my confidence, impelled me to abandon the idea.

I rejoice that the state of your concerns, external as well as internal, no longer renders the pursuit of inclination incompatible with the sentiment of duty or propriety, and am persuaded, whatever partiality may be retained for my services, that, in the present circumstances of our country, you will not disapprove my determination to retire.

The impressions with which I first undertook the arduous trust were explained on the proper occasion.[1] In the discharge of this trust, I will only say, that I have, with good intentions, contributed towards the organization and administration of the government the best exertions of which a very fallible judgment was capable. Not unconscious in the outset of the inferiority of my qualifications, experience in my own eyes, perhaps still more in the eyes of others, has strengthened the motives to diffidence of myself; and every day the increasing weight of years admonishes me more and more that the shade of retirement is as necessary to me as it will be welcome. Satisfied that if any circumstances have given peculiar value to my services, they were temporary, I have the consolation to believe that, while choice and prudence invite me to quit the political scene, patriotism does not forbid it.

In looking forward to the moment which is intended to terminate the career of my public life, my feelings do not permit me to suspend the deep acknowledgment of that debt of gratitude which I owe to my beloved country for the many honors it has conferred upon me; still more for the steadfast confidence with which it has supported me; and for the opportunities I have thence enjoyed of manifesting my inviolable attachment, by services faithful and persevering, though in usefulness unequal to my zeal. If benefits have resulted to our country from these services, let it always be remembered to your praise, and as an instructive example in our annals, that under circumstances in which the passions, agitated in every direction, were liable to mislead, amidst appearances sometimes dubious, vicissitudes of fortune often discouraging, in situations in which not unfrequently want of success has countenanced the spirit of criticism, the constancy of your support was the essential prop of the efforts, and a guarantee of the plans by which they were effected. Profoundly penetrated with this idea, I shall carry it with me to my grave, as a strong incitement to unceasing vows that heaven may continue to you the choicest tokens of its beneficence; that your union and brotherly affection may be perpetual; that the free constitution, which is the work of your hands, may be sacredly maintained; that its administration in every department may be stamped with wisdom and virtue; that, in fine, the happiness of the people of these States, under the auspices of liberty, may be made complete by so careful a preservation and so prudent a use of this blessing as will acquire to them the glory of recommending it to the applause, the affection, and adoption of every nation which is yet a stranger to it.

Here, perhaps, I ought to stop. But a solicitude for your welfare which cannot end but with my life, and the apprehension of danger, natural to that solicitude, urge me, on an occasion like the present, to offer to your solemn contemplation, and to recommend to your frequent review, some sentiments which are the result of much reflection, of no inconsiderable observation, and which appear to me all-important to the permanency of your felicity as a people. These will be offered to you with the more freedom, as you can only see in them the disinterested warnings of a parting friend, who can possibly have no personal motive to bias his counsel. Nor can I forget, as an encouragement to it, your indulgent reception of my sentiments on a former and not dissimilar occasion.

Interwoven as is the love of liberty with every ligament of your hearts, no recommendation of mine is necessary to fortify or confirm the attachment.

The unity of government which constitutes you one people is also now dear to you. It is justly so, for it is a main pillar in the edifice of your real independence, the support of your tranquillity at home, your peace abroad; of your safety; of your prosperity; of that very liberty which you so highly prize. But as it is easy to foresee that, from different causes and from different quarters, much pains will be taken, many artifices employed to weaken in your minds the conviction of this truth; as this is the point in your political fortress against which the batteries of internal and external enemies will be most constantly and actively (though often covertly and insidiously) directed, it is of infinite moment that you should properly estimate the immense value of your national union to your collective and individual happiness; that you should cherish a cordial, habitual, and immovable attachment to it; accustoming yourselves to think and speak of it as of the palladium of your political safety and prosperity; watching for its preservation with jealous anxiety; discountenancing whatever may suggest even a suspicion that it can in any event be abandoned; and indignantly frowning upon the first dawning of every attempt to alienate any portion of our country from the rest, or to enfeeble the sacred ties which now link together the various parts.

For this you have every inducement of sympathy and interest. Citizens, by birth or choice, of a common country, that country has a right to concentrate your affections. The name of American, which belongs to you in your national capacity, must always exalt the just pride of patriotism more than any appellation derived from local discriminations. With slight shades of difference, you have the same religion, manners, habits, and political principles. You have in a common cause fought and triumphed together; the independence and liberty you possess are the work of joint counsels, and joint efforts of common dangers, sufferings, and successes.

But these considerations, however powerfully they address themselves to your sensibility, are greatly outweighed by those, which apply more immediately to your interest. Here every portion of our country finds the most commanding motives for carefully guarding and preserving the Union of the whole.

The North, in an unrestrained intercourse with the South, protected by the equal laws of a common government, finds in the productions of the latter great additional resources of maritime and commercial enterprise and precious materials of manufacturing industry. The South, in the same intercourse, benefiting by the agency of the North, sees its agriculture grow and its commerce expand. Turning partly into its own channels the seamen of the North, it finds its particular navigation invigorated; and, while it contributes, in different ways, to nourish and increase the general mass of the national navigation, it looks forward to the protection of a maritime strength, to which itself is unequally adapted. The East, in a like intercourse with the West, already finds, and in the progressive improvement of interior communications by land and water, will more and more find a valuable vent for the commodities which it brings from abroad, or manufactures at home. The West derives from the East supplies requisite to its growth and comfort, and, what is perhaps of still greater consequence, it must of necessity owe the secure enjoyment of indispensable outlets for its own productions to the weight, influence, and the future maritime strength of the Atlantic side of the Union, directed by an indissoluble community of interest as one nation.

Any other tenure by which the West can hold this essential advantage, whether derived from its own separate strength, or from an apostate and unnatural connexion with any foreign power, must be intrinsically precarious.

While, then, every part of our country thus feels an immediate and particular interest in union, all the parts combined cannot fail to find in the united mass of means and efforts greater strength, greater resource, proportionably greater security from external danger, a less frequent interruption of their peace by foreign nations; and, what is of inestimable value, they must derive from union an exemption from those broils and wars between themselves, which so frequently afflict neighbouring countries not tied together by the same governments, which their own rival ships alone would be sufficient to produce, but which opposite foreign alliances, attachments, and intrigues would stimulate and embitter. Hence, likewise, they will avoid the necessity of those overgrown military establishments which, under any form of government, are inauspicious to liberty, and which are to be regarded as particularly hostile to republican Liberty. In this sense it is, that your union ought to be considered as a main prop of your liberty, and that the love of the one ought to endear to you the preservation of the other.

These considerations speak a persuasive language to every reflecting and virtuous mind, and exhibit the continuance of the Union as a primary object of patriotic desire. Is there a doubt, whether a common government can embrace so large a sphere? Let experience solve it. To listen to mere speculation in such a case were criminal. We are authorized to hope that a proper organization of the whole with the auxiliary agency of governments for the respective subdivisions, will afford a happy issue to the experiment. It is well worth a fair and full experiment. With such powerful and obvious motives to union, affecting all parts of our country, while experience shall not have demonstrated its impracticability, there will always be reason to distrust the patriotism of those who in any quarter may endeavour to weaken its bands.

In contemplating the causes, which may disturb our Union, it occurs as matter of serious concern, that any ground should have been furnished for characterizing parties by geographical discriminations, Northern and Southern, Atlantic and Western; whence designing men may endeavour to excite a belief that there is a real difference of local interests and views. One of the expedients of party to acquire influence within particular districts is to misrepresent the opinions and aims of other districts. You cannot shield yourselves too much against the jealousies and heartburnings which spring from these misrepresentations; they tend to render alien to each other those who ought to be bound together by fraternal affection. The inhabitants of our Western country have lately had a useful lesson on this head; they have seen, in the negotiation by the Executive, and in the unanimous ratification by the Senate, of the treaty with Spain, and in the universal satisfaction at that event, throughout the United States, a decisive proof how unfounded were the suspicions propagated among them of a policy in the General Government and in the Atlantic States unfriendly to their interests in regard to the Mississippi; they have been witnesses to the formation of two treaties, that with Great Britain, and that with Spain, which secure to them everything they could desire, in respect to our foreign relations, towards confirming their prosperity. Will it not be their wisdom to rely for the preservation of these advantages on the Union by which they were procured? Will they not henceforth be deaf to those advisers, if such there are, who would sever them from their brethren, and connect them with aliens?

To the efficacy and permanency of your Union, a government for the whole is indispensable. No alliances, however strict, between the parts can be an adequate substitute; they must inevitably experience the infractions and interruptions which all alliances in all times have experienced. Sensible of this momentous truth, you have improved upon your first essay, by the adoption of a constitution of government better calculated than your former for an intimate union, and for the efficacious management of your common concerns. This government, the offspring of our own choice, uninfluenced and unawed, adopted upon full investigation and mature deliberation, completely free in its principles, in the distribution of its powers, uniting security with energy, and containing within itself a provision for its own amendment, has a just claim to your confidence and your support. Respect for its authority, compliance with its laws, acquiescence in its measures, are duties enjoined by the fundamental maxims of true liberty. The basis of our political systems is the right of the people to make and to alter their constitutions of government. But the Constitution which at any time exists, till changed by an explicit and authentic act of the whole people, is sacredly obligatory upon all. The very idea of the power and the right of the people to establish government presupposes the duty of every individual to obey the established government.

All obstructions to the execution of the laws, all combinations and associations, under whatever plausible character, with the real design to direct, control, counteract, or awe the regular deliberation and action of the constituted authorities, are destructive of this fundamental principle, and of fatal tendency. They serve to organize faction, to give it an artificial and extraordinary force; to put, in the place of the delegated will of the nation, the will of a party, often a small but artful and enterprising minority of the community; and, according to the alternate triumphs of different parties, to make the public administration the mirror of the ill-concerted and incongruous projects of faction, rather than the organ of consistent and wholesome plans digested by common counsels and modified by mutual interests.

However combinations or associations of the above description may now and then answer popular ends, they are likely, in the course of time and things, to become potent engines, by which cunning, ambitious, and unprincipled men will be enabled to subvert the power of the people and to usurp for themselves the reins of government, destroying afterwards the very engines which have lifted them to unjust dominion.

Towards the preservation of your government, and the permanency of your present happy state, it is requisite, not only that you steadily discountenance irregular oppositions to its acknowledged authority, but also that you resist with care the spirit of innovation upon its principles, however specious the pretexts. One method of assault may be to effect, in the forms of the Constitution, alterations which will impair the energy of the system, and thus to undermine what cannot be directly overthrown. In all the changes to which you may be invited, remember that time and habit are at least as necessary to fix the true character of governments as of other human institutions; that experience is the surest standard by which to test the real tendency of the existing constitution of a country; that facility in changes, upon the credit of mere hypothesis and opinion, exposes to perpetual change, from the endless variety of hypothesis and opinion; and remember, especially, that for the efficient management of your common interests, in a country so extensive as ours, a government of as much vigor as is consistent with the perfect security of liberty is indispensable. Liberty itself will find in such a government, with powers properly distributed and adjusted, its surest guardian. It is, indeed, little else than a name, where the government is too feeble to withstand the enterprises of faction, to confine each member of the society within the limits prescribed by the laws, and to maintain all in the secure and tranquil enjoyment of the rights of person and property.

I have already intimated to you the danger of parties in the State, with particular reference to the founding of them on geographical discriminations. Let me now take a more comprehensive view, and warn you in the most solemn manner against the baneful effects of the spirit of party generally.

This spirit, unfortunately, is inseparable from our nature, having its root in the strongest passions of the human mind. It exists under different shapes in all governments, more or less stifled, controlled, or repressed; but, in those of the popular form, it is seen in its greatest rankness, and is truly their worst enemy.

The alternate domination of one faction over another, sharpened by the spirit of revenge, natural to party dissension, which in different ages and countries has perpetrated the most horrid enormities, is itself a frightful despotism. But this leads at length to a more formal and permanent despotism. The disorders and miseries which result gradually incline the minds of men to seek security and repose in the absolute power of an individual; and sooner or later the chief of some prevailing faction, more able or more fortunate than his competitors, turns this disposition to the purposes of his own elevation, on the ruins of public liberty.

Without looking forward to an extremity of this kind, (which nevertheless ought not to be entirely out of sight), the common and continual mischiefs of the spirit of party are sufficient to make it the interest and duty of a wise people to discourage and restrain it.

It serves always to distract the public councils and enfeeble the public administration. It agitates the community with ill-founded jealousies and false alarms, kindles the animosity of one part against another, foments occasionally riot and insurrection. It opens the door to foreign influence and corruption, which find a facilitated access to the government itself through the channels of party passions. Thus the policy and the will of one country are subjected to the policy and will of another.

There is an opinion that parties in free countries are useful checks upon the administration of the government and serve to keep alive the spirit of liberty. This within certain limits is probably true; and in governments of a monarchical cast,[2] patriotism may look with indulgence, if not with favor, upon the spirit of party. But in those of the popular character, in governments purely elective, it is a spirit not to be encouraged. From their natural tendency, it is certain there will always be enough of that spirit for every salutary purpose. And there being constant danger of excess, the effort ought to be by force of public opinion, to mitigate and assuage it. A fire not to be quenched, it demands a uniform vigilance to prevent its bursting into a flame, lest, instead of warming, it should consume.

It is important, likewise, that the habits of thinking in a free country should inspire caution in those entrused with its administration, to confine themselves within their respective constitutional spheres, avoiding in the exercise of the powers of one department to encroach upon another. The spirit of encroachment tends to consolidate the powers of all the departments in one, and thus to create, whatever the form of government, a real despotism. A just estimate of that love of power, and proneness to abuse it, which predominates in the human heart, is sufficient to satisfy us of the truth of this position. The necessity of reciprocal checks in the exercise of political power, by dividing and distributing it into different depositaries, and constituting each the guardian of the public weal against invasions by the others, has been evinced by experiments ancient and modern; some of them in our country and under our own eyes. To preserve them must be as necessary as to institute them. If, in the opinion of the people, the distribution or modification of the constitutional powers be in any particular wrong, let it be corrected by an amendment in the way which the Constitution designates. But let there be no change by usurpation; for, though this, in one instance, may be the instrument of good, it is the customary weapon by which free governments are destroyed. The precedent must always greatly overbalance in permanent evil any partial or transient benefit, which the use can at any time yield.

Of all the dispositions and habits which lead to political prosperity, religion and morality are indispensable supports. In vain would that man claim the tribute of Patriotism, who should labor to subvert these great pillars of human happiness, these firmest props of the duties of men and citizens. The mere politician, equally with the pious man, ought to respect and to cherish them. A volume could not trace all their connexions with private and public felicity. Let it simply be asked: Where is the security for property, for reputation, for life, if the sense of religious obligation desert the oaths which are the instruments of investigation in courts of justice? And let us with caution indulge the supposition that morality can be maintained without religion. Whatever may be conceded to the influence of refined education on minds of peculiar structure, reason and experience both forbid us to expect that national morality can prevail in exclusion of religious principle.

It is substantially true that virtue or morality is a necessary spring of popular government. The rule, indeed, extends with more or less force to every species of free government. Who, that is a sincere friend to it can look with indifference upon attempts to shake the foundation of the fabric?

Promote then, as an object of primary importance, institutions for the general diffusion of knowledge. In proportion as the structure of a government gives force to public opinion, it is essential that public opinion should be enlightened.

As a very important source of strength and security, cherish public credit. One method of preserving it is to use it as sparingly as possible, avoiding occasions of expense by cultivating peace, but remembering also that timely disbursements to prepare for danger frequently prevent much greater disbursements to repel it, avoiding likewise the accumulation of debt, not only by shunning occasions of expense, but by vigorous exertions in time of peace to discharge the debts which unavoidable wars may have occasioned, not ungenerously throwing upon posterity the burthen which we ourselves ought to bear. The execution of these maxims belongs to your representatives, but it is necessary that public opinion should co-operate. To facilitate to them the performance of their duty, it is essential that you should practically bear in mind that towards the payment of debts there must be revenue; that to have revenue there must be taxes; that no taxes can be devised which are not more or less inconvenient and unpleasant; that the intrinsic embarrassment, inseparable from the selection of the proper objects (which is always a choice of difficulties), ought to be a decisive motive for a candid construction of the conduct of the government in making it, and for a spirit of acquiescence in the measures for obtaining revenue, which the public exigencies may at any time dictate.

Observe good faith and justice towards all nations; cultivate peace and harmony with all. Religion and Morality enjoin this conduct; and can it be, that good policy does not equally enjoin it—It will be worthy of a free, enlightened, and at no distant period, a great Nation, to give to mankind the magnanimous and too novel example of a people always guided by an exalted justice and benevolence. Who can doubt that, in the course of time and things, the fruits of such a plan would richly repay any temporary advantages which might be lost by a steady adherence to it? Can it be, that Providence has not connected the permanent felicity of a nation with its virtue? The experiment, at least, is recommended by every sentiment which ennobles human nature. Alas! Is it rendered impossible by its vices?

In the execution of such a plan, nothing is more essential, than that permanent, inveterate antipathies against particular nations, and passionate attachments for others, should be excluded; and that, in place of them, just and amicable feelings towards all should be cultivated. The nation which indulges towards another a habitual hatred or a habitual fondness is in some degree a slave. It is a slave to its animosity or to its affection, either of which is sufficient to lead it astray from its duty and its interest. Antipathy in one nation against another disposes each more readily to offer insult and injury, to lay hold of slight causes of umbrage, and to be haughty and intractable, when accidental or trifling occasions of dispute occur. Hence, frequent collisions, obstinate, envenomed, and bloody contests. The nation, prompted by ill-will and resentment, sometimes impels to war the government, contrary to the best calculations of policy. The government sometimes participates in the national propensity, and adopts through passion what reason would reject; at other times it makes the animosity of the nation subservient to projects of hostility instigated by pride, ambition, and other sinister and pernicious motives. The peace often, sometimes perhaps the liberty, of nations has been the victim.

So likewise, a passionate attachment of one nation for another produces a variety of evils. Sympathy for the favorite nation, facilitating the illusion of an imaginary common interest in cases where no real common interest exists, and infusing into one the enmities of the other, betrays the former into a participation in the quarrels and wars of the latter without adequate inducement or justification. It leads also to concessions to the favorite nation of privileges denied to others which is apt doubly to injure the nation making the concessions; by unnecessarily parting with what ought to have been retained, and by exciting jealousy, ill-will, and a disposition to retaliate, in the parties from whom equal privileges are withheld. And it gives to ambitious, corrupted, or deluded citizens, (who devote themselves to the favorite nation), facility to betray or sacrifice the interests of their own country, without odium, sometimes even with popularity; gilding, with the appearances of a virtuous sense of obligation, a commendable deference for public opinion, or a laudable zeal for public good, the base or foolish compliances of ambition, corruption, or infatuation.

As avenues to foreign influence in innumerable ways, such attachments are particularly alarming to the truly enlightened and independent patriot. How many opportunities do they afford to tamper with domestic factions, to practice the arts of seduction, to mislead public opinion, to influence or awe the public councils. Such an attachment of a small or weak towards a great and powerful nation dooms the former to be the satellite of the latter.

Against the insidious wiles of foreign influence (I conjure you to believe me, fellow-citizens), the jealousy of a free people ought to be constantly awake, since history and experience prove that foreign influence is one of the most baneful foes of republican government. But that jealousy to be useful, must be impartial; else it becomes the instrument of the very influence to be avoided, instead of a defence against it. Excessive partiality for one foreign nation and excessive dislike of another cause those whom they actuate to see danger only on one side, and serve to veil and even second the arts of influence on the other. Real patriots who may resist the intrigues of the favorite are liable to become suspected and odious, while its tools and dupes usurp the applause and confidence of the people, to surrender their interests.

The great rule of conduct for us in regard to foreign nations is in extending our commercial relations, to have with them as little political connexion as possible. So far as we have already formed engagements, let them be fulfilled with perfect good faith. Here let us stop. Europe has a set of primary interests which to us have none; or a very remote relation. Hence she must be engaged in frequent controversies, the causes of which are essentially foreign to our concerns. Hence, therefore, it must be unwise in us to implicate ourselves by artificial ties in the ordinary vicissitudes of her politics, or the ordinary combinations and collisions of her friendships or enmities.

Our detached and distant situation invites and enables us to pursue a different course. If we remain one people, under an efficient government, the period is not far off when we may defy material injury from external annoyance; when we may take such an attitude as will cause the neutrality we may at any time resolve upon to be scrupulously respected; when belligerent nations, under the impossibility of making acquisitions upon us, will not lightly hazard the giving us provocation; when we may choose peace or war, as our interest, guided by justice, shall counsel.

Why forego the advantages of so peculiar a situation? Why quit our own to stand upon foreign ground? Why, by interweaving our destiny with that of any part of Europe, entangle our peace and prosperity in the toils of European ambition, rivalship, interest, humor, or caprice?

It is our true policy to steer clear of permanent alliances with any portion of the foreign world; so far, I mean, as we are now at liberty to do it; for let me not be understood as capable of patronizing infidelity to existing engagements. I hold the maxim no less applicable to public than to private affairs, that honesty is always the best policy. I repeat it, therefore, let those engagements be observed in their genuine sense. But, in my opinion, it is unnecessary and would be unwise to extend them.

Taking care always to keep ourselves by suitable establishments on a respectable defensive posture, we may safely trust to temporary alliances for extraordinary emergencies.

Harmony, liberal intercourse with all nations, are recommended by policy, humanity, and interest. But even our commercial policy should hold an equal and impartial hand; neither seeking nor granting exclusive favors or preferences; consulting the natural course of things; diffusing and diversifying by gentle means the streams of commerce, but forcing nothing; establishing (with powers so disposed, in order to give trade a stable course, to define the rights of our merchants, and to enable the government to support them) conventional rules of intercourse, the best that present circumstances and mutual opinion will permit, but temporary, and liable to be from time to time abandoned or varied, as experience and circumstances shall dictate; constantly keeping in view that it is folly in one nation to look for disinterested favors from another; that it must pay with a portion of its independence for whatever it may accept under that character; that, by such acceptance, it may place itself in the condition of having given equivalents for nominal favors, and yet of being reproached with ingratitude for not giving more. There can be no greater error than to expect or calculate upon real favors from nation to nation. It is an illusion, which experience must cure, which a just pride ought to discard.

In offering to you, my countrymen, these counsels of an old and affectionate friend, I dare not hope they will make the strong and lasting impression I could wish; that they will control the usual current of the passions, or prevent our nation from running the course which has hitherto marked the destiny of nations. But, if I may even flatter myself, that they may be productive of some partial benefit, some occasional good; that they may now and then recur to moderate the fury of party spirit, to warn against the mischiefs of foreign intrigue, to guard against the impostures of pretended patriotism; this hope will be a full recompense for the solicitude for your welfare, by which they have been dictated.

How far in the discharge of my official duties I have been guided by the principles which have been delineated, the public records and other evidences of my conduct must witness to you and to the world. To myself, the assurance of my own conscience is, that I have at least believed myself to be guided by them.

In relation to the still subsisting war in Europe, my Proclamation of the twenty-second of April 1793,[3] is the index to my plan. Sanctioned by your approving voice, and by that of your representatives in both houses of Congress, the spirit of that measure has continually governed me, uninfluenced by any attempts to deter or divert me from it.

After deliberate examination, with the aid of the best lights I could obtain, I was well satisfied that our country, under all the circumstances of the case, had a right to take, and was bound in duty and interest to take, a neutral position. Having taken it, I determined, as far as should depend upon me, to maintain it, with moderation, perseverance, and firmness.

The considerations which respect the right to hold this conduct, it is not necessary on this occasion to detail. I will only observe that, according to my understanding of the matter, that right, so far from being denied by any of the belligerent powers, has been virtually admitted by all.

The duty of holding a neutral conduct may be inferred, without any thing more, from the obligation which justice and humanity impose on every nation, in cases in which it is free to act, to maintain inviolate the relations of peace and amity towards other nations.

The inducements of interest for observing that conduct will best be referred to your own reflections and experience. With me a predominant motive has been to endeavour to gain time to our country to settle and mature its yet recent institutions, and to progress without interruption to that degree of strength and consistency which is necessary to give it, humanly speaking, the command of its own fortunes.

Though, in reviewing the incidents of my administration, I am unconscious of intentional error, I am nevertheless too sensible of my defects not to think it probable that I may have committed many errors. Whatever they may be, I fervently beseech the Almighty to avert or mitigate the evils to which they may tend. I shall also carry with me the hope, that my country will never cease to view them with indulgence; and that, after forty-five years of my life dedicated to its service with an upright zeal, the faults of incompetent abilities will be consigned to oblivion, as myself must soon be to the mansions of rest.

Relying on its kindness in this as in other things, and actuated by that fervent love towards it, which is so natural to a man, who views it in the native soil of himself and his progenitors for several generations, I anticipate with pleasing expectation that retreat in which I promise myself to realize, without alloy, the sweet enjoyment of partaking, in the midst of my fellow-citizens, the benign influence of good laws under a free government, the ever-favorite object of my heart, and the happy reward, as I trust, of our mutual cares, labors, and dangers.

注释：

1. 本句中的on the proper occasion和impression指1789年就职演说第一段中提到的诚惶诚恐。
2. in governments of a monarchical cast：在君主制政府下。
3. my Proclamation of the twenty-second of April 1793：指在英法交战中华盛顿政府发表的中立申明。

思考题：

1. George Washington voluntarily resigned a third presidency in 1796. Was this important in American history? Why?
2. What had caused George Washington to offer those advices in his farewell address?
3. Where did American isolationism originate and how did it change in history? What is the essence of American isolationism?

9. First Inaugural Address (1801)①

Thomas Jefferson

导读：

托马斯·杰斐逊（Thomas Jefferson, 1743—1826）是美国第三任总统，也是美国开国元勋之一。在美国人民心中，他与乔治·华盛顿、亚伯拉罕·林肯和富兰克林·罗斯福齐名，是美国历史上最杰出的总统之一。杰斐逊享有如此高的声望不仅因为他是《独立宣言》（1776）的主要起草人，而且也因为他的民主思想对美国人民及美国社会产生了深远的影响。深受自然权利学说的影响，他认为在自然法则面前，每个人都是独立的、平等的；他主张精神的绝对自由，提倡言论自由、出版自由、宗教自由和人身自由，且第一次将这些思想写进了官方文件。在其起草的《独立宣言》中，杰斐逊提出："人人生而平等，造物主赋予他们若干不可剥夺的权利，其中包括生存权、自由权和追求幸福的权利。"②《独立宣言》获得批准之后，回到弗吉尼亚州任州议员的杰斐逊又向议会提出《弗吉尼亚宗教自由法案》（"Virginia Statute for Religious Freedom", 1779, 1786）。他指出："不得强迫任何人举行任何宗教礼拜仪式，或资助任何圣地或牧师，也不得由于其宗教见解或信仰而对其人身或财产施加限制、强制或折磨，一切人均可自由表明并通过说理坚持其宗教见解，决不可因此而缩小、扩大或影响其公民权。"（No man shall be compelled to frequent or support any religious worship, place or ministry whatsoever, nor shall be enforced, restrained, molested, or burthened in his body or goods, nor shall otherwise suffer on account of his religious opinions or belief; but that all men shall be free to profess, and by argument to maintain, their opinions in matters of religion, and that the same

---

① George Washington, et al., *The Inaugural Address of the U.S. Presidents* (Beijing: Central Compilation & Translation Press, 2009): 13−17.

② http://www.archives.gov/exhibits/charters/declaration_transcript.html (accessed Oct. 10, 2021).

shall in no wise diminish, enlarge, or affect their civil capacities.）[1]杰斐逊认为信仰纯粹是个人的事情，国家不应该干涉。之后，他因对1787年《宪法》中缺少保障人民自由权利的条款不满而奔走呼吁，要求把保障人民自由的“权利法案”加到宪法中去，主张在法案中规定一系列人民的自由以保证其生存权、自由权和追求幸福的权力。1791年，第一至十条修正案获得通过，成为现在所称的《权利法案》（“Bill of Rights”，又称《人权法案》）。1800年，杰斐逊击败与其竞选的前任总统亚当斯当选美国第三任总统，成为美国历史上唯一担任过副总统后又竞选上总统且任满两届任期的人。他上任之后，立即废除了诸如《移民归化法》（“Immigration and Naturalization Act”）、《客籍法和镇压叛乱法》（“Alien and Sedition Acts”）、《敌对外侨法》（“Alien Enemies Act”）等不合理的联邦法令，保障了人民的基本权利。杰斐逊的胜利标志着联邦主义的衰败和共和主义的兴起。[2]

杰斐逊的这篇就职演讲是其民主思想的充分写照，也体现出浓厚的人文主义色彩。他在承认多数人意志起决定性作用的同时指出少数人也享有同等权利，力图实行人人平等和公正、公平的制度。他向联邦党人伸出橄榄枝，号召大家同心同德，团结起来，因为个人的自由是建立在社会和谐以及人与人之间和睦友爱的基础之上的。他指出：“并不是每一种意见分歧都是原则分歧。我们就曾经用不同的名称去称呼持有相同原则的兄弟。我们都是共和党人，我们都是联邦党人。”[3]这种杰斐逊式的民主并非一味迁就联邦党人，也并非无原则的和解，而是希望联邦党人摒弃原有的错误思想和主张，团结到共和党人的旗帜下，共同创立一个和平、自由、平等、安全的国度，实现民主政治。杰斐逊在此演讲中丰富和发展了自己的民主思想，在强调平等、自由及人民的各项权利

---

① 原文请参见Thomas Jefferson, *Notes on the State of Virginia,* ed., Frank C. Shuffelton (New York: Penguin Group Inc., 1999): 232。译文见托马斯·杰斐逊著，朱曾汶译，《杰斐逊选集》，北京：商务印书馆，1999年，第297页。

② 在乔治·华盛顿担任美国第一任总统期间，美国的两大政党逐渐形成——由财政部长亚历山大·汉密尔顿领导的联邦党和国务卿托马斯·杰斐逊领导的共和党。联邦党主张建立强大的联邦政府，增强政府的权力，认为国家应该由有权有势的人统治。相反，共和党则反对让政府享有无限的权力，他们认为政治权力应该分配给民众。18世纪90年代，联邦党在内阁的势力很大，甚至连总统华盛顿和亚当斯都受其影响。然而，1801年杰斐逊当选总统之后重组内阁，大批联邦党人被免除职务，因此杰斐逊的竞选成功标志着联邦主义的衰败和共和主义的兴起。

③ 托马斯·杰斐逊著，朱曾汶译，《杰斐逊选集》，北京：商务印书馆，1999年，第306页。

的同时，坚定了一个贤明政府的信念，为美国民主的形成奠定了坚实的基础，使其成为美国历史上最具影响力的演讲之一。

Friends and Fellow-Citizens: —

Called upon to undertake the duties of the first executive office of our country, I avail myself of the presence of that portion of my fellow citizens which is here assembled, to express my grateful thanks for the favor with which they have been pleased to look toward me, to declare a sincere consciousness that the task is above my talents, and that I approach it with those anxious and awful presentiments which the greatness of the charge and the weakness of my powers so justly inspire. A rising nation, spread over a wide and fruitful land, traversing all the seas with the rich productions of their industry, engaged in commerce with nations who feel power and forget right, advancing rapidly to destinies beyond the reach of mortal eye—when I contemplate these transcendent objects, and see the honor, the happiness, and the hopes of this beloved country committed to the issue and the auspices of this day, I shrink from the contemplation, and humble myself before the magnitude of the undertaking. Utterly indeed, should I despair did not the presence of many whom I here see remind me, that in the other high authorities[1] provided by our constitution, I shall find resources of wisdom, of virtue, and of zeal, on which to rely under all difficulties. To you, then, gentlemen, who are charged with the sovereign functions of legislation, and to those associated with you, I look with encouragement for that guidance and support which may enable us to steer with safety the vessel in which we are all embarked amid the conflicting elements of a troubled world.

During the contest of opinion through which we have passed, the animation of discussions and of exertions has sometimes worn an aspect which might impose on strangers unused to think freely and to speak and to write what they think; but this being now decided by the voice of the nation, announced according to the rules of the constitution, all will, of course, arrange themselves under the will of the law, and unite in common efforts for the common good. All, too, will bear in mind this sacred principle, that though the will of the majority is in all cases to prevail, that will, to be rightful, must be reasonable; that the minority possess their equal rights, which equal law must protect, and to violate which would be oppression. Let us, then, fellow citizens, unite with one heart and one mind. Let us restore to social intercourse that harmony and affection without which liberty and even life itself are but dreary things. And let us reflect that having banished from our land that religious intolerance under which mankind so long bled and suffered, we have yet gained little if we countenance a political intolerance as despotic, as wicked, and capable of as bitter and bloody persecutions. During the throes and convulsions of the ancient world, during the agonizing spasms of infuriated man, seeking through blood and slaughter his long-lost liberty, it was not wonderful that the agitation of the billows should reach even this distant and peaceful shore; that this should be more felt and feared by some and less by others; and this should divide opinions as to measures of safety. But every difference of opinion is not a difference of principle. We have called by different names brethren of the same principle. We are all republicans—we are all federalists. If there be any among us who would wish to dissolve this Union or to change its republican form, let them stand undisturbed as monuments of the safety with which error of opinion may be tolerated where reason is left free to combat it. I know, indeed, that some honest men fear that a republican government can not be strong; that this government is not strong enough. But would the honest patriot, in the full tide of successful experiment, abandon a government which has so far kept us free and firm, on the theoretic and visionary fear that this government, the world's best hope, may by possibility want energy to preserve itself? I trust not. I believe this, on the contrary, the strongest government on earth. I believe it is the only one where every man, at the call of the laws, would fly to the standard of the law, and would meet invasions of the public order as his own personal concern. Sometimes it is said that man can not be trusted with the government of himself. Can he, then, be trusted with the government of others? Or have we found angels in the forms of kings to govern him? Let history answer this question.

Let us, then, with courage and confidence pursue our own federal and republican principles, our attachment to union and representative government. Kindly separated by nature and a wide ocean from the exterminating havoc of one quarter of the globe;[2] too high-minded to endure the degradations of the others; possessing a chosen country, with room enough for our descendants to the thousandth and thousandth generation; entertaining a due sense of our equal right to the use of our own faculties, to the acquisitions of our industry, to honor and confidence from our fellow citizens, resulting not from birth, but from our actions and their sense of them; enlightened by a benign religion, professed, indeed, and practiced in various forms, yet all of them including honesty, truth, temperance, gratitude, and the love of man; acknowledging and adoring an overruling Providence, which by all its dispensations proves that it delights in the happiness of man here and his greater happiness hereafter; with all these blessings, what more is necessary to make us a happy and a prosperous people? Still one thing more, fellow citizens—a wise and frugal government, which shall restrain men from injuring one another, shall leave them otherwise free to regulate their own pursuits of industry and improvement, and shall not take from the mouth of labor the bread it has earned. This is the sum of good government, and this is necessary to close the circle of our felicities.

About to enter, fellow citizens, on the exercise of duties which comprehend everything dear and valuable to you, it is proper you should understand what I deem the essential principles of our government, and consequently those which ought to shape its administration. I will compress them within the narrowest compass they will bear, stating the general principle, but not all its limitations. Equal and exact justice to all men, of whatever state or persuasion, religious or political; peace, commerce, and honest friendship, with all nations—entangling alliances with none; the support of the state governments in all their rights, as the most competent administrations for our domestic concerns and the surest bulwarks against anti-republican tendencies; the preservation of the general government in its whole constitutional vigor, as the sheet anchor of our peace at home and safety abroad; a jealous care of the right of election by the people—a mild and safe corrective of abuses which are lopped by the sword of revolution where peaceable remedies are unprovided; absolute acquiescence in the decisions of the majority—the vital principle of republics, from which is no appeal but to force, the vital principle and immediate parent of despotism; a well-disciplined militia—our best reliance in peace and for the first moments of war, till regulars may relieve them; the supremacy of the civil over the military authority; economy in the public expense, that labor may be lightly burthened; the honest payment of our debts and sacred preservation of the public faith; encouragement of agriculture, and of commerce as its handmaid;[3] the diffusion of information and arraignment of all abuses at the bar of the public reason; freedom of religion; freedom of the press; freedom of person under the protection of the *habeas corpus*; and trial by juries impartially selected—these principles form the bright constellation which has gone before us, and guided our steps through an age of revolution and reformation. The wisdom of our sages and the blood of our heroes have been devoted to their attainment. They should be the creed of our political faith—the text of civic instruction—the touchstone by which to try the services of those we trust; and should we wander from them in moments of error or of alarm, let us hasten to retrace our steps and to regain the road which alone leads to peace, liberty, and safety.

I repair, then, fellow citizens, to the post you have assigned me. With experience enough in subordinate offices to have seen the difficulties of this, the greatest of all, I have learnt to expect that it will rarely fall to the lot of imperfect man to retire from this station with the reputation and the favor which bring him into it. Without pretensions to that high confidence reposed in our first and greatest revolutionary character[4], whose preeminent services had entitled him to the first place in his country's love and destined for him the fairest page in the volume of faithful history, I ask so much confidence only as may give firmness and effect to the legal administration of your affairs. I shall often go wrong through defect of judgment. When right, I shall often be thought wrong by those whose positions will not command a view of the whole ground. I ask your indulgence for my own errors, which will never be intentional; and your support against the errors of others, who may condemn what they would not if seen in all its parts. The approbation implied by your suffrage is a consolation to me for the past; and my future solicitude will be to retain the good opinion of those who have bestowed it in advance, to conciliate that of others by doing them all the good in my power, and to be instrumental to the happiness and freedom of all.

Relying, then, on the patronage of your good will, I advance with obedience to the work, ready to retire from it whenever you become sensible how much better choice it is in your power to make. And may that Infinite Power which rules the destinies of the universe, lead our councils to what is best, and give them a favorable issue for your peace and prosperity.

注释:

1. the other high authorities：指立法部门国会两院（参议院和众议院）以及司法部门，体现出美国联邦政府在行政、立法、司法上三权分立的思想。
2. 此句指1789年法国大革命后欧洲出现的长期战争和动荡局面。
3. 当时的美国以农业为主，杰斐逊也希望美国成为一个以农业为主的国家。他认为美国地理条件得天独厚，而且自由平等和独立的农民是民主政治的最好基础；相反，工业资本主义的发展将破坏民主政治的基础。
4. our first and greatest revolutionary character：第一任美国总统乔治·华盛顿。

思考题：

1. Why did Thomas Jefferson believe that not federal but republican government was the strongest government on earth?
2. What was the difference between Federal Party and Republican Party in their political faith? When the two parties struggled for power in the late eighteenth century, what did Jefferson mean by saying "Federal and Republic principles"?
3. How did Thomas Jefferson help build the concept of "democracy" in America, and what is the difference between Jeffersonian democracy and American democracy afterward?
4. What contribution did Thomas Jefferson make to the overall success of equal right of election by all men?

10. The Monroe Doctrine (1823)①

James Monroe

导读：

詹姆斯·门罗（James Monroe, 1758—1831）的生平与美国第三任总统托马斯·杰斐逊相似：两人都出生于弗吉尼亚州，就读于威廉玛丽学院（College of William & Mary），先后担任弗吉尼亚州议员、州长、美国国务卿和美国总统，并参与路易斯安那购地②。1816年，詹姆斯·门罗以绝对优势战胜了联邦党候选人鲁弗斯·金（Rufus King），成为美国第五任总统，1820年获得连任。门罗在位期间，阿根廷、智利、秘鲁等国相继打败了殖民军并宣布独立。然而，欧洲神圣同盟③却企图干涉拉丁美洲的独立运动，以维护其在拉丁美洲的殖民统治。当时

① 选自詹姆斯·门罗1823年向国会提出的国情咨文（the Seventh Annual Message to Congress）。文中所述观点起初并未得名"门罗主义"（Monroe Doctrine），而被称为"门罗宣言"（Monroe Declaration）。后来，"门罗宣言"一直被视为美国外交政策的重要准则。1845年，美国第11任总统詹姆斯·诺克斯·波尔克（James Knox Polk, 1795—1849）宣布必须严格遵守门罗主义，如此一来，"门罗主义"一词才得以广泛使用。文献来源：*Journal of the Senate of the United States of America, Being the First Session of the Eighteenth Congress*, Washington: Gales and Seaton, 1823: 12, 21-22.

② 路易斯安那购地（Louisiana Purchase）：1801年，杰斐逊总统派遣罗伯特·利文斯顿（Robert Livingston）前往巴黎与拿破仑政府商讨购地事宜。美方准备出价200万美元收购新奥尔良，但利文斯顿的购地提议并未被法国方面接受；1802年，皮埃尔·塞缪尔·杜邦·德·内穆尔（Pierre Samuel du Pont de Nemours）应美方邀请协助谈判，他向拿破仑提出一个规模更大的路易斯安那购地方案；1803年，杰斐逊派遣詹姆斯·门罗前往巴黎加入谈判，一番讨价还价之后，美国最终以1500万美元（相当于8000万法郎）的价格从法国购买了超过529 911 680英亩（约2 144 476平方公里）的土地，大约每英亩3美分。此次购地使美国领土增加了近一倍。

③ 神圣同盟（Holy Alliance）：1815年9月，在俄国沙皇亚历山大一世（Alexander Ⅰ, 1777—1825）的倡议下，奥地利皇帝弗朗西斯一世（Francis Ⅰ of Austria, 1768—1835）、普鲁士国王腓特烈·威廉三世（Friedrich Wilhelm Ⅲ, 1770—1840）与沙皇在巴黎签署《神圣同盟宣言》，成立了维护君主专制的君主互助同盟——神圣同盟。同年11月，法国国王路易十八（Louis Stanislas Xavier, 1755—1824）加入同盟。后来，欧洲其他各国君主也纷纷加盟。神圣同盟旨在维护君主政体，反对法国大革命在欧洲所传播的革命思想，先后镇压了意大利革命和西班牙革命。神圣同盟诸国还曾干涉拉丁美洲的独立运动，企图维护各同盟国在拉丁美洲的殖民统治，但其行为遭到了美国的强烈反对。

的美国还是一个相对较弱的新兴国家，没有后来的经济实力和军事实力，所以美国政府尽量避免卷入欧洲大国的纷争；面对欧洲各国之间的争端，以及各国与其美洲殖民地之间的战事，美国保持中立。但是，倘若这些新兴的独立国家再度沦为他国的殖民地，便会影响美国在拉丁美洲的经济发展和势力扩张，甚至美国的独立地位也会受到威胁。因此，出于自身利益的考量，美国公开承认已经宣布独立的国家，并且宣称如果欧洲列强再在这些国家夺取殖民地，美国将视之为敌对行为。1823年，门罗总统在向国会提出的国情咨文中明确表明了这一立场。他说："对于欧洲国家现有殖民地和附属国，我们没有，也不会干涉。但是对于那些已经宣布了并保持独立的国家，对于那些其独立已经过我们的仔细斟酌并按照公正原则予以承认的国家，那么，对于任何欧洲国家旨在镇压它们或以其他任何方式控制它们的命运而进行的一切干涉，我们便只能视为是对美国不友好意向的表示。"[①]他还提出：美洲大陆，由于它已获得独立，从此可以保持自由状态，此后不能再被认为是任何欧洲国家用来当作殖民地的地方。这就是人们所熟知的"门罗宣言"。

"门罗宣言"包含三条重要原则。一是不准欧洲国家在美洲夺取殖民地的原则。二是美洲体系的原则：门罗指出，欧洲的政治制度与美洲的政治制度在本质上不同，欧洲列强把它们的政治制度扩展到西半球的任何企图都将危及美国的和平与安全。三是互不干涉的原则：美国不介入欧洲事务，欧洲列强也不能干涉美洲事务。这三条原则既表达了美国对自身和平与安全的维护，也隐含了美国欲在美洲建立霸权的野心。"门罗宣言"的发表对美国制定拉美政策产生了很大影响，并逐渐成为美国在美洲进行侵略扩张的工具。比如：1845年，总统波尔克（James Knox Polk, 1795—1849）在国情咨文中重申"美洲体系原则"，其在外交政策中的地位大大提升。次年，美国就打着门罗主义的旗号，夺取了墨西哥一半以上的国土[②]。1904年，罗斯福总统（Theodore Roosevelt,

① 王建华：《美国历届总统执政与告别演说精选》，南昌：江西人民出版社，1999年，第151页。

② 即墨西哥战争（1846—1848）。

1858—1919）将著名的罗斯福推论①补充到门罗主义中，使美国在西半球堂而皇之地充当国际警察，干涉拉美国家事务。虽然，门罗之后的美国领导人不断根据新的国际国内形势调整外交政策，为“门罗主义”注入新的内容，但是“门罗主义”作为美国制定拉美政策的基本原则和指导思想的地位始终没有改变。

The occasion has been judged proper for asserting, as a principle in which the rights and interests of the United States are involved, that the American continents, by the free and independent condition which they have assumed and maintain, are henceforth not to be considered as subjects for future colonization by any European powers….

Of events in that quarter of the globe (Europe),[1] with which we have so much intercourse and from which we derive our origin, we have always been anxious and interested spectators.

The citizens of the United States cherish sentiments the most friendly in favor of the liberty and happiness of their fellowmen on that side of the Atlantic. In the wars of the European powers in matters relating to themselves we have never taken any part, nor does it comport with our policy so to do. It is only when our rights are invaded or seriously menaced that we resent injuries or make preparation for our defense. With the movements in this hemisphere we are of necessity more immediately connected, and by causes which must be obvious to all enlightened and impartial observers. The political system of the allied powers is essentially different in this respect from that of America. This difference proceeds from that which exists in their respective Governments; and to the defence of our own, which has been achieved by the loss of so much blood and

① 罗斯福推论（Roosevelt Corollary）是美国总统西奥多·罗斯福对“门罗主义”的一次重要补充。在1904年的国情咨文中，罗斯福宣称：“长期的不法行为，或导致文明社会关系普遍松动的软弱无能，在美洲，如同在其他地方一样，最终将需要某一文明国家的干涉，而在西半球美国坚守的‘门罗主义’可能迫使美国不论多么不情愿仍不得不对这些臭名昭著的不法行为或软弱无能行使其国际警察的权利。”（Chronic wrongdoing, or an impotence which results in a general loosening of the ties of civilized society, may in America, as elsewhere, ultimately require intervention by some civilized nation, and in the Western Hemisphere the adherence of the United States to the Monroe Doctrine may force the United States, however reluctantly, in flagrant cases of such wrongdoing or impotence, to the exercise of an international police power.）详见http://www.infoplease.com/t/hist/state-of-the-union/116.html union/116.html (accessed Sept. 4, 2013).

treasure, and matured by the wisdom of their most enlightened citizens, and under which we have enjoyed unexampled felicity, this whole nation is devoted.

We owe it, therefore, to candor and to the amicable relations existing between the United States and those powers to declare that we should consider any attempt on their part to extend their system to any portion of this hemisphere as dangerous to our peace and safety. With the existing colonies or dependencies of any European power we have not interfered and shall not interfere. But with the Governments who have declared their independence and maintained it, and whose independence we have, on great consideration and on just principles, acknowledged, we could not view any interposition for the purpose of oppressing them, or controlling in any other manner their destiny, by any European power in any other light than as the manifestation of an unfriendly disposition towards the United States.

In the war between those new Governments[2] and Spain we declared our neutrality at the time of their recognition, and to this we have adhered and shall continue to adhere, provided no change shall occur which, in the judgment of the competent authorities of this Government, shall make a corresponding change on the part of the United States indispensable to their security.

The late events in Spain and Portugal[3] shew that Europe is still unsettled. Of this important fact no stronger proof can be adduced than that the allied powers should have thought it proper, on any principle satisfactory to themselves, to have interposed by force in the internal concerns of Spain. To what extent such interposition may be carried, on the same principle, is a question in which all independent powers whose governments differ from theirs are interested, even those most remote, and surely none more so than the United States.

Our policy in regard to Europe, which was adopted at an early stage of the wars which have so long agitated that quarter of the globe, nevertheless remains the same, which is, not to interfere in the internal concerns of any of its powers; to consider the government *de facto*[4] as the legitimate government for us; to cultivate friendly relations with it, and to preserve those relations by a frank, firm, and manly policy, meeting in all instances the just claims of every power, submitting to injuries from none. But in regard to those continents circumstances are eminently and conspicuously different. It is impossible that the allied powers should extend their political system to any portion of either continent without endangering our peace and happiness; nor can anyone believe that our southern brethren, if left to themselves, would adopt it of their own accord. It is equally impossible, therefore, that we should behold such interposition in any form with indifference. If we look to the comparative strength and resources of Spain and those new Governments, and their distance from each other, it must be obvious that she can never subdue them. It is still the true policy of the United States to leave the parties to themselves, in the hope that other powers will pursue the same course….

注释：

1. that quarter of the globe：欧洲大陆。
2. the war between new Governments：指1810年爆发的拉丁美洲人民反对西班牙殖民统治的独立战争。战争一直持续到1826年，涉及西班牙在拉丁美洲的多个殖民地。新政府则指打败西班牙殖民军并宣布独立的委内瑞拉、巴拉圭、墨西哥、阿根廷、智利、秘鲁等国。
3. 19世纪初期，葡萄牙、西班牙先后遭到拿破仑的进攻，大片土地被法国控制，国内动荡不安。
4. *de facto*：拉丁语，相当于英语“in fact”。

思考题：

1. Why was Monroe Doctrine so influential in helping Latin American countries gain independence and avoid colonialism, while the UK and France were much stronger and more powerful than the newly-established US at that time?
2. Did the later American leaders change James Monroe’s principle or is Monroe’s statement the cornerstone of American hegemonism at its very start?

11. David Walker's Appeal (1829)①

David Walker

导读：

大卫·沃克（David Walker, 1785—1830）出生在北卡罗来纳州的威尔明顿（Wilmington）。他虽然是一名自由黑人，但是从小就亲眼看见黑人奴隶的悲惨遭遇和奴隶主的残酷行径，因而对奴隶制深恶痛绝。1827年，由于不堪忍受白人对黑人的压迫，沃克离开南方到波士顿定居。他说："如果我继续待在这片血腥的土地，我将活不长久……我无法待在这里，不断地听着奴隶的脚镣声，还得遭受伪善奴隶主的凌辱。"（If I remain in this bloody land, I will not live long... I cannot remain where I must hear slaves' chains continually and where I must encounter the insults of their hypocritical enslavers.②）沃克在波士顿开了一家二手服装店，同时也为美国历史上第一份黑人报纸《自由报》（*Freedom's Journal*）工作和写作。沃克渐渐参与许多民间废奴运动，在此期间他通过发表演讲、出版小册子来传播他的废奴主义思想。他认为，奴隶制不仅降低了黑人的身份，使他们遭受非人的待遇，还迫害他们的身躯，摧残他们的灵魂。1829年，沃克出版了《对全世界有色公民的呼吁》（*An Appeal to the Coloured Citizens of the World*）。书中他强烈反对奴隶制和白人特权，呼吁黑人同胞不惜一切代价反抗奴隶主的压迫，拒绝不公正的待遇，追求自由并捍卫自己的权利。沃克所生活的年代是黑人被剥夺教育权利的年代。白人阻止黑人学习，因为他们害怕黑人受到启蒙和开导后会违抗他们。他们把黑人的无知当作欺压和奴役黑人的有力保障。沃克的呼吁不仅揭露了白人的伪善本质，而且指出了南方奴隶主们一手握《圣经》、一手握长鞭的矛盾。

自1776年托马斯·杰斐逊等人发表《独立宣言》到1863年亚伯拉罕·林肯发表《解放奴隶宣言》，奴隶制的存在无疑是对美国民主的最

① David Walker, *David Walker's Appeal to the Coloured Citizens of the World* (New York: Hall and Wang, Inc., 1965): 1-6.

② http://docsouth.unc.edu/nc/walker/bio.html (accessed Oct. 4, 2013).

大讽刺，而“美国民主”只是美国白人的民主。为了让黑人看清自己的处境，沃克在《对全世界有色公民的呼吁》中一针见血地指出，奴隶制与《圣经》中“上帝面前人人平等”的观点相悖，也违背了《独立宣言》中托马斯·杰斐逊提出的“人人生而平等，造物主赋予他们若干不可剥夺的权利，其中包括生存权、自由权和追求幸福的权利”。沃克认为奴隶制度、愚昧无知、基督教传教和殖民主义是导致黑人悲惨遭遇的四大原因；他强烈谴责白人对黑人的压迫奴役和愚民政策，呼吁民众不仅要解放黑奴，还要让黑人在工作、政治、经济、教育等方面获得与白人同等的地位与权利。

本文为《对全世界有色公民的呼吁》一书的《序言》。该书的出版引起了美国南方的恐慌与不安，尤其是佐治亚州、弗吉尼亚州和沃克的家乡北卡罗来纳州。它激发了黑人民族主义者的思考，让废奴运动从早期贵格会①的温和劝说转向斗志昂扬的抗议革命，成为美国内战前种族关系的转折点和黑人民主运动的源泉。

My dearly beloved Brethren and Fellow Citizens.

Having travelled over a considerable portion of these United States, and having, in the course of my travels, taken the most accurate observations of things as they exist—the result of my observations has warranted the full and unshaken conviction, that we, (coloured people of these United States,) are the most degraded, wretched, and abject set of beings that ever lived since the world began; and I pray God that none like us ever may live again until time shall be no more. They tell us of the Israelites in Egypt,[1] the Helots in Sparta,[2] and of the Roman Slaves,[3] which last were made up from almost every nation under heaven, whose sufferings under those ancient and heathen nations, were, in comparison with ours, under this enlightened and Christian nation, no more than a cypher—or, in other words, those heathen nations of antiquity, had

① 贵格会（Quakers）又称教友派（Religious Society of Friends），是基督教新教的一个派别，公元17世纪由乔治·福克斯（George Fox, 1624—1691）创立于英国，后传播到美国和肯尼亚等地。贵格会没有成文的教义，但是贵格会教徒坚持与人为善，主张和平与宗教自由，反对奴隶制。利瓦伊·科芬（Levi Coffin, 1798—1877），一个曾多次帮助很多黑奴获得自由的贵格会教徒就说过：“《圣经》上只是要我们给饥者以食物，无衣者以衣衫，但是没提到过肤色的事。”（The Bible, in bidding us to feed the hungry and clothe the naked, said nothing about color.）1775年，贵格会在费城成立了美国第一个废奴主义协会，其后又开展了一系列民主活动，在美国废奴运动中扮演了重要的角色。

but little more among them than the name and form of slavery; while wretchedness and endless miseries were reserved, apparently in a phial, to be poured out upon our fathers, ourselves and our children, by *Christian* Americans!

These positions I shall endeavour, by the help of the Lord, to demonstrate in the course of this *Appeal*, to the satisfaction of the most incredulous mind—and may God Almighty, who is the Father of our Lord Jesus Christ, open your hearts to understand and believe the truth.

The *causes*, my brethren, which produce our wretchedness and miseries, are so very numerous and aggravating, that I believe the pen only of a Josephus[4] or a Plutarch,[5] can well enumerate and explain them. Upon subjects, then, of such incomprehensible magnitude, so impenetrable, and so notorious, I shall be obliged to omit a large class of, and content myself with giving you an exposition of a few of those, which do indeed rage to such an alarming pitch, that they cannot but be a perpetual source of terror and dismay to every reflecting mind.

I am fully aware, in making this appeal to my much afflicted and suffering brethren, that I shall not only be assailed by those whose greatest earthly desires are, to keep us in abject ignorance and wretchedness, and who are of the firm conviction that Heaven has designed us and our children to be slaves and *beasts of burden* to them and their children. I say, I do not only expect to be held up to the public as an ignorant, impudent and restless disturber of the public peace, by such avaricious creatures, as well as a mover of insubordination—and perhaps put in prison or to death, for giving a superficial exposition of our miseries, and exposing tyrants. But I am persuaded, that many of my brethren, particularly those who are ignorantly in league with slave-holders or tyrants, who acquire their daily bread by the blood and sweat of their more ignorant brethren—and not a few of those too, who are too ignorant to see an inch beyond their noses, will rise up and call me cursed—Yea,[6] the jealous ones among us will perhaps use more abject subtlety, by affirming that this work is not worth perusing, that we are well situated, and there is no use in trying to better our condition, for we cannot. I will ask one question here.—Can our condition be any worse?—Can it be more mean and abject? If there are any changes, will they not be for the better, though they may appear for the worst at first? Can they get us any lower? Where can they get us? They are afraid to treat us worse, for they know well, the day they do it they are gone. But against all accusations which may or can be preferred against me, I appeal to Heaven for my motive in writing—who knows that my object is, if possible, to awaken in the breasts of my afflicted, degraded and slumbering brethren, a spirit of inquiry and investigation respecting our miseries and wretchedness in this *Republican Land of Liberty!!!!!!*

The sources from which our miseries are derived, and on which I shall comment, I shall not combine in one, but shall put them under distinct heads and expose them in their turn; in doing which, keeping truth on my side, and not departing from the strictest rules of morality, I shall endeavour to penetrate, search out, and lay them open for your inspection. If you cannot or will not profit by them, I shall have done *my* duty to you, my country and my God.

And as the inhuman system of *slavery*, is the *source* from which most of our miseries proceed, I shall begin with that *curse to nations*, which has spread terror and devastation through so many nations of antiquity, and which is raging to such a pitch at the present day in Spain and in Portugal.[7] It had one tug in England, in France, and in the United States of America; yet the inhabitants thereof, do not learn wisdom, and erase it entirely from their dwellings and from all with whom they have to do. The fact is, the labour of slaves comes so cheap to the avaricious usurpers, and is (as they think) of such great utility to the country where it exists, that those who are actuated by sordid avarice only, overlook the evils, which will as sure as the Lord lives, follow after the good. In fact, they are so happy to keep in ignorance and degradation, and to receive the homage and the labour of the slaves, they forget that God rules in the armies of heaven and among the inhabitants of the earth, having his ears continually open to the cries, tears and groans of his oppressed people; and being a just and holy Being will at one day appear fully in behalf of the oppressed, and arrest the progress of the avaricious oppressors; for although the destruction of the oppressors God may not effect by the oppressed, yet the Lord our God will bring other destructions upon them—for not unfrequently will he cause them to rise up one against another, to be split and divided, and to oppress each other, and sometimes to open hostilities with sword in hand. Some may ask, what is the matter with this united and happy people?—Some say it is the cause of political usurpers, tyrants, oppressors, &c. But has not the Lord an oppressed and suffering people among them? Does the Lord condescend to hear their cries and see their tears in consequence of oppression? Will he let the oppressors rest comfortably and happy always? Will he not cause the very children of the oppressors to rise up against them, and oftimes[8] put them to death? "God works in many ways his wonders to perform."

I will not here speak of the destructions which the Lord brought upon Egypt,[9] in consequence of the oppression and consequent groans of the oppressed—of the hundreds and thousands of Egyptians whom God hurled into the Red Sea[10] for afflicting his people in their land—of the Lord's suffering people in Sparta or Lacedaemon,[11] the land of the truly famous Lycurgus[12]—nor have I time to comment upon the cause which produced the fierceness with which Sylla[13] usurped the title, and absolutely acted as dictator of the Roman people—the conspiracy of Cataline[14]—the conspiracy against, and murder of Cæsar in the Senate house—the spirit with which Marc Antony[15] made himself master of the commonwealth—his associating Octavius[16] and Lipidus[17] with himself in power—their dividing the provinces of Rome among themselves—their attack and defeat, on the plains of Phillippi,[18] of the last defenders of their liberty, (Brutus[19] and Cassius[20])—the tyranny of Tiberius,[21] and from him to the final overthrow of Constantinople by the Turkish Sultan, Mahomed Ⅱ. A. D. 1453.[22] I say, I shall not take up time to speak of the *causes* which produced so much wretchedness and massacre among those heathen nations, for I am aware that you know too well, that God is just, as well as merciful![23]—I shall call your attention a few moments to that *Christian* nation, the Spaniards—while I shall leave almost unnoticed, that avaricious and cruel people, the Portuguese, among whom all true hearted Christians and lovers of Jesus Christ, must evidently see the judgments of God displayed. To show the judgments of God upon the Spaniards, I shall occupy but a little time, leaving a plenty of room for the candid and unprejudiced to reflect.

All persons who are acquainted with history, and particularly the Bible, who are not blinded by the God of this world, and are not actuated solely by avarice—who are able to lay aside prejudice long enough to view candidly and impartially, things as they were, are, and probably will be—who are willing to admit that God made man to serve Him *alone*, and that man should have no other Lord or Lords but Himself—that God Almighty is the *sole proprietor* or *master* of the WHOLE human family, and will not on any consideration admit of a colleague, being unwilling to divide his glory with another—and who can dispense with prejudice long enough to admit that we are *men*, notwithstanding our *improminent noses* and *woolly heads*, and believe that we feel for our fathers, mothers, wives and children, as well as the whites do for theirs.—I say, all who are permitted to see and believe these things, can easily recognize the judgments of God among the Spaniards. Though others may lay the cause of the fierceness with which they cut each other's throats, to some other circumstance, yet they who believe that God is a God of justice, will believe that SLAVERY *is the principal cause.*

While the Spaniards are running about upon the field of battle cutting each other's throats, has not the Lord an afflicted and suffering people in the midst of them, whose cries and groans in consequence of oppression are continually pouring into the ears of the God of justice? Would they not cease to cut each other's throats, if they could? But how can they? The very support which they draw from government to aid them in perpetrating such enormities, does it not arise in a great degree from the wretched victims of oppression among them? And yet they are calling for *Peace!—Peace!!* Will any peace be given unto them? Their destruction may indeed be procrastinated awhile, but can it continue long, while they are oppressing the Lord's people? Has He not the hearts of all men in His hand? Will he suffer one part of his creatures to go on oppressing another like brutes always, with impunity? And yet, those avaricious wretches are calling for *Peace!!!!* I declare, it does appear to me, as though some nations think God is asleep, or that he made the Africans for nothing else but to dig their mines and work their farms, or they cannot believe history, sacred or profane. I ask every man who has a heart, and is blessed with the privilege of believing—Is not God a God of justice to *all* his creatures? Do you say he is? Then if he gives peace and tranquillity to tyrants, and permits them to keep our fathers, our mothers, ourselves and our children in eternal ignorance and wretchedness, to support them and their families, would he be to us a God of *justice*? I ask, O ye *Christians!!!* who hold us and our children in the most abject ignorance and degradation, that ever a people were afflicted with since the world began—I say, if God gives you peace and tranquillity, and suffers you thus to go on afflicting us, and our children, who have never given you the least provocation—would he be to us *a God of justice*? If you will allow that we are MEN, who feel for each other, does not the blood of our fathers and of us their children, cry aloud to the Lord of Sabaoth[24] against you, for the cruelties and murders with which you have, and do continue to afflict us. But it is time for me to close my remarks on the suburbs, just to enter more fully into the interior of this system of cruelty and oppression.

注释：

1. 以色列人（《圣经》中希伯来人的后裔）移民到埃及后繁衍生息，但是逐渐增多的以色列人对埃及构成了潜在威胁，所以埃及法老下令将以色列人所生的男孩丢进河里，而成年的以色列人则被迫为奴。《圣经·出埃及记》讲述的便是摩西受神的旨意带领不堪忍受压迫与奴役的以色列人走出埃及的故事。
2. Helots in Sparta：古斯巴达奴隶希洛人。斯巴达是古希腊城邦之一，而奴隶希洛人归城邦所有。
3. Roman Slaves：古罗马奴隶，其中大多数为罗马对外侵略时俘获的外族奴隶。
4. Josephus：约瑟夫斯是犹太历史学家和军人，在一次反对罗马的犹太起义中战败投降，后前往罗马，著有《犹太战争史》（*History of the Jewish War*）、《犹太古事记》（*Antiquities of the Jews*）等关于犹太历史和宗教的书籍。
5. Plutarch：普鲁塔克是罗马传记文学家，其著作《希腊罗马名人传》（*Parallel Lives*）、《掌故清谈录》（*Moralia*）等是脍炙人口的传世佳作，对后世影响深远。
6. Yea：同yes。
7. 西班牙和葡萄牙是早期的殖民国家，在美洲拥有殖民地。它们起初强迫印第安人为其开采矿产、种植农作物，后来由于大多数印第安人死于疾病和劳累，西班牙人和葡萄牙人便开始从非洲带黑人来殖民地做苦工。英国、法国和荷兰也采用同样的方式。早在1619年，第一批黑人就由荷兰人从几内亚运送到弗吉尼亚当奴隶，这便是美洲奴隶制的起源。
8. oftimes：同oftentimes。
9. 据《圣经·出埃及记》，上帝为惩罚埃及法老压迫以色列人并证明只有他是唯一的神而连降十灾（尼罗河变血之灾、青蛙之灾、虱子之灾、苍蝇之灾、畜疫之灾、生疮之灾、冰雹和火之灾、蝗虫之灾、三天黑暗之灾和杀长子之灾）。然而，摩西受神的旨意让以色列人把羊羔的血涂在自家门框上，神的审判（Judgments of God）便越过以色列人的家而不降灾于他们，这就是以色列人逾越节的由来。
10. 据《圣经·出埃及记》，埃及法老派兵追击出走埃及的以色列人时，上帝让以色列人穿过红海，而将埃及人淹死在海中。
11. Lacedaemon：古斯巴达的别称。
12. Lycurgus：莱格古士，传说中公元前8世纪斯巴达的国王。
13. Sulla：路西乌斯·科尔涅利乌斯·苏拉（Lucius Cornelius Sulla, 公元前138—公元前78）是古罗马著名的统帅、贵族政治家和独裁者，希腊文化中也称他Sylla。
14. the conspiracy of Cataline：罗马共和国末期没落贵族喀提林企图夺取政权的阴谋。
15. Marc Antony：马克·安东尼（约公元前83—公元前30）是古罗马政治家、军事家和凯撒大帝的支持者，也是凯撒最重要的军队指挥官和管理人员之一；凯撒死后，安东尼与屋大维（Octavius）、雷必达（Lipidus）结成政治同盟，史称后三头同盟。

16. Octavius：屋大维（公元前63—公元14）原名盖乌斯·屋大维乌斯·图里努斯（Gaius Octavius Thurinus），其母亲是凯撒大帝的侄女。后来凯撒领养了屋大维并指定其为继承人，将其更名为盖乌斯·尤利乌斯·凯撒·屋大维乌斯（Gaius Julius Caesar Octavius）。屋大维是罗马帝国的开国君主，他结束了罗马共和国内战，并改组罗马政府，实行元首制，使罗马帝国进入了和平与繁荣的辉煌时期。公元前27年他被元老院赐予"奥古斯都"（Augustus）的称号。

17. Lipidus：马库斯·埃米利乌斯·雷必达（Marcus Aemilius Lipidus，约公元前89—公元前13或公元前12）是古罗马政治家和骑兵长官，也是凯撒大帝的追随者。公元前43年，雷必达与安东尼、屋大维结成同盟共治罗马帝国。

18. Phillippi：菲利皮是马其顿王国东部城市，公元前356年由菲利普二世（Philip Ⅱ）建立。公元前42年，布鲁图斯（Brutus）和卡西乌斯（Cassius）率兵占领菲利皮城，安东尼和屋大维为消灭共和派势力领兵进攻菲利皮，这就是著名的菲利皮之战。战争以布鲁图斯和卡西乌斯的失败而告终。

19. Brutus：马库斯·布鲁图斯（Marcus Junius Brutus Caepio, 公元前85—公元前42），罗马贵族世家出身，由于不满凯撒的独裁统治，于公元前44年密谋并参与了刺杀凯撒的行动。公元前42年，布鲁图斯死于菲利皮之战。

20. Cassius：盖乌斯·卡西乌斯·朗基努斯（Gaius Cassius Longinus, 早于公元前85—公元前42）是罗马共和国末期将领，同布鲁图斯一起参加了密谋刺杀凯撒的行动和菲利皮之战。

21. Tiberius：提贝里乌斯·克劳狄乌斯·尼禄（Tiberius Claudius Nero Caesar, 公元前42—公元37），又称提比略，是罗马最伟大的将领之一，曾率兵征服了潘诺尼亚、达尔马提亚和雷蒂，后继屋大维之位成为罗马帝国第二任皇帝。

22. Mahomed Ⅱ：穆罕默德二世（Fatih Sultan Mehmed, 1432—1481）是奥斯曼土耳其帝国第七代君主，也被称为土耳其苏丹（苏丹是伊斯兰教头衔）。1453年，穆罕默德二世率军攻占君士坦丁堡，灭亡了拜占庭帝国，并将君士坦丁堡更名为伊斯坦布尔，作为奥斯曼帝国的首都。

23.《圣经》中有多处"上帝是公正的和仁慈的"的说法，参见《但以理书》［"the Lord our God is just in all he has done" (9: 14)］、《申命记》［"he is a merciful God" (4: 31)］、《历代记》［"The Lord your God is merciful and compassionate" (30: 9)］等。

24. Lord of Sabaoth：指上帝。

思考题：

1. What was David Walker's purpose of citing the judgments of God?
2. According to Walker, what led to the wretchedness and miseries of both free and enslaved American blacks?
3. Why is *David Walker's Appeal* regarded as one of the most provocative political documents in the abolitionist movement in America?

12. Indian Removal Act (1830)①

Andrew Jackson

导读：

安德鲁·杰克逊（Andrew Jackson, 1767—1845）是美国第七任总统，也是美国历史上备受争议的一位总统。究其原因，大多与杰克逊政府对印第安人的态度和政策有关。19世纪20年代，战后②的美国工业发展迅速③，大批欧洲移民涌入美国，而白人移民与印第安人之间矛盾重重——土地争夺、文化冲突、种族歧视，这些都使美国政府与印第安部落的关系日益恶化。1830年5月28日，安德鲁·杰克逊总统签署了《印第安人迁移法》（"Indian Removal Act"），希望通过这种残酷的方式永远解决这个难题。该法案授权总统与居住在密西西比河以东地区的印第安部落谈判，美国政府用密西西比河以西的土地交换印第安人在东部各州境内的土地，要求密西西比河以东的印第安部落全部迁移到密西西比河以西，并拨款50万美元作为迁移资金。该法案一公布便招致许多印第安人与一些白人民主人士的反对，但是，南方各州渴望得到"文明化五部族"（Five Civilized Tribes）④的土地，因而极力支持。而时任总统杰克逊一方面为了夺取印第安人的土地资源来为白人谋利益，另一方面为了在两年后的第二次总统竞选中得到南方各州的选票，也支持

① Richard E. Ellis, *Andrew Jackson* (Washington, D.C.: CQ Press, a division of Congressional Quarterly Inc., 2003): 110-114.

② 指1812年战争（War of 1812），1812至1815年间美国与英国之间的战争，也称为美国第二次独立战争。1792至1815年间，拿破仑四处作战，欧洲动荡不安，而英法两国为争夺各自在欧洲的政治和经济地位展开了激烈的斗争。英国力图阻止美国在战争期间与法国的贸易；为了捍卫自己作为中立国与各国自由贸易的权利，美国于1812年向英国宣战。但是大部分印第安人由于不满美国人掠夺他们的土地资源支持英国，而英国也支持印第安部落抵抗美国的土地扩张。印第安人卷入这场战争，无疑使他们与美国政府之间的冲突日益加剧。

③ 战争切断了美国与英国的贸易，美国不得不自己生产原本需要进口的商品，因而大力发展制造业，美国的工业化进程由此得以推动。

④ 指切罗基族（Cherokee）、乔克托族（Choctaw）、克里克族（Creek）、奇克索族（Chickasaw）和西米诺尔族（Seminole）。

印第安人西迁。经过数次谈判与战争，大多数印第安部落同意西迁并签订了迁移条约。其中第一个便是1830年9月27日签订的《舞兔克里克条约》（“Treaty of Dancing Rabbit Creek”），随后还有《新埃可塔条约》（“Treaty of New Echota”，1835）等。而这些条约无论是自愿还是被诱导或被胁迫签订的，其结果都导致成千上万的印第安人被迫离开他们世世代代生活的故乡，被强制驱逐到西部贫瘠的荒凉之地。迁移过程中，大批印第安人死于疾病、饥饿或冻伤，仅切罗基人就有30%死于迁往俄克拉荷马的途中。而当他们到达所谓的印第安人保留地（Indian Territory）后，又因赞同迁移者与反对迁移者之间的冲突而处于长期的动乱之中。因此，印第安人的迁移之路又被称为美国历史上的“血泪之路”（Trail of Tears），而那些不愿意迁移的部落则遭到了美国军方的残酷屠杀。

虽然印第安人迁移政策自路易斯安那购地（Louisiana Purchase）之后便开始逐渐成形[①]，包括詹姆斯·门罗（James Monroe）和约翰·昆西·亚当斯（John Quincy Adams）在内的多位领导人都极力推行该政策，但是最终将其写进法律并付诸实践的是安德鲁·杰克逊。《印第安人迁移法》是美国对印第安人政策中重要的一部分，也引起了很多争议。可以说它帮助印第安人摆脱了原始落后的生活方式，解决了印第安人与白人之间的土地纷争，推动了美国的城市化进程，促进了社会的文明进步；也可以说它是蔑视人权的种族隔离，给印第安人带来了致命的灾难，泯灭了古老的部族文化，造就了“美国民主”即“白人的民主”的错误观念。有学者认为，对印第安人的迁移政策，“不能轻易地视之为失败或成功，恶毒或仁慈，它两者兼而有之”[②]。

本文节选自安德鲁·杰克逊的第二次国情咨文（The Second Annual Message to Congress），其中针对印第安人迁移的内容与《印第安人迁移法》的出台密切相关，充分表露出在印第安人迁移这个问题上美国主流社会的贪婪与伪善。

It gives me pleasure to announce to Congress that the benevolent policy of the

①路易斯安那购地让美国获得了密西西比河以西的大片土地，也为解决印第安人的问题提供了契机；美国用从法国购买的土地交换印第安人在东部的土地，迫使印第安人往西迁移。

②威尔科姆·E. 沃什伯恩著，陆毅译，《美国印第安人》，北京：商务印书馆，1997年，第183页。

Government, steadily pursued for nearly thirty years, in relation to the removal of the Indians beyond the white settlements is approaching to a happy consummation. Two important tribes[1] have accepted the provision made for their removal at the last session of Congress, and it is believed that their example will induce the remaining tribes also to seek the same obvious advantages.

The consequences of a speedy removal will be important to the United States, and to the Indians themselves. The pecuniary advantages which it promises to the Government are the least of its recommendations. It puts an end to all possible danger of collision between the authorities of the General and State Governments on account of the Indians. It will place a dense and civilized population in large tracts of country now occupied by a few savage hunters. By opening the whole territory between Tennessee on the north and Louisiana on the south to the settlement of the whites it will incalculably strengthen the southwestern frontier and render the adjacent States strong enough to repel future invasions without remote aid. It will relieve the whole State of Mississippi and the western part of Alabama of Indian occupancy, and enable those States to advance rapidly in population, wealth, and power. It will separate the Indians from immediate contact with settlements of whites; free from the power of the States; enable them to pursue happiness in their own way and under their own rude institutions; will retard the progress of decay, which is lessening their numbers, and perhaps cause them gradually, under the protection of the Government and through the influence of good counsels, to cast off their savage habits and become an interesting, civilized, and Christian community.[2] These consequences, some of them so certain and the rest so probable, make the complete execution of the plan sanctioned by Congress at their last session an object of much solicitude.

Toward the aborigines of the country no one can indulge a more friendly feeling than myself, or would go further in attempting to reclaim them from their wandering habits and make them a happy, prosperous people. I have endeavored to impress upon them my own solemn convictions of the duties and powers of the General Government in relation to the State authorities. For the justice of the laws passed by the States within the scope of their reserved powers they are not responsible to this government. As individuals we may entertain and express our opinions of their acts, but as a Government we have as little right to control them as we have to prescribe laws for other nations.

With a full understanding of the subject, the Choctaw and the Chickasaw tribes have with great unanimity determined to avail themselves of the liberal offers presented by the act of Congress, and have agreed to remove beyond the Mississippi River. Treaties have been made with them, which in due season will be submitted for consideration. In negotiating these treaties they were made to understand their true condition, and they have preferred maintaining their independence in the Western forests to submitting to the laws of the States in which they now reside. These treaties, being probably the last which will ever be made with them, are characterized by great liberality on the part of the Government. They give the Indians a liberal sum in consideration of their removal, and comfortable subsistence on their arrival at their new homes. If it be their real interest to maintain a separate existence, they will there be at liberty to do so without the inconveniences and vexations to which they would unavoidably have been subject in Alabama and Mississippi.

Humanity has often wept over the fate of the aborigines of this country, and Philanthropy has been long busily employed in devising means to avert it, but its progress has never for a moment been arrested, and one by one have many powerful tribes disappeared from the earth. To follow to the tomb the last of his race and to tread on the graves of extinct nations excite melancholy reflections. But true Philanthropy reconciles the mind to these vicissitudes as it does to the extinction of one generation to make room for another. In the monuments and fortresses of an unknown people, spread over the extensive regions of the West, we behold the memorials of a once powerful race, which was exterminated or has disappeared to make room for the existing savage tribes. Nor is there anything in this which, upon a comprehensive view of the general interests of the human race, is to be regretted. Philanthropy could not wish to see this continent restored to the condition in which it was found by our forefathers. What good man would prefer a country covered with forests and ranged by a few thousand savages to our extensive Republic, studded with cities, towns, and prosperous farms, embellished with all the improvements which art can devise or industry execute, occupied by more than 12,000,000 happy people, and filled with all the blessings of liberty, civilization, and religion?

The present policy of the Government is but a continuation of the same progressive change by a milder process. The tribes which occupied the countries now constituting the Eastern States were annihilated or have melted away to make room for the whites. The waves of population and civilization are rolling to the westward, and we now propose to acquire the countries occupied by the red men of the South and

West by a fair exchange, and, at the expense of the United States, to send them to a land where their existence may be prolonged and perhaps made perpetual.[3] Doubtless it will be painful to leave the graves of their fathers; but what do they more than our ancestors did or than our children are now doing? To better their condition in an unknown land our forefathers left all that was dear in earthly objects. Our children by thousands yearly leave the land of their birth to seek new homes in distant regions. Does Humanity weep at these painful separations from everything, animate and inanimate, with which the young heart has become entwined? Far from it. It is rather a source of joy that our country affords scope where our young population may range unconstrained in body or in mind, developing the power and faculties of man in their highest perfection. These remove hundreds and almost thousands of miles at their own expense, purchase the lands they occupy, and support themselves at their new homes from the moment of their arrival. Can it be cruel in this Government when, by events which it can not control, the Indian is made discontented in his ancient home to purchase his lands, to give him a new and extensive territory, to pay the expense of his removal, and support him a year in his new abode? How many thousands of our own people would gladly embrace the opportunity of removing to the West on such conditions! If the offers made to the Indians were extended to them, they would be hailed with gratitude and joy.

And is it supposed that the wandering savage has a stronger attachment to his home than the settled, civilized Christian? Is it more afflicting to him to leave the graves of his fathers than it is to our brothers and children? Rightly considered, the policy of the General Government toward the red man is not only liberal, but generous. He is unwilling to submit to the laws of the States and mingle with their population. To save him from his alternative, or perhaps utter annihilation, the General Government kindly offers him a new home, and proposes to pay the whole expense of his removal and settlement.

In the consummation of a policy originating at an early period and steadily pursued by every Administration within the present century—so just to the States and so generous to the Indians—the Executive feels it has a right to expect the cooperation of Congress and all good and disinterested men. The States, moreover, have a right to demand it. It was substantially a part of the compact which made them members of our Confederacy. With Georgia there is an express contract; with the new States an implied one of equal obligation. Why, in authorizing Ohio, Indiana, Illinois, Missouri,

Mississippi, and Alabama to form constitutions and become separate States, did Congress include within their limits extensive tracts of Indian lands, and, in some instances, powerful Indian tribes? Was it not understood by both parties that the power of the States was to be coextensive with their limits, and that with all convenient dispatch the General Government should extinguish the Indian title and remove every obstruction to the complete jurisdiction of the State governments over the soil? Probably not one of those States would have accepted a separate existence—certainly it would never have been granted by Congress—had it been understood that they were to be confined forever to those small portions of their nominal territory the Indian title to which had at the time been extinguished.

It is, therefore, a duty which this Government owes to the new States to extinguish as soon as possible the Indian title to all lands which congress themselves have included within their limits. When this is done the duties of the General Government in relation to the States and the Indians within their limits are at an end. The Indians may leave the State or not, as they choose. The purchase of their lands does not alter in the least their personal relations with the State government. No act of the General Government has ever been deemed necessary to give the States jurisdiction over the persons of the Indians. That they possess by virtue of their sovereign power within their own limits in as full a manner before as after the purchase of the Indian lands; nor can this Government add to or diminish it.

May we hope, therefore, that all good citizens, and none more zealously than those who think the Indians oppressed by subjection to the laws of the States, will unite in attempting to open the eyes of those children of the forest to their true condition, and by a speedy removal to relieve them from all the evils, real or imaginary, present or prospective, with which they may be supposed to be threatened.

注释:

1. Two important tribes：指乔克托族（Choctaw）和奇克索族（Chickasaw）。
2. 在对印第安人进行“文明开化”和民族同化的过程中，美国白人希望印第安人不仅放弃原有的“野蛮生活方式”，也放弃原有的信仰而改信基督教。
3. 美国政府并没有遵守这个诺言，之后又通过各种方式剥夺印第安人的土地。1854年美国国会通过了《堪萨斯-内布拉斯加法案》（“Kansas-Nebraska Act”），迫使印第安人割让大片土地；1887年美国国会通过了《印第安人土地专有权法》即《道斯法案》（“The Dawes Act”），强制实行土地私有化，印第安人的土地又一次被掠夺了。

思考题：

1. What are the influences of the "Indian Removal Act" on the history and culture of Native Americans?
2. Do you accept Andrew Jackson's rhetoric that the object of the American government to remove Native Americans was to save them from "utter annihilation"?
3. What aspect of American democracy can we see from the "Indian Removal Act"?

13. Self-Reliance (1841)①

Ralph Waldo Emerson

导读：

拉尔夫·瓦尔多·爱默生（Ralph Waldo Emerson, 1803—1882）是美国著名思想家、文学家、诗人，也是超验主义学说的创始人。爱默生出身于波士顿的一个牧师家庭，8岁时父亲去世，由母亲抚养成人。他14岁入读哈佛大学，毕业后一边任教，一边从事神学研究。1825年，爱默生又进入哈佛大学神学院学习，在完成学业之后被任命为波士顿第二教堂牧师，开始了和父亲相同的神职工作。然而，爱默生崇尚自然，强调精神的重要性，认为人与自然在精神上是统一的；他相信“超灵”的存在，并认为万事万物（包括人）都有灵魂，且万事万物的灵魂与“超灵”是一致的，因而主张人可以依靠自己的直觉直接解读上帝的启示，直接认识真理而不需要通过任何中介。这样的超验主义思想与传统的基督教信条格格不入，而爱默生倡导的自立、自助、独立自主的精神也颠覆了上帝的权威，打破了神学教条的束缚，这让当时的宗教人士极为不满。于是，1832年爱默生辞去牧师职务，开始以演讲和写作为生。殊不知这样的改变却造就了美国思想史、文学史上的一颗璀璨之星。

本文选自1841年爱默生发表的《自助》（“Self-Reliance”），文章处处体现出他的超验主义思想与自立创新的精神。文章开头引用了一句拉丁语点明主题——“Ne te quaesiveris extra”，即“不要在你自身之外寻找你自己”②。文中，爱默生宣扬人的自我价值和内心直觉的重要性，他不断告诉读者要相信自己，相信自己的思想，尤其是内心深处最真实的声音。他说：“一个人应当学会发现和观察从内部闪过他心灵的微光，而不是诗人和圣贤的太空里的光彩。”③由此看来，爱默生爱上帝，但他更爱内心的神圣，更爱真理。他认为：“除了你自己心灵的

① Ralph Waldo Emerson, *Selected Works of Ralph Waldo Emerson* (Shanghai: World Publishing Corporation, 2010): 71–96.

② 爱默生著，蒲隆译，《爱默生随笔》，上海：上海译文出版社，2010年，第72页。

③ 同上，第74页。

完善，没有什么神圣之物。”① 基于自我的神圣性，他反对权威，反对人们做顺民，反对向束缚人们的传统教条和社会体制投降，并号召人们依靠自己，依靠直觉来与上帝沟通，从而直接认识真理。他这种不顺从（nonconformity）的思想打破了传统教条的束缚，鼓励人们勇敢地按自己的想法生活，保持自己的个性，大声地说出真理。此外，爱默生还反对一成不变的一致。他认为：“如果强求一成不变，伟大的灵魂就一事无成。”② 对不一致（inconsistency）的推崇使我们敢于否定昨天的自己，推翻过去的错误理论，不卑不亢，追求真理与创新。

爱默生的这篇文章是美国文化与美国精神的缩影，其蕴含的超验主义思想和自立主张不仅影响了一代又一代的优秀作家（如梭罗、惠特曼），而且在美国的思想文化领域引起了巨大的震动，推动了美国文明的发展。

I read the other day some verses written by an eminent painter which were original and not conventional. The soul always hears an admonition in such lines, let the subject be what it may. The sentiment they instil is of more value than any thought they may contain. To believe your own thought, to believe that what is true for you in your private heart is true for all men—that is genius. Speak your latent conviction, and it shall be the universal sense; for the inmost in due time becomes the outmost, and our first thought is rendered back to us by the trumpets of the Last Judgment[1]. Familiar as the voice of the mind is to each, the highest merit we ascribe to Moses[2], Plato[3], and Milton[4] is that they set at naught books and traditions, and spoke not what men, but what *they* thought. A man should learn to detect and watch that gleam of light which flashes across his mind from within, more than the lustre of the firmament of bards and sages. Yet he dismisses without notice his thought, because it is his. In every work of genius we recognize our own rejected thoughts; they come back to us with a certain alienated majesty. Great works of art have no more affecting lesson for us than this. They teach us to abide by our spontaneous impression with good-humored inflexibility then most when the whole cry of voices is on the other side. Else to-morrow a stranger will say with masterly good sense precisely what we have thought and felt all the time, and we shall be forced to take with shame our own opinion from another.

① 爱默生著，蒲隆译，《爱默生随笔》，上海：上海译文出版社，2010年，第77页。
② 同上，第81页。

There is a time in every man's education when he arrives at the conviction that envy is ignorance; that imitation is suicide; that he must take himself for better, for worse, as his portion; that though the wide universe is full of good, no kernel of nourishing corn can come to him but through his toil bestowed on that plot of ground which is given to him to till. The power which resides in him is new in nature, and none but he knows what that is which he can do, nor does he know until he has tried. Not for nothing one face, one character, one fact, makes much impression on him, and another none. This sculpture in the memory is not without preestablished harmony. The eye was placed where one ray should fall, that it might testify of that particular ray. We but half express ourselves, and are ashamed of that divine idea which each of us represents. It may be safely trusted as proportionate and of good issues, so it be faithfully imparted, but God will not have his work made manifest by cowards. A man is relieved and gay when he has put his heart into his work and done his best; but what he has said or done otherwise shall give him no peace. It is a deliverance which does not deliver. In the attempt his genius deserts him; no muse befriends; no invention, no hope.

Trust thyself:[5] every heart vibrates to that iron string. Accept the place the divine providence has found for you, the society of your contemporaries, the connection of events. Great men have always done so, and confided themselves childlike to the genius of their age, betraying their perception that the absolutely trustworthy was seated at their heart, working through their hands, predominating in all their being. And we are now men, and must accept in the highest mind the same transcendent destiny; and not minors and invalids in a protected corner, not cowards fleeing before a revolution, but guides, redeemers and benefactors, obeying the Almighty effort and advancing on Chaos and the Dark.

....

These are the voices which we hear in solitude, but they grow faint and inaudible as we enter into the world. Society everywhere is in conspiracy against the manhood of every one of its members. Society is a joint-stock company, in which the members agree, for the better securing of his bread to each shareholder, to surrender the liberty and culture of the eater. The virtue in most request is conformity. Self-reliance is its aversion. It loves not realities and creators, but names and customs.

Whoso would be a man, must be a nonconformist. He who would gather immortal palms must not be hindered by the name of goodness, but must explore if it be goodness. Nothing is at last sacred but the integrity of your own mind. Absolve you to yourself, and you shall have the suffrage of the world. I remember an answer which when quite young I was prompted to make to a valued adviser who was wont to importune me with the dear old doctrines of the church. On my saying, "What have I to do with the sacredness of traditions, if I live wholly from within?" my friend suggested—"But these impulses may be from below, not from above." I replied, "They do not seem to me to be such; but if I am the Devil's child, I will live then from the Devil." No law can be sacred to me but that of my nature. Good and bad are but names very readily transferable to that or this; the only right is what is after my constitution; the only wrong what is against it. A man is to carry himself in the presence of all opposition as if every thing were titular and ephemeral but he. I am ashamed to think how easily we capitulate to badges and names, to large societies and dead institutions. Every decent and well-spoken individual affects and sways me more than is right. I ought to go upright and vital, and speak the rude truth in all ways...

What I must do is all that concerns me, not what the people think. This rule, equally arduous in actual and in intellectual life, may serve for the whole distinction between greatness and meanness. It is the harder because you will always find those who think they know what is your duty better than you know it. It is easy in the world to live after the world's opinion; it is easy in solitude to live after our own; but the great man is he who in the midst of the crowd keeps with perfect sweetness the independence of solitude.

The objection to conforming to usages that have become dead to you is that it scatters your force. It loses your time and blurs the impression of your character. If you maintain a dead church, contribute to a dead Bible-society, vote with a great party either for the government or against it, spread your table like base housekeepers—under all these screens I have difficulty to detect the precise man you are: and of course so much force is withdrawn from your proper life. But do your work, and I shall know you. Do your work, and you shall reinforce yourself. A man must consider what a blind-man's-buff is this game of conformity. If I know your sect I anticipate your argument. I hear a preacher announce for his text and topic the expediency of one of the institutions of his church. Do I not know beforehand that not possibly can he say a new and spontaneous word?... Well, most men have bound their eyes with one or another handkerchief, and attached themselves to some one of these communities of opinion. This conformity makes them not false in a few particulars, authors of a few lies, but false in all particulars. Their every truth is not quite true. Their two is not the real two, their four not the real four; so that every word they say chagrins us and we know not where to begin to set them right. Meantime nature is not slow to equip us in the prison-uniform of the party to which we adhere. We come to wear one cut of face and figure, and acquire by degrees the gentlest asinine expression. There is a mortifying experience in particular, which does not fail to wreak itself also in the general history; I mean "the foolish face of praise,"[6] the forced smile which we put on in company where we do not feel at ease, in answer to conversation which does not interest us. The muscles, not spontaneously moved but moved by a low usurping wilfulness, grow tight about the outline of the face, with the most disagreeable sensation.

For nonconformity the world whips you with its displeasure. And therefore a man must know how to estimate a sour face. The by-standers look askance on him in the public street or in the friend's parlor. If this aversation had its origin in contempt and resistance like his own he might well go home with a sad countenance; but the sour faces of the multitude, like their sweet faces, have no deep cause, but are put on and off as the wind blows and a newspaper directs. Yet is the discontent of the multitude more formidable than that of the senate and the college. It is easy enough for a firm man who knows the world to brook the rage of the cultivated classes. Their rage is decorous and prudent, for they are timid, as being very vulnerable themselves. But when to their feminine rage the indignation of the people is added, when the ignorant and the poor are aroused, when the unintelligent brute force that lies at the bottom of society is made to growl and mow, it needs the habit of magnanimity and religion to treat it godlike as a trifle of no concernment.

The other terror that scares us from self-trust is our consistency; a reverence for our past act or word because the eyes of others have no other data for computing our orbit than our past acts, and we are loath to disappoint them.

But why should you keep your head over your shoulder? Why drag about this corpse of your memory, lest you contradict somewhat you have stated in this or that public place? Suppose you should contradict yourself; what then? It seems to be a rule of wisdom never to rely on your memory alone, scarcely even in acts of pure memory, but to bring the past for judgment into the thousand-eyed present, and live ever in a new day. In your metaphysics you have denied personality to the Deity, yet when the devout motions of the soul come, yield to them heart and life, though they should clothe God with shape and color. Leave your theory, as Joseph his coat in the hand of the harlot, and flee.[7]

A foolish consistency is the hobgoblin of little minds, adored by little statesmen and philosophers and divines. With consistency a great soul has simply nothing to do. He may as well concern himself with his shadow on the wall. Speak what you think now in hard words and to-morrow speak what to-morrow thinks in hard words again, though it contradict every thing you said to-day.—"Ah, so you shall be sure to be misunderstood."—Is it so bad then to be misunderstood? Pythagoras[8] was misunderstood, and Socrates,[9] and Jesus, and Luther, and Copernicus,[10] and Galileo,[11] and Newton, and every pure and wise spirit that ever took flesh. To be great is to be misunderstood…

注释：

1. the Last Judgment："最后的审判"，也叫"末日审判"，是一种宗教思想，指在世界末日时神会出现，对世人进行审判裁决，好人得以永生，坏人则受到惩罚。这种观点最初起源于琐罗亚斯德教的教义，它认为创世的阿胡拉·玛兹达将会在末日时审判世界。后来，犹太教、基督教、伊斯兰教等宗教也继承了这一思想。《圣经》中《马太福音》（*Matthew*）和《启示录》（*Revelation*）对末日审判均有记述，在世界终结前，上帝和耶稣要对世人进行审判，凡信仰上帝和耶稣基督并行善者可升入天堂，反之，则得不到救赎，要下地狱接受惩罚。
2. Moses：摩西，犹太教、基督教和伊斯兰教等宗教信奉的一位伟大的先知。根据《圣经·出埃及记》（*Exodus*）的记述，公元前13世纪，摩西受上帝耶和华（Yahweh）之命，率领被奴役的希伯来人（又称以色列人）逃离古埃及，前往一块富饶的应许之地。在摩西的带领下，希伯来人迁徙到巴勒斯坦，摆脱了悲惨的奴隶生活，并成为历史上首个尊奉单一神宗教的民族。
3. Plato：柏拉图（约公元前427—公元前347），古希腊著名的哲学家和思想家，他与他的老师苏格拉底、学生亚里士多德被并称为西方哲学的奠基者。他写下了许多哲学对话录，并且在雅典创办了著名的学院，代表作有《伊壁鸠鲁篇》（*Euthyphro*）、《苏格拉底的申辩》（*The Defence of Socrates*）、《理想国》（*The Republic*）等。
4. Milton：弥尔顿（John Milton, 1608—1674），英国著名的诗人和思想家，也是清教徒文学界的代表人物，因其史诗《失乐园》（*Paradise Lost*）和反对书报审查制的《论出版自由》（*Areopagitica: A speech of Mr. John Milton for the liberty of unlicensed printing to the Parliament of England*）而闻名于后世。
5. thyself：同yourself。
6. "the foolish face of praise"：参见英国诗人亚历山大·蒲柏（Alexander Pope, 1688—

1744）的《与阿勃斯诺特医生书》（“Epistle to Dr. Arbuthnot”）。
7. 此句参见《圣经·创世记》（*Genesis*）39: 7–20。
8. Pythagoras：毕达哥拉斯（公元前572—公元前497），古希腊数学家和哲学家，发现了著名的毕达哥拉斯定理，即勾股定理。
9. Socrates：苏格拉底（公元前469—公元前399），古希腊杰出的思想家、哲学家和教育家。
10. Copernicus：哥白尼（Nicolas Copernicus，1473—1543），波兰天文学家，因发表“日心说”被罗马天主教会认为违反《圣经》而开除教籍。
11. Galileo：伽利略（Galileo Galilei, 1564—1642），意大利伟大的物理学家和天文学家，他的天文学发现及其著作明显地体现出哥白尼“日心说”的观点，他后来因此受到教会的残酷迫害。

思考题：

1. According to Emerson, what are the major aspects of self-reliance?
2. What is Emerson’s influence on American individualism?
3. Is there any difference between the “soul” and the “spirit” according to Emerson’s transcendentalism?

14. Civil Disobedience (1848)①

Henry David Thoreau

导读：

亨利·大卫·梭罗（Henry David Thoreau, 1817—1862）是美国颇具影响力的思想家、哲学家和作家。他从小生活在知识分子云集的文化小镇康科德（Concord），其思想深受超验主义学说创始人爱默生的影响。梭罗崇尚自然，向往心灵的自由，提倡简朴的生活方式，是一位超验主义实践家。1845年，他借了一柄斧头，独自来到离康科德镇不远的瓦尔登湖畔，在湖边的山林里砍白松，造房子，开始了两年零两个月的隐居生活。后来，他把自己这段时间的亲身体验与思想感悟写进了《瓦尔登湖》一书。他说："我走近丛林，是因为我想带着明确的目的去生活，以图直面生命的本质，以验证我是否无法领会它给予的启示，以免在我弥留之际，发现自己没有真正地生活过。"（I went to the woods because I wished to live deliberately, to front only the essential facts of life, and see if I could not learn what it had to teach, and not, when I came to die, discover that I had not lived.）②因而，梭罗的隐居并非是消极地退隐山林、远离尘嚣、逃避生活，而是通过回归自然的方式探索人生，积极地向世人展现一种简单纯朴而又轻松愉快的生活。

梭罗所生活的年代，正值西方第一次工业革命③空前发展之际。当时，工业和农业齐头并进，使美国迅速积累了许多物质财富④；"西进

① Henry David Thoreau, *Walden and "Civil Disobedience"* (New York: New American Library, 1999): 265-288.

② 原文请参见Henry David Thoreau, *Walden and "Civil Disobedience"* (New York: New American Library, 1999): 72；译文见梭罗著，仲泽译，《瓦尔登湖》，成都：四川文艺出版社，2011年，第117页。

③ 第一次工业革命：18世纪60年代至19世纪40年代。

④ 当时美国北方以工业为主，南方以农业、种植业为主。

运动”[①]大幅扩张了美国的疆域。当所有的土地都有了主人的时候，需要更多土地蓄奴种植棉花的奴隶主们便把目光投向墨西哥，挑起了美国和墨西哥的战争。而一向追求正义与公平的梭罗则通过拒绝交税来表达自己对奴隶制和墨西哥战争的抗议。在瓦尔登湖生活期间，梭罗因拒交“人头税”（poll tax）而被捕入狱，虽然他只在狱中待了一个晚上，但这一夜却激发了他对国家、社会和个人的许多思考。出狱后，他把自己对理想国家和政府的认识与对美国内政外交的批判结合在一起写成了这篇著名的《抵制国民政府》（“Resistance to Civil Government”，后改名为“Civil Disobedience”，译为《论公民的不服从》）。文中，梭罗指出“管得最少的政府是最好的政府”，当这个警句迅速且系统地得到实施之后，其最终结果将是——“一事不管的政府才是最好的政府”。他还认为一个理想的国家应该是一个“对所有人都主持正义，人人都能像邻居一样相互尊重”的国家。然而，理想与现实总是相去甚远。面对不公，面对压迫，梭罗告诉人们“尊重法律不如尊重正义”，因为“我们首先是人，其后才是公民”。人们应该用良知来判断正误，来抵制不公，而不是盲目地少数服从多数。梭罗所宣扬的这些思想使美国的民主、自由、平等的观念有了新的诠释，而这种非暴力抵抗非正义力量的方式也对印度的民族领袖甘地[②]领导的印度民族独立运动和美国黑人领袖马丁·路德·金[③]领导的民权运动产生了极大的影响。

I heartily accept the motto,—“That government is best which governs least”; and

---

① 西进运动（Westward Movement）始于18世纪末，终于19世纪末20世纪初，是指美国东部居民向西部地区迁移和开发西部的运动。西进运动使美国的疆土扩张七倍之多，促进了美国经济的发展。但是，随着西进运动的进行，大批印第安人遭到屠杀，其他的则被强迫迁移到西部更为荒凉贫瘠的地区。1830年5月，安德鲁·杰克逊总统签署了《印第安人迁移法》（“Indian Removal Act”），把印第安人押送出密西西比河以东地区。

② 莫罕达斯·卡拉姆昌德·甘地（Mohandas Karamchand Gandhi, 1869—1948），尊称圣雄甘地（Mahatma Gandhi），是印度民族解放运动的领导人。他把梭罗的政治思想发展成“非暴力不合作”（non-violence），主张以和平的方式抵制政府，反对压迫，他的“非暴力不合作运动”（Satyagraha Movement）使印度摆脱了英国的殖民统治而走向独立。

③ 马丁·路德·金（Martin Luther King Jr., 1929—1968），著名的美国民权运动领袖，组织了多次为黑人争取工作机会和平等权利的游行与罢工。1963年8月28日他在林肯纪念堂前发表了著名演讲《我有一个梦想》（“I Have a Dream”），并在演讲中呼吁团结，呼吁正义，呼吁人人平等。1964年他获得诺贝尔和平奖。

I should like to see it acted up to more rapidly and systematically. Carried out, it finally amounts to this, which also I believe,—"That government is best which governs not at all"; and when men are prepared for it, that will be the kind of government which they will have. Government is at best but an expedient; but most governments are usually, and all governments are sometimes, inexpedient. The objections which have been brought against a standing army, and they are many and weighty, and deserve to prevail, may also at last be brought against a standing government. The standing army is only an arm of the standing government. The government itself, which is only the mode which the people have chosen to execute their will, is equally liable to be abused and perverted before the people can act through it. Witness the present Mexican war,[1] the work of comparatively a few individuals using the standing government as their tool; for, in the outset, the people would not have consented to this measure.

This American government, —what is it but a tradition, though a recent one, endeavoring to transmit itself unimpaired to posterity, but each instant losing some of its integrity? It has not the vitality and force of a single living man; for a single man can bend it to his will. It is a sort of wooden gun to the people themselves. But it is not the less necessary for this; for the people must have some complicated machinery or other, and hear its din, to satisfy that idea of government which they have. Governments show thus how successfully men can be imposed on, even impose on themselves, for their own advantage. It is excellent, we must all allow. Yet this government never of itself furthered any enterprise, but by the alacrity with which it got out of its way. *It* does not keep the country free. *It* does not settle the West. *It* does not educate. The character inherent in the American people has done all that has been accomplished; and it would have done somewhat more, if the government had not sometimes got in its way. For government is an expedient by which men would fain succeed in letting one another alone; and, as has been said, when it is most expedient, the governed are most let alone by it. Trade and commerce, if they were not made of India-rubber, would never manage to bounce over the obstacles which legislators are continually putting in their way; and, if one were to judge these men wholly by the effects of their actions and not partly by their intentions, they would deserve to be classed and punished with those mischievous persons who put obstructions on the railroads.

But, to speak practically and as a citizen, unlike those who call themselves no-government men, I ask for, not at once no government, but *at once* a better government. Let every man make known what kind of government would command his respect, and that will be one step toward obtaining it.

After all, the practical reason why, when the power is once in the hands of the people, a majority are permitted, and for a long period continue, to rule, is not because they are most likely to be in the right, nor because this seems fairest to the minority, but because they are physically the strongest. But a government in which the majority rule in all cases cannot be based on justice, even as far as men understand it. Can there not be a government in which majorities do not virtually decide right and wrong, but conscience?—in which majorities decide only those questions to which the rule of expediency is applicable? Must the citizen ever for a moment, or in the least degree, resign his conscience to the legislator? Why has every man a conscience, then? I think that we should be men first, and subjects afterward. It is not desirable to cultivate a respect for the law, so much as for the right. The only obligation which I have a right to assume is to do at any time what I think right…

How does it become a man to behave toward this American government to-day? I answer, that he cannot without disgrace be associated with it. I cannot for an instant recognize that political organization as *my* government which is the *slave's* government also.

All men recognize the right of revolution; that is, the right to refuse allegiance to, and to resist the government, when its tyranny or its inefficiency are great and unendurable. But almost all say that such is not the case now. But such was the case, they think, in the Revolution of '75.[2] If one were to tell me that this was a bad government because it taxed certain foreign commodities brought to its ports, it is most probable that I should not make an ado about it, for I can do without them. All machines have their friction; and possibly this does enough good to counterbalance the evil. At any rate, it is a great evil to make a stir about it. But when the friction comes to have its machine, and oppression and robbery are organized, I say, let us not have such a machine any longer. In other words, when a sixth of the population of a nation which has undertaken to be the refuge of liberty are slaves, and a whole country is unjustly overrun and conquered by a foreign army, and subjected to military law, I think that it is not too soon for honest men to rebel and revolutionize. What makes this duty the more urgent is the fact, that the country so overrun is not our own, but ours is the invading army…[3]

Practically speaking, the opponents to a reform in Massachusetts are not a hundred thousand politicians at the South, but a hundred thousand merchants and farmers here, who are more interested in commerce and agriculture than they are in humanity, and are not prepared to do justice to the slave and to Mexico, *cost what it may*. I quarrel not with far-off foes, but with those who, near at home, coöperate with, and do the bidding of those far away, and without whom the latter would be harmless. We are accustomed to say, that the mass of men are unprepared; but improvement is slow, because the few are not materially wiser or better than the many. It is not so important that many should be as good as you, as that there be some absolute goodness somewhere; for that will leaven the whole lump. There are thousands who are *in opinion* opposed to slavery and to the war, who yet in effect do nothing to put an end to them; who, esteeming themselves children of Washington and Franklin, sit down with their hands in their pockets, and say that they know not what to do, and do nothing; who even postpone the question of freedom to the question of free-trade, and quietly read the prices-current along with the latest advices from Mexico, after dinner, and, it may be, fall asleep over them both…

Unjust laws exist; shall we be content to obey them, or shall we endeavor to amend them, and obey them until we have succeeded, or shall we transgress them at once? Men generally, under such a government as this, think that they ought to wait until they have persuaded the majority to alter them. They think that, if they should resist, the remedy would be worse than the evil. But it is the fault of the government itself that the remedy *is* worse than the evil. *It* makes it worse. Why is it not more apt to anticipate and provide for reform? Why does it not cherish its wise minority? Why does it cry and resist before it is hurt? Why does it not encourage its citizens to be on the alert to point out its faults, and *do* better than it would have them? Why does it always crucify Christ, and excommunicate Copernicus and Luther[4], and pronounce Washington and Franklin rebels?…

If the injustice is part of the necessary friction of the machine of government, let it go, let it go: perchance it will wear smooth,—certainly the machine will wear out. If the injustice has a spring, or a pulley, or a rope, or a crank, exclusively for itself, then perhaps you may consider whether the remedy will not be worse than the evil; but if it is of such a nature that it requires you to be the agent of injustice to another, then, I say, break the law. Let your life be a counter friction to stop the machine. What I have to do is to see, at any rate, that I do not lend myself to the wrong which I condemn.

As for adopting the ways which the State has provided for remedying the evil, I know not of such ways. They take too much time, and a man's life will be gone. I have other affairs to attend to. I came into this world, not chiefly to make this a good place to live in, but to live in it, be it good or bad. A man has not everything to do, but something; and because he cannot do *everything*, it is not necessary that he should do *something* wrong. It is not my business to be petitioning the Governor or the Legislature any more than it is theirs to petition me; and, if they should not hear my petition, what should I do then? But in this case the state has provided no way: its very Constitution is the evil. This may seem to be harsh and stubborn and unconciliatory; but it is to treat with the utmost kindness and consideration the only spirit that can appreciate or deserve it. So is all change for the better, like birth and death, which convulse the body.

I do not hesitate to say, that those who call themselves Abolitionists should at once effectually withdraw their support, both in person and property, from the government of Massachusetts and not wait till they constitute a majority of one, before they suffer the right to prevail through them. I think that it is enough if they have God on their side, without waiting for that other one. Moreover, any man more right than his neighbors constitutes a majority of one already…

注释：

1. Mexican war：墨西哥战争，指1846至1848年间美国和墨西哥之间爆发的一场战争。双方于1848年1月开始和谈，2月签订和约，美国获得了得克萨斯、新墨西哥和加利福尼亚等州的大片土地，而废奴主义者们则认为美国想借此拓宽疆域蓄奴种植，进而把奴隶制推进到更多地方。
2. the Revolution of '75：1775年，美国人民在列克星敦（Lexington）与康科德（Concord）打响了独立战争的第一枪，拉开了美国独立战争的序幕。此次革命使北美13个州脱离了英国的殖民统治，并且创立了美利坚合众国。
3. 此句指美国入侵墨西哥，发动墨西哥战争。
4. Luther：马丁·路德（Martin Luther, 1483—1546）：16世纪欧洲宗教改革的倡导者及基督教新教路德教派的创始人。

思考题：

1. Do you agree that "That government is best which governs not at all"? Please justify your

point with examples from reality, especially, by comparing the performance of Chinese government and American government in face of great disasters.

2. What was Thoreau's attitude toward the existing unjust laws?

15. Declaration of Sentiments and Resolutions (1848)①

Elizabeth Cady Stanton

导读：

伊丽莎白·卡迪·斯坦顿（Elizabeth Cady Stanton, 1815—1902）出生于美国纽约州的约翰斯敦（Johnstown）。其父丹尼尔·卡迪（Daniel Cady）是著名律师，曾担任国会议员（1814—1817）。他不仅让伊丽莎白从小接受良好的教育，学习拉丁文、希腊文等课程，还将法律带进了伊丽莎白的生活，这让她很早就意识到妇女在法律上的不平等地位。后来，伊丽莎白在参与禁酒运动和废奴运动时结识了兼任记者和废奴主义演说家的亨利·布鲁斯特·斯坦顿（Henry Brewster Stanton, 1805—1887），两人于1840年结为夫妻。婚后，伊丽莎白深受丈夫废奴主义思想的影响，欲与其一同参加在伦敦召开的第一次国际废奴大会。然而，这些当时最开明、最激进的废奴主义者在为黑人奴隶争取平等权利的同时却忽视了妇女的平等权利。他们不给妇女正式代表资格，不允许妇女发言，这引起了包括伊丽莎白在内的很多妇女的强烈不满。② 因此，她们决定开展女权运动，为自己争取平等权利。1848年7月，伊丽莎白在柳克丽霞·莫特（Lucretia Mott）的协助下在塞尼卡福尔斯（Seneca Falls）召开了美国历史上第一次女权大会。会上，伊丽莎白发表了这篇《感伤宣言与决议》（"Declaration of Sentiments and Resolutions"），她也因此成为美国早期女权运动的领导人。

这篇由伊丽莎白·卡迪·斯坦顿起草的宣言开篇便模仿《独立宣言》来道出其中心思想："我们认为下面这些真理是不言而喻的：男人与女人生而平等；造物者赋予她们若干不可剥夺的权利，其中包括生命权、自由权和追求幸福的权利。"接着，宣言指出，"人类的历史是一

① Mari Jo and Paul Buhle, eds., *The Concise History of Woman Suffrage* (Urbana: University of Illinois Press, 1978): 94-97.

② 在第一次国际废奴大会上，参会代表对妇女的态度让她们非常诧异，此时妇女们意识到在这个男权至上的社会里原来自己也是"奴隶"。因此，她们便开始了为自己争取平等权利的斗争。大多数女权主义者都曾是和男性一起参与废奴运动的废奴主义者，而当时也有些废奴主义组织排斥女性的加入。

部男人对妇女不断伤害与掠夺的历史”，因为男人剥夺了女人的选举权、财产权、自由权、受教育的权利、离婚权以及离婚后的子女监护权，并且让女人在贸易、商业、宗教等诸多方面遭受不公平的待遇。接下来的12条决议则针对女性受歧视的不公平现象提出男女平等、妇女应享有和男人同等权利的观点，如妇女享有和男人同等的选举权，在各行各业和社交活动中妇女享有与男人同样的参与权，在道德和举止谈吐等方面对男人和妇女应提出同等要求等。

伊丽莎白·卡迪·斯坦顿起草的宣言与决议让19世纪只拥有少数法律知识和政治权利的妇女从被压迫与歧视中觉醒，为妇女争取自由和平等权利的斗争拉开了序幕，掀起了美国女权运动①的第一次浪潮。在经过长达72年的不懈努力后，1920年美国国会通过了第19条宪法修正案，美国妇女终于获得了投票选举权。

Declaration of Sentiments

When, in the course of human events, it becomes necessary for one portion of the family of man to assume among the people of the earth a position different from that which they have hitherto occupied, but one to which the laws of nature and of nature's God entitle them, a decent respect to the opinions of mankind requires that they should declare the causes that impel them to such a course.

We hold these truths to be self-evident: that all men and women are created equal; that they are endowed by their Creator with certain inalienable rights; that among these are life, liberty, and the pursuit of happiness; that to secure these rights governments are instituted, deriving their just powers from the consent of the governed. Whenever any form of government becomes destructive of these ends, it is the right of those who suffer from it to refuse allegiance to it, and to insist upon the institution of a new government, laying its foundation on such principles, and organizing its powers in such form, as to them shall seem most likely to effect their safety and happiness. Prudence, indeed, will dictate that governments long established should not be changed

① 美国女权运动兴起于19世纪40年代，其标志则是1848年在塞尼卡福尔斯召开的美国第一次女权大会。早期参与女权运动的妇女并不称自己为女权主义者（Feminist），而自称为妇女权利的支持者（Advocate of women's rights）或妇女政权论者（Suffragist）。女权运动的第二次浪潮出现在20世纪60年代，第三次浪潮始于20世纪80年代。

for light and transient causes; and accordingly all experience hath shown that mankind are more disposed to suffer, while evils are sufferable, than to right themselves by abolishing the forms to which they were accustomed. But when a long train of abuses and usurpations, pursuing invariably the same object evinces a design to reduce them under absolute despotism, it is their duty to throw off such government, and to provide new guards for their future security. Such has been the patient sufferance of the women under this government, and such is now the necessity which constrains them to demand the equal station to which they are entitled.

The history of mankind is a history of repeated injuries and usurpations on the part of man toward woman, having in direct object the establishment of an absolute tyranny over her. To prove this, let facts be submitted to a candid world.

He has never permitted her to exercise her inalienable right to the elective franchise.

He has compelled her to submit to laws, in the formation of which she had no voice.

He has withheld from her rights which are given to the most ignorant and degraded men—both natives and foreigners.

Having deprived her of this first right of a citizen, the elective franchise, thereby leaving her without representation in the halls of legislation, he has oppressed her on all sides.

He has made her, if married, in the eye of the law, civilly dead.

He has taken from her all right in property, even to the wages she earns.

He has made her, morally, an irresponsible being, as she can commit many crimes with impunity, provided they be done in the presence of her husband. In the covenant of marriage, she is compelled to promise obedience to her husband, he becoming, to all intents and purposes, her master—the law giving him power to deprive her of her liberty, and to administer chastisement.

He has so framed the laws of divorce, as to what shall be the proper causes, and in case of separation, to whom the guardianship of the children shall be given, as to be wholly regardless of the happiness of women—the law, in all cases, going upon a false supposition of the supremacy of man, and giving all power into his hands.

After depriving her of all rights as a married woman, if single, and the owner of property, he has taxed her to support a government which recognizes her only when her property can be made profitable to it.

He has monopolized nearly all the profitable employments, and from those she is permitted to follow, she receives but a scanty remuneration. He closes against her all the avenues to wealth and distinction which he considers most honorable to himself. As a teacher of theology, medicine, or law, she is not known.

He has denied her the facilities for obtaining a thorough education, all colleges being closed against her.

He allows her in Church, as well as State, but a subordinate position, claiming Apostolic authority for her exclusion from the ministry, and, with some exceptions, from any public participation in the affairs of the Church.

He has created a false public sentiment by giving to the world a different code of morals for men and women, by which moral delinquencies which exclude women from society, are not only tolerated, but deemed of little account in man.

He has usurped the prerogative of Jehovah[1] himself, claiming it as his right to assign for her a sphere of action, when that belongs to her conscience and to her God.

He has endeavored, in every way that he could, to destroy her confidence in her own powers, to lessen her self-respect, and to make her willing to lead a dependent and abject life.

Now, in view of this entire disfranchisement of one-half the people of this country, their social and religious degradation—in view of the unjust laws above mentioned, and because women do feel themselves aggrieved, oppressed, and fraudulently deprived of their most sacred rights, we insist that they have immediate admission to all the rights and privileges which belong to them as citizens of the United States.

In entering upon the great work before us, we anticipate no small amount of misconception, misrepresentation, and ridicule; but we shall use every instrumentality within our power to effect our object. We shall employ agents, circulate tracts, petition the State and National legislatures, and endeavor to enlist the pulpit and the press in our behalf. We hope this Convention will be followed by a series of Conventions embracing every part of the country.

Resolutions

Whereas, the great precept of nature is conceded to be, that "man shall pursue his own true and substantial happiness." Blackstone[2] in his Commentaries remarks, that this law of Nature being coeval with mankind, and dictated by God himself, is of course superior in obligation to any other. It is binding over all the globe, in all countries and at all times; no human laws are of any validity if contrary to this, and such of them as are valid, derive all their force, and all their validity, and all their authority, mediately and immediately, from this original; therefore,

Resolved, That such laws as conflict, in any way, with the true and substantial happiness of woman, are contrary to the great precept of nature and of no validity, for this is "superior in obligation to any other."

Resolved, That all laws which prevent woman from occupying such a station in society as her conscience shall dictate, or which place her in a position inferior to that of man, are contrary to the great precept of nature, and therefore of no force or authority.

Resolved, That woman is man's equal—was intended to be so by the Creator, and the highest good of the race demands that she should be recognized as such.

Resolved, That the women of this country ought to be enlightened in regard to the laws under which they live, that they may no longer publish their degradation by declaring themselves satisfied with their present position, nor their ignorance, by asserting that they have all the rights they want.

Resolved, That inasmuch as man, while claiming for himself intellectual superiority, does accord to woman moral superiority, it is pre-eminently his duty to encourage her to speak and teach, as she has an opportunity, in all religious assemblies.

Resolved, That the same amount of virtue, delicacy, and refinement of behavior that is required of woman in the social state, should also be required of man, and the same transgressions should be visited with equal severity on both man and woman.

Resolved, That the objection of indelicacy and impropriety, which is so often brought against woman when she addresses a public audience, comes with a very ill-grace from those who encourage, by their attendance, her appearance on the stage, in the concert, or in feats of the circus.

Resolved, That woman has too long rested satisfied in the circumscribed limits which corrupt customs and a perverted application of the Scriptures[3] have marked out for her, and that it is time she should move in the enlarged sphere which her great Creator has assigned her.

Resolved, That it is the duty of the women of this country to secure to themselves their sacred right to the elective franchise.

Resolved, That the equality of human rights results necessarily from the fact of the identity of the race in capabilities and responsibilities.

Resolved, *therefore*, That, being invested by the Creator with the same capabilities, and the same consciousness of responsibility for their exercise, it is demonstrably the right and duty of woman, equally with man, to promote every righteous cause by every righteous means; and especially in regard to the great subjects of morals and religion, it is self-evidently her right to participate with her brother in teaching them, both in private and in public, by writing and by speaking, by any instrumentalities proper to be used, and in any assemblies proper to be held; and this being a self-evident truth growing out of the divinely implanted principles of human nature, any custom or authority adverse to it, whether modern or wearing the hoary sanction of antiquity, is to be regarded as a self-evident falsehood, and at war with mankind.

Resolved, That the speedy success of our cause depends upon the zealous and untiring efforts of both men and women, for the overthrow of the monopoly of the pulpit, and for the securing to woman an equal participation with men in the various trades, professions, and commerce.

注释：

1. Jehovah：耶和华，指上帝。
2. Blackstone：威廉·布莱克斯通爵士（Sir William Blackstone, 1723—1780），英国法学家、法官。他认为一切法律应遵守自然法和神法，其主要著作《英国法释义》系统地阐述了英国法，对英国和美国的法律界和法律研究影响深远。
3. the Scriptures：《圣经》。

思考题：

1. Why did Elizabeth Cady Stanton deliberately model the "Declaration of Sentiments" on "The Declaration of Independence"?
2. What's in the "Declaration of Sentiments"?
3. Do you think the sentiments expressed here include those of African American women and Native American women?

16. Address to the Ohio Women's Rights Convention (1851)[①]

Sojourner Truth

导读：

索杰纳·特鲁斯（Sojourner Truth, 1797—1883）原名伊莎贝拉·鲍姆弗里（Isabella Baumfree），是美国著名的黑人废奴主义者和妇女权利的倡导者。她出生于纽约州阿尔斯特县的一个奴隶家庭。1826年年底，纽约州废除奴隶制前夕，她为自己争得了自由。[②]她目不识丁，却谙熟圣经，1843年，在宗教信仰的启迪下，改名为索杰纳·特鲁斯[③]。之后她人如其名，积极投身传教工作，同时宣传废奴和女权主义的思想。南北战争期间，特鲁斯致力护理伤员，募集给养，并于1864年10月受到亚伯拉罕·林肯总统的接见。

特鲁斯是一名优秀的演说家，她以自己近三十年的北方奴隶经历慷慨激昂地控诉奴隶制的种种罪恶，激发公众的反奴隶制觉悟。她是

① James Daley, ed., *Great Speeches by African Americans: Frederick Douglass, Sojourner Truth, Dr. Martin Luther King, Jr., Barack Obama, and Others* (Mineola, New York: Dover Publications, Inc., 2006): 11-12. 索杰纳·特鲁斯在1851年5月俄亥俄州妇女权利大会上发表的演讲有两种记载。一种是由编辑塞勒姆市的《反奴号角》的白人男性马里厄斯·鲁宾逊（Marius Robinson）记录的，用的是准确的英语表达，于1851年6月发表在该报上。另一种记载是用方言写成的，于1863年4月发表在纽约《独立报》上，记录者是此次会议的组织者、白人女性作家弗朗西斯·达纳·盖奇（Frances Dana Gage）。为了便于理解，这里选用的是翻译成标准英语的盖奇的记载。

② 1799年纽约州通过了逐步解放奴隶法，规定奴隶主释放1799年7月4日以后出生的奴隶儿童以及年满28周岁的男性奴隶和25周岁的女性奴隶。1817年又出台一项法律，规定奴隶主在1827年7月4日前释放所有年满28周岁的奴隶。1825年，特鲁斯当时的主人约翰·杜蒙（John Dumont）与其达成协议，如果特鲁斯更加努力工作，他将提前一年释放她。一年以后，杜蒙拒绝履行承诺。但特鲁斯认为自己已经自由，所以她逃离庄园，投奔教友会教徒冯·瓦格纳（Van Wageners）。杜蒙追到瓦格纳家后，瓦格纳买下特鲁斯，并即刻宣布她自由。还有种说法，瓦格纳直到1827年7月4日才释放特鲁斯，但一直让她像一个自由人一样生活。

③ 特鲁斯改名后的姓Truth是“真理”的意思，名Sojourner是“旅居者”的意思。她之所以选择这个名字是因为她觉得主召唤她“周游全国，向人们指明他们的罪孽，并向他们昭示神的旨意”。

第一位将废除奴隶制的事业与争取女性平等权利的事业融为一体并为之四处演讲宣传的黑人女性。哈里雅特·比彻·斯托（Harriet Beecher Stowe, 1811—1896）称赞特鲁斯为“利比亚女先知”[①]。如今，特鲁斯的半身塑像陈列在美国国会大厦，她是首位享此殊荣的美国黑人女性。

19世纪上半叶，美国社会掀起了一次社会改革高潮，各个社会改良运动尤其是废奴运动中不断涌现出大批女性活动家，甚至是女性领袖。她们在改革中日益接受性别平等观念，在为黑人奴隶争取自由的同时逐渐意识到妇女自身受歧视、被限制的处境，从而开始转入争取女性自身权利的运动之中。从40年代起，妇女逐渐发起了争取财产权、子女监护权、教育权、选举权等运动。1848年7月，在纽约北部的塞尼卡福尔斯召开了美国历史上第一次妇女权利大会，会上讨论并签署了《感伤宣言与决议》，明确提出了妇女选举权的问题。这次大会的召开标志着美国女权运动向组织化、规模化方向迈进。自1850年起的十年间，有许多州代表参加的大型集会几乎年年举行，小城镇里类似的集会屡见不鲜。1851年在俄亥俄州阿克伦举行的妇女权利大会就是其中之一。正是在这次会议上，特鲁斯发出了质问：“难道我不是一个女人吗？”

会上先于特鲁斯发言的有几位男教士，他们高唱男女平等的反调，理由不外乎老生常谈的几条：女人天生就是弱者；耶稣是男人；女人犯了原罪，决定了她的从属地位。特鲁斯一一驳斥了他们的观点。她用切身经历撕碎了女人身上“弱者”的标签，又以子之矛，攻子之盾，巧妙而有力地击破了其他几个伪命题。特鲁斯是与会的唯一黑人，许多与会者反对她发言，担心她会把女权运动和黑人解放运动扯在一起。特鲁斯演讲前，会场一片嘘声，演讲结束后，会场爆发出雷鸣般的掌声。特鲁斯这篇即席演讲体现了她的一贯风格：言语犀利，角度新颖，一针见血，雄辩有力，为刚刚起步的女权运动打赢了漂亮的一仗。而她在会场上的质问也在美国女权运动史上留下了永久的回声。

Well, children,[1] where there is so much racket there must be something out of

① 《解放奴隶宣言》正式发布后没几天，特鲁斯中风了，不久就传出她去世的谣言。哈里雅特·比彻·斯托得知后信以为真，写了篇题为《索杰纳·特鲁斯：利比亚女先知》（“Sojourner Truth, the Libyan Sibyl”）的文章，缅怀特鲁斯一生的功绩，发表在《大西洋月刊》上。之后特鲁斯就常被人称为“利比亚女先知”。

kilter. I think that 'twixt the Negroes of the South and the women at the North, all talking about rights, the white men will be in a fix pretty soon. But what's all this here talking about?

That man over there says that women need to be helped into carriages, and lifted over ditches, and to have the best place everywhere. Nobody ever helps me into carriages, or over mud-puddles, or gives me any best place! And ain't I a woman? Look at me! Look at my arm! I have ploughed and planted, and gathered into barns, and no man could head me! And ain't I a woman? I could work as much and eat as much as a man—when I could get it—and bear the lash as well! And ain't I a woman? I have borne thirteen children,[2] and seen most all sold off to slavery, and when I cried out with my mother's grief, none but Jesus heard me! And ain't I a woman?

Then they talk about this thing in the head; what's this they call it? [member of audience whispers, "intellect"] That's it, honey. What's that got to do with women's rights or Negroes' rights? If my cup won't hold but a pint, and yours holds a quart, wouldn't you be mean not to let me have my little half measure full?

Then that little man in black there, he says women can't have as much rights as men, 'cause Christ wasn't a woman! Where did your Christ come from? Where did your Christ come from? From God and a woman! Man had nothing to do with Him.

If the first woman God ever made was strong enough to turn the world upside down all alone, these women together ought to be able to turn it back, and get it right side up again! And now they is asking to do it, the men better let them.

Obliged to you for hearing me, and now old Sojourner ain't got nothing more to say.

注释：

1. 这是特鲁斯演讲时常用的开场白。
2. 特鲁斯只有五个孩子，这里特鲁斯是用自己的口吻讲述她母亲的经历。

思考题：

1. What were the connotations of Sojourner Truth's famous question "Ain't I a woman"?
2. What aspects of American society were revealed by Sojourner Truth's question "Ain't I a woman"?

17. Independence Day Speech at Rochester (1852)[①]

Frederick Douglass

导读:

弗雷德里克·道格拉斯（Frederick Douglass, 1818—1895）是19世纪美国黑人解放运动中杰出的黑人领袖，著名的人道主义者、演说家。生而为奴的他有幸掌握了读写技能[②]，研读了不少著名演讲[③]，年少时就充满了对奴隶制的仇恨和对自由的向往。1838年道格拉斯逃往北方，随后积极投身废奴运动，逐渐成长为废奴运动的骨干和领导者。1847年道格拉斯独立创办反奴报纸——《北极星》报（*North Star*）[④]，开辟了废奴运动的一个重要宣传阵地。美国南北战争期间，道格拉斯积极推动并号召黑人踊跃参军，同时努力为黑人士兵争取平等权利和公平待遇。奴隶制被废除后，道格拉斯继续领导黑人争取公民权和选举权，并取得了成功。

道格拉斯一生致力争取黑人平等权利和彻底解放，他同时也是女权运动的坚定支持者，为妇女解放事业做出了巨大的努力。道格拉斯还是一位著名的作家，先后出版了三部自传[⑤]，为19世纪美国黑人文学做出了

---

① James Daley, ed., *Great Speeches by African Americans: Frederick Douglass, Sojourner Truth, Dr. Martin Luther King, Jr., Barack Obama, and Others* (Mineola, New York: Dover Publications, Inc., 2006): 13-34.

② 1827年，道格拉斯在巴尔的摩做家僮时，女主人索菲娅·奥尔德曾教道格拉斯字母，男主人休·奥尔德得知后大发雷霆。索菲亚从此不仅不再教他识字，而且禁止他看书读报。休·奥尔德夫妇的阻碍反而激起道格拉斯更大的学习热情，他刻苦自学，最终掌握了良好的读写技能。

③ 道格拉斯13岁时得到一本《哥伦比亚演说家》。该书由一名马萨诸塞反对奴隶制的牧师在1797年编辑而成，其中不仅有乔治·华盛顿和英国政治家威廉·皮特的讲稿，还收录了古希腊罗马时期的演说。道格拉斯从这本书中不仅看到了前辈对奴隶制的大胆谴责和对人权的有力维护，还学会了雄辩术。

④ 1851年该报与《自由党报》合并，改为《弗雷德里克·道格拉斯报》，1860年6月，因经济困难，改为《道格拉斯月报》。

⑤ 即1845年出版的《弗雷德里克·道格拉斯：一个美国奴隶的叙述，由他本人撰写》（*Narrative of the Life of Frederick Douglass, an American Slave, Written by Himself*）、1855年出版的《我的奴隶生涯和我的自由》（*My Bondage and My Freedom*），以及1881年出版（1892年增订）的《弗雷德里克·道格拉斯的生平和时代》（*The Life and Times of Frederick Douglass*）。

杰出的贡献。

1847年道格拉斯从英国回到美国后①，居住在纽约的罗切斯特。因为他的到来及《北极星》报的诞生，罗切斯特成为废奴运动的一个大本营。1852年道格拉斯被邀请在罗切斯特的美国独立纪念日集会上演讲。美国独立纪念日演说是美国由来已久的政治传统，演讲内容一般是追忆开国元勋的丰功伟绩，讴歌美国建国历史。此类演说年年举行，但能被后人记住的并不多，道格拉斯这篇演说就是其中之一。

演讲之初道格拉斯按照惯例赞美了美国开国元勋众所周知的功绩，随后话锋一转，用"尖刻无情的嘲笑、粉碎一切的谴责、摧枯拉朽的讽刺、声色俱厉的训斥"控诉了当时仍在美国南方盛行的奴隶制。道格拉斯从一开始就特意将听众与他及400万黑人奴隶区分开来，最终发出了全美国都应为之汗颜的质问："对于美国的奴隶来说，你们的7月4日到底意味着什么？"与其他谴责奴隶制的檄文不同的是，道格拉斯并未将焦点放在奴隶制的邪恶或是奴隶主的残暴上，而是质疑美国的国家品格，斥责美国人的虚伪本性，指出他们在颂扬他们引以为傲的《独立宣言》的同时肆意践踏宣言中倡导的自由平等的思想和原则。在对奴隶制进行淋漓尽致的谴责之后，道格拉斯表达了对奴隶制灭亡的坚定信心以及对美国未来的美好憧憬。

道格拉斯发表演说时的美国社会正因奴隶制的问题争论不休。《1850年妥协案》（"Compromise of 1850"）②虽暂时缓和了南部脱离联邦的危局，但《逃亡奴隶法》却激起了更广泛的反对奴隶制的斗争，使南北之间的矛盾更加激化。1852年3月，哈里雅特·比彻·斯托的小

① 1845年道格拉斯出版了他的第一部自传，他担心这本书出版后自己将被当作逃亡奴隶，因而前往英国继续宣传废奴运动。1846年英国废奴主义朋友用募得的资金替道格拉斯赎回自由。1847年道格拉斯回到美国。

②《1850年妥协案》（"Compromise of 1850"）是美国国会就有关奴隶制问题于1850年9月通过的几个主要法案的统称。1848年美墨战争结束后，美国攫得墨西哥一半国土。紧接着，加利福尼亚出现了淘金热，致使该地区人口骤增。在这些新获得的领土上究竟是禁止奴隶制还是允许实行奴隶制引起了南北双方的激烈争论。鉴于南部各州以脱离联邦相威胁，辉格党领袖亨利·克莱等人自1850年初先后向国会提出一系列妥协性议案。经过激烈争论与折中后，国会在1850年9月通过以下几个主要法案：加利福尼亚作为自由州加入联邦；新墨西哥和犹他组成领地，在奴隶制问题上由其自行决定；首都哥伦比亚特区禁止奴隶贸易；重新制定一部更严峻的逃奴缉捕法。

说《汤姆叔叔的小屋》以书本形式出版①，揭露了奴隶制的罪恶，引发了人们对奴隶制的深刻反省。正是在这种背景下，道格拉斯发表了这篇演说，并将其印成小册子，使其得以广泛传播。这篇演说对推动美国人民的反奴隶制情绪、促进废奴运动的发展起到了重要的作用。

… Fellow citizens, I am not wanting in respect for the fathers of this republic. The signers of the Declaration of Independence were brave men. They were great men, too—great enough to give frame to a great age. It does not often happen to a nation to raise, at one time, such a number of truly great men. The point from which I am compelled to view them is not, certainly, the most favorable; and yet I cannot contemplate their great deeds with less than admiration. They were statesmen, patriots and heroes, and for the good they did, and the principles they contended for, I will unite with you to honor their memory…

Fellow citizens, pardon me, allow me to ask, why am I called upon to speak here today? What have I, or those I represent, to do with your national independence? Are the great principles of political freedom and of natural justice, embodied in that Declaration of Independence, extended to us? and am I, therefore, called upon to bring our humble offering to the national altar and to confess the benefits and express devout gratitude for the blessings resulting from your independence to us?

Would to God, both for your sakes and ours, that an affirmative answer could be truthfully returned to these questions! Then would my task be light and my burden easy and delightful. For *who* is there so cold that a nation's sympathy could not warm him? Who so obdurate and dead to the claims of gratitude that would not thankfully acknowledge such priceless benefits? Who so stolid and selfish that would not give his voice to swell the hallelujahs of a nation's jubilee, when the chains of servitude had been torn from his limbs? I am not that man. In a case like that, the dumb might eloquently speak, and the "lame man leap as an hart."

But such is not the state of the case. I say it with a sad sense of the disparity between us. I am not included within the pale of this glorious anniversary! Your high

① 《汤姆叔叔的小屋》最初发表在废奴主义者杂志《国家时代》（*National Era*）上。从1851年6月5日起，总共连载40周。1852年3月20日，这部小说开始以书的形式出版，其第一版很快便被抢购一空，并最终成为19世纪全世界最畅销的小说以及仅次于《圣经》的第二畅销书。

independence only reveals the immeasurable distance between us. The blessings in which you, this day, rejoice, are not enjoyed in common. The rich inheritance of justice, liberty, prosperity and independence, bequeathed by your fathers, is shared by you, not by me. The sunlight that brought light and healing to you, has brought stripes and death to me. This Fourth of July is *yours*, not *mine*. *You* may rejoice, *I* must mourn. To drag a man in fetters into the grand illuminated temple of liberty and call upon him to join you in joyous anthems were inhuman mockery and sacrilegious irony. Do you mean, citizens, to mock me, by asking me to speak today? If so, there is a parallel to your conduct. And let me warn you that it is dangerous to copy the example of a nation whose crimes, towering up to heaven, were thrown down by the breath of the Almighty, burying that nation in irrecoverable ruin! I can today take up the plaintive lament of a peeled and woe-smitten people!

"By the rivers of Babylon, there we sat down. Yea! we wept when we remembered Zion. We hanged our harps upon the willows in the midst thereof. For there they that carried us away captive required of us a song; and they who wasted us required of us mirth, saying, Sing us one of the songs of Zion. How shall we sing the Lord's song in a strange land? If I forget thee, O Jerusalem, let my right hand forget her cunning. If I do not remember thee, let my tongue cleave to the roof of my mouth."[1]

Fellow citizens; above your national, tumultuous joy I hear the mournful wail of millions! whose chains, heavy and grievous yesterday, are today rendered more intolerable by the jubilee shouts that reach them. If I do forget, if I do not faithfully remember those bleeding children of sorrow this day, "may my right hand forget her cunning, and may my tongue cleave to the roof of my mouth!" To forget them, to pass lightly over their wrongs and to chime in with the popular theme would be treason most scandalous and shocking and would make me a reproach before God and the world. My subject, then, fellow citizens, is American slavery. I shall see this day and its popular characteristics from the slave's point of view. Standing there identified with the American bondman, making his wrongs mine, I do not hesitate to declare, with all my soul, that the character and conduct of this nation never looked blacker to me than on this Fourth of July. Whether we turn to the declarations of the past or to the professions of the present, the conduct of the nation seems equally hideous and revolting. America is false to the past, false to the present, and solemnly binds herself to be false to the future. Standing with God and the crushed and bleeding slave on this occasion, I will, in the name of humanity which is outraged, in the name of liberty which is fettered, in the name of the Constitution and the Bible which are disregarded and trampled upon, dare to call in question and to denounce, with all the emphasis I can command, everything that serves to perpetuate slavery—the great sin and shame of America! "I will not equivocate; I will not excuse";[2] I will use the severest language I can command; and yet not one word shall escape me that any man, whose judgment is not blinded by prejudice, or who is not at heart a slaveholder, shall not confess to be right and just.

But I fancy I hear some one of my audience say, "It is just in this circumstance that you and your brother abolitionists fail to make a favorable impression on the public mind. Would you argue more and denounce less, would you persuade more and rebuke less, your cause would be much more likely to succeed." But, I submit, where all is plain there is nothing to be argued. What point in the antislavery creed would you have me argue? On what branch of the subject do the people of this country need light? Must I undertake to prove that the slave is a man? That point is conceded already. Nobody doubts it. The slaveholders themselves acknowledge it in the enactment of laws for their government. They acknowledge it when they punish disobedience on the part of the slave. There are seventy-two crimes in the state of Virginia which, if committed by a black man (no matter how ignorant he be), subject him to the punishment of death; while only two of the same crimes will subject a white man to the like punishment. What is this but the acknowledgement that the slave is a moral, intellectual and responsible being? The manhood of the slave is conceded. It is admitted in the fact that Southern statute books are covered with enactments forbidding, under severe fines and penalties, the teaching of the slave to read or to write. When you can point to any such laws in reference to the beasts of the field, then I may consent to argue the manhood of the slave. When the dogs in your streets, when the fowls of the air, when the cattle on your hills, when the fish of the sea and the reptiles that crawl shall be unable to distinguish the slave from a brute, *then* will I argue with you that the slave is a man!

For the present, it is enough to affirm the equal manhood of the Negro race. Is it not astonishing that, while we are plowing, planting and reaping, using all kinds of mechanical tools, erecting houses, constructing bridges, building ships, working in metals of brass, iron, copper, silver and gold; that, while we are reading, writing and ciphering, acting as clerks, merchants and secretaries, having among us lawyers, doctors, ministers, poets, authors, editors, orators and teachers; that, while we are engaged in all manner of enterprises common to other men, digging gold in California, capturing the whale in the Pacific, feeding sheep and cattle on the hillside, living, moving, acting, thinking, planning, living in families as husbands, wives and children, and, above all, confessing and worshipping the Christian's God and looking hopefully for life and immortality beyond the grave, we are called upon to prove that we are men!

Would you have me argue that man is entitled to liberty? that he is the rightful owner of his own body? You have already declared it. Must I argue the wrongfulness of slavery? Is that a question for republicans? Is it to be settled by the rules of logic and argumentation, as a matter beset with great difficulty, involving a doubtful application of the principle of justice, hard to be understood? How should I look today, in the presence of Americans, dividing and subdividing a discourse, to show that men have a natural right to freedom, speaking of it relatively and positively, negatively and affirmatively? To do so would be to make myself ridiculous and to offer an insult to your understanding. There is not a man beneath the canopy of heaven that does not know that slavery is wrong *for him*.

What, am I to argue that it is wrong to make men brutes, to rob them of their liberty, to work them without wages, to keep them ignorant of their relations to their fellow men, to beat them with sticks, to flay their flesh with the lash, to load their limbs with irons, to hunt them with dogs, to sell them at auction, to sunder their families, to knock out their teeth, to burn their flesh, to starve them into obedience and submission to their masters? Must I argue that a system thus marked with blood and stained with pollution is *wrong?* No! I will not. I have better employments for my time and strength than such arguments would imply.

What, then, remains to be argued? Is it that slavery is not divine; that God did not establish it; that our doctors of divinity are mistaken? There is blasphemy in the thought. That which is inhuman, cannot be divine! *Who* can reason on such a proposition? They that can, may; I cannot. The time for such argument is passed.

At a time like this, scorching irony, not convincing argument, is needed. O! had I the ability, and could I reach the nation's ear, I would, today, pour out a fiery stream of biting ridicule, blasting reproach, withering sarcasm and stern rebuke. For it is not light that is needed, but fire; it is not the gentle shower, but thunder. We need the storm, the whirlwind, and the earthquake. The feeling of the nation must be quickened; the conscience of the nation must be roused; the propriety of the nation must be startled;

the hypocrisy of the nation must be exposed; and its crimes against God and man must be proclaimed and denounced.

What, to the American slave, is your Fourth of July? I answer: a day that reveals to him, more than all other days in the year, the gross injustice and cruelty to which he is the constant victim. To him, your celebration is a sham; your boasted liberty an unholy license; your national greatness swelling vanity; your sounds of rejoicing are empty and heartless; your denunciations of tyrants brass-fronted impudence; your shouts of liberty and equality hollow mockery; your prayers and hymns, your sermons and thanksgivings, with all your religious parade and solemnity, are to Him mere bombast, fraud, deception, impiety and hypocrisy—a thin veil to cover up crimes which would disgrace a nation of savages. There is not a nation on the earth guilty of practices more shocking and bloody than are the people of the United States at this very hour.

Go where you may, search where you will, roam through all the monarchies and despotisms of the Old World, travel through South America, search out every abuse, and when you have found the last, lay your facts by the side of the everyday practices of this nation, and you will say with me, that, for revolting barbarity and shameless hypocrisy, America reigns without a rival…

Allow me to say, in conclusion, notwithstanding the dark picture I have this day presented, of the state of the nation, I do not despair of this country. There are forces in operation which must inevitably work the downfall of slavery. "The arm of the Lord is not shortened,"[3] and the doom of slavery is certain. I, therefore, leave off where I began, with hope. While drawing encouragement from "the Declaration of Independence," the great principles it contains and the genius of American institutions, my spirit is also cheered by the obvious tendencies of the age. Nations do not now stand in the same relation to each other that they did ages ago. No nation can now shut itself up from the surrounding world and trot round in the same old path of its fathers without interference. The time was when such could be done. Long-established customs of hurtful character could formerly fence themselves in and do their evil work with social impunity. Knowledge was then confined and enjoyed by the privileged few, and the multitude walked on in mental darkness. But a change has now come over the affairs of mankind. Walled cities and empires have become unfashionable. The arm of commerce has borne away the gates of the strong city. Intelligence is penetrating the darkest corners of the globe. It makes its pathway over and under the sea, as well as on the earth. Wind, steam and lightning are its chartered agents. Oceans no longer divide, but link nations together. From Boston to London is now a holiday excursion. Space is comparatively annihilated. Thoughts expressed on one side of the Atlantic are distinctly heard on the other.

The far-off and almost fabulous Pacific rolls in grandeur at our feet. The Celestial Empire, the mystery of ages, is being solved. The fiat of the Almighty, "Let there be Light," has not yet spent its force. No abuse, no outrage, whether in taste, sport or avarice, can now hide itself from the all-pervading light. The iron shoe and crippled foot of China must be seen in contrast with nature. Africa must rise and put on her yet unwoven garment. "Ethiopia shall stretch out her hand unto God."[4] In the fervent aspirations of William Lloyd Garrison, I say, and let every heart join in saying it,

God speed the year of jubilee
The wide world o'er!
When from their galling chains set free,
Th'oppress'd shall vilely bend the knee,
And wear the yoke of tyranny
Like brutes no more.
That year will come, and freedom's reign,
To man his plundered rights again
Restore.

God speed the day when human blood
Shall cease to flow!
In every clime be understood,
The claims of human brotherhood,
And each return for evil, good,
Not blow for blow;
That day will come all feuds to end,
And change into a faithful friend
Each foe.

God speed the hour, the glorious hour,
When none on earth

Shall exercise a lordly power,
Nor in a tyrant's presence cower;
But all to manhood's stature tower,
By equal birth!
That hour will come, to each, to all,
And from his prison-house, the thrall
Go forth.

Until that year, day, hour, arrive,
With head, and heart, and hand I'll strive,
To break the rod, and rend the gyve,
The spoiler of his prey deprive—
So witness Heaven!
And never from my chosen post,
Whate'er the peril or the cost,
Be driven.

注释：

1. 该段引自《圣经·诗篇》第137篇第1至第6节，此处道格拉斯将美国黑人奴隶比作被巴比伦人奴役的犹太人。
2. 这两句话出自威廉·劳埃德·加里森（William Lloyd Garrison）为1831年出版的第一期《解放者》（*The Liberator*）周报撰写的《发刊词》。
3. 出自《圣经·以赛亚书》第59章第1节。原文为："Behold, the Lord's hand is not shortened, that it cannot save; neither his ear heavy, that it cannot hear."
4. 出自《圣经·诗篇》第68篇第31节。

思考题：

1. What was Douglass's opinion of the Founding Fathers and the "Declaration of Independence"?
2. Which part of the speech is the most eloquent and powerful? Why?
3. How did Douglass relate the freedom of African Americans with the progress of the American empire?

18. Liberty and Equal Rights (1859)①

Carl Schurz

导读：

卡尔·舒尔茨（Carl Schurz, 1829—1906）是美国著名的德裔政治家、新闻工作者、演说家。舒尔茨在波恩大学求学时参加了德国1848年革命②，革命失败后逃离德国，最终于1852年移居美国。舒尔茨在美国继续施展他的政治抱负，先后担任美国驻西班牙大使、联邦军志愿军少将、国会参议员、内政部长、全国文官制度改革同盟主席等职务。舒尔茨在新闻业和写作方面也颇有建树，曾任《底特律邮报》（*Detroit Post*）和德文版《圣路易斯西方邮报》（*St. Louis Westliche Post*）编辑，编印《纽约晚邮报》（*New York Evening Post*）和《民族报》（*The Nation*），为《哈泼斯周刊》（*Harper's Weekly*）撰写社论，并撰写名人传记③和个人回忆录。

舒尔茨在美国政界十分活跃，是“1848年志士”④中的著名人物，是第一位进入美国参议院的德裔美国人，也是继亚历山大·汉密尔顿（Alexander Hamilton, 1757—1804）⑤之后唯一在19世纪的美国政府担任高级官职的外来移民。

1859年，马萨诸塞州立法机关批准向选民提交一项修正案，这一修正案要求外来移民在归化后必须等待两年才能获得投票权。当时共和党

① Carl Schurz, *Speeches of Carl Schurz* (Philadelphia: J. B. Lippincott & Co., 1865): 51-75.

② 1848年2月底到3月初，在法国革命的影响下，德国各邦先后爆发了一系列抗议和起义，统称为德国1848年革命。这次革命的主要任务是维护国家统一，发展资本主义，但最后以失败告终。

③ 舒尔茨1887年出版了《亨利·克莱传》（*Henry Clay*），1889年出版了《亚伯拉罕·林肯传》（*Abraham Lincoln*）。

④ 德国1848年革命之后，一批政治避难者来到美国，这些人被称为“1848年志士”。他们当中有许多人成为支持共和党和林肯的中坚分子，在美国南北战争时为拯救联邦、废除奴隶制做出了贡献。

⑤ 美国开国元勋之一亚历山大·汉密尔顿是来自西印度群岛的移民，他于1772年迁居波士顿。在独立战争时期，他以卓越的才华和出色的表现深受华盛顿的赏识。华盛顿就任总统后，汉密尔顿出任财政部部长。

正因党内有许多排外主义者而受到民主党不遗余力的攻击。这一歧视外来移民的修正案势必会影响共和党在第二年的大选中赢得当时已成为一支重要政治力量的德国移民的选票。虽然共和党内有许多排外主义者，但是排外思想在党内留下的痕迹并不多，一些重要的共和党人都谴责这项修正案。为了洗清民主党对共和党的指控，打消德裔美国人对共和党的猜疑，共和党人借举办托马斯·杰斐逊诞辰①纪念宴会之机邀请当时堪称德国移民代言人的舒尔茨来到波士顿。舒尔茨在随后为他举行的欢迎会上发表了这篇关于自由与平等权利的著名演说。

在演说中，舒尔茨认为，美国精神应当是改革时代的杰出代表、人性尊严的伟大捍卫者、受苦人类最后希望的主要寄托，强调美国民族特性的本质不是源自"一个家族、一个部落，或者一个国家"，而是吸收了"世界上所有文明国家的活力元素"，正是"自由"那"同化一切的力量"将这些元素融合在一起，成就了美国。所以在舒尔茨看来，无论是针对新移民的排外主义，还是针对美国黑人的奴隶制，都严重违背了美国精神。要解决上述问题，那就应该让"自由和平等权利，像空气一样为人类所共有——自由和平等权利，统一而不可分割"！

舒尔茨真切地希望《独立宣言》中"人人生而自由和平等，并被赋予若干不可剥夺的权利"这句名言"铭刻在共和国领土内每一根门柱上"。舒尔茨用他自己的方式践行着这一理想。他坚决主张维护黑人权利，推行有进步意义的印第安人政策，提倡宗教宽容，反对帝国主义。

遗憾的是，在舒尔茨发表其关于自由与平等权利这一著名演讲163年之后的今天，在美国，自由与平等权利仍然是一个尚待实现的理想，排外主义、种族歧视、种族仇恨、白人至上主义等仍然很有市场。比如新冠疫情期间，美国国内针对亚裔族群的歧视和仇恨事件频频发生。再如2022年5月14日发生在纽约州水牛城一家超市的枪击案就是种族主义导致的暴力事件。该事件造成10人死亡，3人受伤，13名受害人中有11名是非洲裔美国人。凶手在事件发生前曾公开发表一篇白人至上主义宣言，在实施枪击的过程中高喊种族诽谤口号，其手持的半自动步枪上则写着白人至上的口号。水牛城发生的这一枪击事件绝非偶然事件，它不过是美国社会众多种族仇恨犯罪中的一例。可以说，舒尔茨在其演讲中宣扬的关于平等与自由权利的观点对于今天的美国社会而言，仍然很有现实意义。

① 托马斯·杰斐逊是美国第三任总统，其生日是4月13日。舒尔茨发表这篇演说的时间是4月18日。

Mr. President and gentlemen: —

A few days ago I stood on the cupola of your Statehouse, and overlooked for the first time this venerable city[1] and the country surrounding it. Then the streets, and hills, and waters around me began to teem with the life of historical recollections, recollections dear to all mankind, and a feeling of pride arose in my heart, and I said to myself, I, too, am an American citizen. There was Bunker Hill, there Charlestown, Lexington, and Dorchester Heights not far off; there the harbor into which the British tea was sunk; there the place where the old liberty-tree stood; there John Hancock's house; there Benjamin Franklin's birth-place… And here, with all these glorious memories crowding upon my heart, I will offer mine…

That was the first time that I heard of America, and my childish imagination took possession of a land covered partly with majestic trees, partly with flowery prairies, immeasurable to the eye, and intersected with large rivers and broad lakes—a land where everybody could do what he thought best, and where nobody need be poor, because everybody was free.

And later, when I was old enough to read, and descriptions of this country and books on American history fell into my hands, the offspring of my imagination acquired the colors of reality, and I began to exercise my brain with the thought what man might be and become, when left perfectly free to himself. And still later, when ripening into manhood, I looked up from my school-books into the stir and bustle of the world, and the trumpet-tones of struggling humanity struck my ear and thrilled my heart, and I saw my nation[2] shake her chains in order to burst them, and I heard a gigantic, universal shout for Liberty rising up to the skies; and at last, after having struggled manfully and drenched the earth of Fatherland with the blood of thousands of noble beings, I saw that nation crushed down again, not only by overwhelming armies, but by the dead weight of customs and institutions and notions and prejudices, which past centuries had heaped upon them, and which a moment of enthusiasm, however sublime, could not destroy; then I consoled an almost despondent heart with the idea of a youthful people and of original institutions clearing the way for an untrammeled development of the ideal nature of man. Then I turned my eyes instinctively across the Atlantic Ocean, and America and Americanism, as I fancied them, appeared to me as the last depositories of the hopes of all true friends of humanity.

… Was it but a wild delusion when we thought that man has the faculty to be free and to govern himself? Have we been fighting, were we ready to die, for a mere phantom, for a mere product of a morbid imagination? This question downtrodden humanity cries out into the world, and from this country it expects an answer.

As its advocate I speak to you. I will speak of Americanism as the great representative of the reformatory age, as the great champion of the dignity of human nature, as the great repository of the last hopes of suffering mankind. I will speak of the ideal mission of this country and of this people…

… Every people, every creed, every class of society has contributed its share to that wonderful mixture out of which is to grow the great nation of the new world. It is true, the Anglo-Saxon establishes and maintains his ascendancy, but without absolutely absorbing the other national elements. They modify each other, and their peculiar characteristics are to be blended together by the all-assimilating power of freedom. This is the origin of the American nationality, which did not spring from one family, one tribe, one country, but incorporates the vigorous elements of all civilized nations on earth…

Thus, I say, was founded the colony of free humanity on virgin soil. The youthful elements which constitute people of the new world, cannot submit to rules which are not of their own making; they must throw off the fetters which bind them to an old decrepit order of things. They resolve to enter the great family of nations as an independent member. And in the colony of free humanity, whose mother-country is the world, they establish *the Republic of equal rights, where the title of manhood is the title to citizenship*…

Sir, I wish the words of the Declaration of Independence, "that all men are created free and equal, and are endowed with certain inalienable rights," were inscribed upon every gate-post within the limits of this Republic. From this principle the Revolutionary Fathers derived their claim to independence; upon this they founded the institutions of this country, and the whole structure was to be the living incarnation of this idea. This principle contains the programme of our political existence. It is the most progressive, and at the same time the most conservative one; the most progressive, for it takes even the lowliest members of the human family out of their degradation, and inspires them with the elevating consciousness of equal human dignity; the most conservative, for it makes a common cause of individual rights. From the equality of rights springs identity of our highest interests; you cannot subvert your neighbor's rights without striking a dangerous blow at your own. And when the rights of one cannot be infringed without finding a ready defense in all others who defend their own rights in defending his, then, and only then, are the rights of all safe against the usurpations of governmental authority…

Shall I point out to you the consequences of a deviation from this principle? Look at the Slave States. There is a class of men who are deprived of their natural rights. But this is not the only deplorable feature of that peculiar organization of society. Equally deplorable is it, that there is another class of men who keep the former in subjection. That there are slaves is bad; but almost worse is it, that there are masters. Are not the masters freemen? No, sir! Where is their liberty of the press? Where is their liberty of speech? Where is the man among them who dares to advocate openly principles not in strict accordance with the ruling system? They speak of a republican form of government—they speak of democracy, but the despotic spirit of slavery and mastership combined pervades their whole political life like a liquid poison. They do not dare to be free, lest the spirit of liberty become contagious. The system of slavery has enslaved them all, master as well as slave. What is the cause of all this? It is that you cannot deny one class of society the full measure of their natural rights without imposing restraints upon your own liberty. If you want to be free, there is but one way; it is to guarantee an equally full measure of liberty to all your neighbors. There is no other…

It is an old dodge of the advocates of despotism throughout the world, that the people who are not experienced in self-government, are not fit for the exercise of self-government, and must first be educated under the rule of a superior authority. But at the same time the advocates of despotism will never offer them an opportunity to acquire experience in self-government, lest they suddenly become fit for its independent exercise. To this treacherous sophistry the fathers of this republic opposed the noble doctrine, that liberty is the best school for liberty, and that self-government cannot be learned but by practising it. This, sir, is a truly American idea; this is true Americanism, and to this I pay the tribute of my devotion.

… As to religious fanaticism, it will prosper under oppression; it will feed on persecution; it will grow strong by proscription; but it is powerless against genuine democracy. It may indulge in short-lived freaks of passion, or in wily intrigues, but it will die of itself, for its lungs are not adapted to breathe the atmosphere of liberty. It is like the shark of the sea; drag him into the air, and the monster will perhaps struggle fearfully and frighten timid people with the powerful blows of his tail, and the terrible array of his teeth, but leave him quietly to die and he will die. But engage with him in a hand to hand struggle even then, and the last of his convulsions may fatally punish your rash attempt. Against fanaticism genuine democracy wields an irresistible weapon—it is *Toleration*. Toleration will not strike down the fanatic, but it will quietly and gently disarm him. But fight fanaticism *with* fanaticism, and you will restore it to its own congenial element…

I have already called your attention to the despotic tendency of the slaveholding system. I need not enlarge upon it; I need not describe how the existence of slavery in the South affected and demoralized even the political life of the Free States; how they attempted to press us, you and me, into the posse of the slave-catcher by that abominable act, which, worse than the "alien and sedition laws,"[3] still disgraces our statute-book; how the ruling party, which has devoted itself to the service of that despotic interest, shrinks from no violation of good faith, from no adulteration of the constitutional compact, from no encroachment upon natural right, from no treacherous abandonment of fundamental principles. And I do not hesitate to prophesy, that if the theories engendered by the institution of slavery be suffered to outgrow the equalizing tendency of true democracy, the American Republic will, at no distant day, crumble down under the burden of the laws and measures which the ruling interest will demand for its protection, and its name will be added to the sad catalogue of the broken hopes of humanity.

But the mischief does not come from that side alone; it is in things of small beginnings, but fearful in their growth. One of these is the propensity of men *to lose sight of fundamental principles, when passing abuses are to be corrected.*

Is it not wonderful how nations who have won their liberty by the severest struggles, become so easily impatient of the small inconveniences and passing difficulties, which are almost inseparably connected with the practical working of general self-government? How they so easily forget that rights may be abused, and yet remain inalienable rights? Europe has witnessed many an attempt for the establishment of democratic institutions; some of them were at first successful, and the people were free, but the abuses and inconveniences connected with liberty became at once apparent. Then the ruling classes of society, in order to get rid of the abuses, restricted liberty; they did, indeed, get rid of the abuses, but they got rid of liberty at the same time. You heard liberal governments there speak of protecting and regulating the liberty of the press; and, in order to prevent that liberty from being abused, they adopted measures, apparently harmless at first, which ultimately resulted in an absolute censorship. Would it be much better if we, recognizing the right of man to the exercise of self-government, should, in order to protect the purity of the ballot-box, restrict the right of suffrage?…

Another danger for the safety of our institutions, and perhaps the most formidable one, arises from the general propensity of political parties and public men to act on a policy of mere expediency, and to sacrifice principle to local and temporary success. And here, sir, let me address a solemn appeal to the consciences of those with whom I am proud to struggle side by side against human thraldom.

You hate kingcraft, and you would sacrifice your fortunes and your lives in order to prevent its establishment on the soil of this Republic. But let me tell you that the rule of political parties which sacrifice principle to expediency, is no less dangerous, no less disastrous, no less aggressive, of no less despotic a nature, than the rule of monarchs. Do not indulge in the delusion, that in order to make a government fair and liberal, the only thing necessary is to make it elective. When a political party in power, however liberal their principles may be, have once adopted the policy of knocking down their opponents instead of voting them down, there is an end of justice and equal rights…

Remember the shout of indignation that went all over the Northern States when we heard that the border ruffians of Kansas had crowded the free-state men away from the polls and had not allowed them to vote. That indignation was just, not only because the men who were thus terrorized were free-state men and friends of liberty, but because they were deprived of their right of suffrage, and because the government of that territory was placed on the basis of force, instead of equal rights. Sir, if ever the party of liberty should use their local predominance for the purpose of disarming their opponents instead of convincing them, they will but follow the example set by the ruffians of Kansas, although legislative enactments may be a genteeler weapon than the revolver and bowie knife. They may perhaps achieve some petty local success, they may gain some small temporary advantage, but they will help to introduce a system of action into our politics which will gradually undermine the very foundations upon which our republican edifice rests. Of all the dangers and difficulties that beset us, there is none more horrible than the hideous monster, whose name is "Proscription for opinion's sake". I am an anti-slavery man, and I have a right to my opinion in South Carolina just as well as in Massachusetts. My neighbor is a pro-slavery man; I may be sorry for it, but I solemnly acknowledge his right to his opinion in Massachusetts as well as in South Carolina. You tell me, that for my opinion they would mob me in

South Carolina? Sir, there is the difference between South Carolina and Massachusetts. There is the difference between an anti-slavery man, who is a freeman, and a slaveholder, who is himself a slave.

Our present issues will pass away. The slavery question will be settled, liberty will be triumphant, and other matters of difference will divide the political parties of this country. What if we, in our struggle against slavery, had removed the solid basis of equal rights, on which such new matters of difference may be peaceably settled? …

Force instead of right, privilege instead of equality, expediency instead of principle, being once the leading motives of your policy, you will have no power to stem the current. There will be new abuses to be corrected, new inconveniences to be remedied, new supposed dangers to be obviated, new equally exacting ends to be subserved, and your encroachments upon the natural rights of your opponents now, will be used as welcome precedents for the mutual oppression of parties then. Having once knowingly disregarded the doctrine of equal rights, the ruling parties will soon accustom themselves to consult only their interests where fundamental principles are at stake. Those who lead us into this channel will be like the sorcerer who knew the art of making a giant snake. And when he had made it, he forgot the charm-word that would destroy it again. And the giant snake threw its horrid coils around him, and the unfortunate man was choked to death by the monster of his own creation…

… Under this banner, all the languages of civilized mankind are spoken, every creed is protected, every right is sacred. There stands every element of Western society, with enthusiasm for a great cause, with confidence in each other, with honor to themselves. This is the banner floating over the glorious valley which stretches from the Western slope of the Alleghanies to the Rocky Mountains—that Valley of Jehoshaphat, where the nations of the world assemble to celebrate the resurrection of human freedom. The inscription on that banner is not "Opposition to the Democratic party for the sake of placing a new set of men into office;" for this battle-cry of speculators our hearts have no response. Nor is it "Restriction of slavery and restriction of the right of suffrage," for this—believe my words, I entreat you—this would be the signal of deserved, inevitable and disgraceful defeat. But the inscription is "Liberty and equal rights, common to all as the air of Heaven—Liberty and equal rights, one and inseparable!"

With this banner we stand before the world. In this sign—in this sign alone, and no other—there is victory. And thus sir, we mean to realize the great cosmopolitan idea, upon which the existence of the American nation rests. Thus we mean to fulfill the great mission of true Americanism—thus we mean to answer the anxious question of down-trodden humanity—"Has *man* the faculty to be free and to govern himself?" The answer is a triumphant "Aye," thundering into the ears of the despots of the old world that "a man is a man for all that;" proclaiming to the oppressed that they are held in subjection on false pretences; cheering the hearts of the despondent friends of man with consolation and renewed confidence.

This is true Americanism, clasping mankind to its great heart. Under its banner we march; let the world follow.

注释：

1. this venerable city：指波士顿。
2. my nation：指德国。
3. 1798年6至7月，美国国会相继通过了针对外国侨民和本国公民的四项法令，即《归化法》（"The Naturalization Act"）、《客籍法》（"The Alien Act"）、《敌对外侨法》（"The Alien Enemies Act"）、《惩治煽动叛乱法案》（"The Sedition Act"），统称为《客籍法和镇压叛乱法》（"The Alien and Sedition Acts"）。该法令规定，凡是发表有关反对政府、国会或总统的"虚假的、诽谤的、恶意的"言论和文章，目的是诋毁他们，损害他们的声誉，或是激起人民对他们的仇恨，都是一种犯罪行为。当时，美国和法国剑拔弩张，法令的支持者旨在打压国内的亲法言论。这项法令侵犯了人民的言论和出版自由，遭到了当时身为副总统的托马斯·杰斐逊的强烈谴责。杰斐逊在1801年当选总统后，有关的法律条文随后不是失效就是被废。

思考题：

1. In Carl Schurz's opinion, what was the "true Americanism"?
2. How did Carl Schurz defend his argument that slavery was harmful to both the slave and the master?
3. According to Carl Schurz, what was the relationship between liberty and equal rights?

19. First Inaugural Address (1861)[①]

Abraham Lincoln

导读：

亚伯拉罕·林肯（Abraham Lincoln, 1809—1865）是美国第16任总统，也是首位共和党籍总统，美国南北战争贯穿其整个任期[②]。他出身贫寒，未受过任何正规教育，但他做出的杰出贡献使其在美国历史上与开国元勋乔治·华盛顿齐名。他颁布了著名的《解放奴隶宣言》（"The Emancipation Proclamation"），废除了奴隶制度，扫清了美国资本主义发展的最大障碍，为以后美国经济的迅速发展创造了条件；他领导了美国南北战争并取得了最终胜利，维护了联邦的统一，为美国成为世界强国奠定了坚实的基础。1864年11月8日，林肯再度当选为总统。1865年4月14日，就在南方军队投降后第五天，林肯在华盛顿福特剧院遇刺，翌日清晨与世长辞。

1860年的总统大选，共和党推选林肯为总统候选人。在这次竞选中，共和党提出了比较符合时代潮流的政治纲领[③]，林肯顺利当选。早在总统大选前夕，北方资本主义制度和南方奴隶制之间的矛盾就日趋激化。林肯当选后不久，南卡罗来纳等南部七州[④]相继脱离联邦，宣布成立"美利坚邦联国"（Confederate State of America），简称"南部联盟"。南部七州脱离联邦后，北方出现了多种声音。共和党激进派以及工人和农民中坚定的奴隶制反对者坚决主张严厉镇压叛乱者；共和党保守派即大资产阶级只管如何保全自己的既得利益，而不关心奴隶制的存

① Abraham Lincoln, *Abraham Lincoln: Selected Speeches and Writings* (Library of America, 2009): 284-293.

② 林肯任期：1861年3月4日—1865年4月15日。美国南北战争时间：1861年4月12日—1865年4月9日。

③ 1860年5月，共和党第一次全国代表大会在芝加哥召开。大会制定的政治纲领重申了反对向任何新领地扩展奴隶制的一贯立场，但不干涉各州的奴隶制，强调实行国内改革、保护关税和宅地法，并提出了言论自由、土地自由、劳动自由和人身自由的政治口号。这个纲领具有进步意义，获得了工人和农民的广泛支持。

④ 南部七州即南卡罗来纳、密西西比、佛罗里达、阿拉巴马、佐治亚、路易斯安那、得克萨斯。

废问题；北部民主党人却在很大程度上同情叛乱，煽动反战情绪，甚至鼓动叛乱。

林肯正是在这种复杂形势下就任联邦总统的。1861年3月4日，林肯宣誓就职并发表了这篇演说，阐述了他面对当时重大政治争端所持的观点和态度。林肯首先设法消除南方的疑虑和恐惧，他保证“无意直接或间接干涉蓄奴州的奴隶制度”，承诺联邦政府“不会使任何地区的财产、和平和安全受到威胁”，表示要继续执行《逃亡奴隶法》。然后，林肯进入他演说最重要的主题：反对联邦分裂，维护国家统一。林肯从宪法、法律以及地缘的角度论证了联邦是“永存”的，是“不可分裂”的。他极力呼吁和平，宣布联邦政府不会首先采取军事行动，要求南部分离分子不要发动内战。

此时的林肯仍然坚持：南北的对立不一定非动用武力解决不可，只要能保持国家完整，维护联邦统一，采用某种温和的、妥协的办法也是可行的。所以在不放弃他的宪法责任的前提下，林肯愿意做出一切可能的让步，希望与南方达成和解。

Fellow citizens of the United States:

In compliance with a custom as old as the government itself, I appear before you to address you briefly, and to take, in your presence, the oath prescribed by the Constitution of the United States, to be taken by the President “before he enters on the execution of his office.”

I do not consider it necessary, at present, for me to discuss those matters of administration about which there is no special anxiety, or excitement.

Apprehension seems to exist among the people of the Southern States, that by the accession of a Republican Administration, their property, and their peace, and personal security, are to be endangered. There has never been any reasonable cause for such apprehension. Indeed, the most ample evidence to the contrary has all the while existed, and been open to their inspection. It is found in nearly all the published speeches of him who now addresses you. I do but quote from one of those speeches when I declare that “I have no purpose, directly or indirectly, to interfere with the institution of slavery in the States where it exists. I believe I have no lawful right to do so, and I have no inclination to do so.” Those who nominated and elected me did so with full knowledge that I had made this, and many similar declarations, and had never recanted them. And more than this, they placed in the platform, for my acceptance, and as a law to themselves, and to me, the clear and emphatic resolution which I now read:

"*Resolved*, That the maintenance inviolate of the rights of the States, and especially the right of each State to order and control its own domestic institutions according to its own judgment exclusively, is essential to that balance of power on which the perfection and endurance of our political fabric depend; and we denounce the lawless invasion by armed force of the soil of any State or Territory, no matter under what pretext, as among the gravest of crimes."

I now reiterate these sentiments: and in doing so, I only press upon the public attention the most conclusive evidence of which the case is susceptible, that the property, peace and security of no section are to be in anywise endangered by the now incoming Administration. I add too, that all the protection which, consistently with the Constitution and the laws, can be given, will be cheerfully given to all the States when lawfully demanded, for whatever cause—as cheerfully to one section, as to another.

There is much controversy about the delivering up of fugitives[1] from service or labor. The clause I now read is as plainly written in the Constitution as any other of its provisions:

"No person held to service or labor in one State, under the laws thereof, escaping into another, shall, in consequence of any law or regulation therein, be discharged from such service or labor, but shall be delivered up on claim of the party to whom such service or labor may be due."

It is scarcely questioned that this provision was intended by those who made it, for the reclaiming of what we call fugitive slaves; and the intention of the law-giver is the law. All members of Congress swear their support to the whole Constitution—to this provision as much as to any other. To the proposition, then, that slaves whose cases come within the terms of this clause, "shall be delivered up," their oaths are unanimous. Now, if they would make the effort in good temper, could they not, with nearly equal unanimity, frame and pass a law, by means of which to keep good that unanimous oath?

There is some difference of opinion whether this clause should be enforced by national or by state authority; but surely that difference is not a very material one. If the slave is to be surrendered, it can be of but little consequence to him, or to others, by which authority it is done. And should any one, in any case, be content that his oath shall go unkept, on a merely unsubstantial controversy as to *how* it shall be kept?

Again, in any law upon this subject, ought not all the safeguards of liberty known in civilized and humane jurisprudence to be introduced, so that a free man be not, in any case, surrendered as a slave? And might it not be well, at the same time, to provide by law for the enforcement of that clause in the Constitution which guarranties that "The citizens of each State shall be entitled to all privileges and immunities of citizens in the several States?"

I take the official oath to-day, with no mental reservations, and with no purpose to construe the Constitution or laws, by any hypercritical rules. And while I do not choose now to specify particular acts of Congress as proper to be enforced, I do suggest, that it will be much safer for all, both in official and private stations, to conform to, and abide by, all those acts which stand unrepealed, than to violate any of them, trusting to find impunity in having them held to be unconstitutional.

It is seventy-two years since the first inauguration of a President under our national Constitution. During that period fifteen different and greatly distinguished citizens, have, in succession, administered the executive branch of the government. They have conducted it through many perils; and, generally, with great success. Yet, with all this scope for precedent, I now enter upon the same task for the brief constitutional term of four years, under great and peculiar difficulty. A disruption of the Federal Union heretofore only menaced, is now formidably attempted.

I hold, that in contemplation of universal law, and of the Constitution, the Union of these States is perpetual. Perpetuity is implied, if not expressed, in the fundamental law of all national governments. It is safe to assert that no government proper, ever had a provision in its organic law for its own termination. Continue to execute all the express provisions of our national Constitution, and the Union will endure forever—it being impossible to destroy it, except by some action not provided for in the instrument itself.

Again, if the United States be not a government proper, but an association of States in the nature of contract merely, can it, as a contract, be peaceably unmade, by less than all the parties who made it? One party to a contract may violate it—break it, so to speak; but does it not require all to lawfully rescind it?

Descending from these general principles, we find the proposition that, in legal contemplation, the Union is perpetual, confirmed by the history of the Union itself. The Union is much older than the Constitution. It was formed in fact, by the Articles of Association in 1774. It was matured and continued by the Declaration of Independence in 1776. It was further matured and the faith of all the then thirteen States expressly plighted and engaged that it should be perpetual, by the Articles of Confederation in 1778. And finally, in 1787, one of the declared objects for ordaining and establishing the Constitution, was *"to form a more perfect union."*

But if destruction of the Union, by one, or by a part only, of the States, be lawfully possible, the Union is *less* perfect than before the Constitution, having lost the vital element of perpetuity.

It follows from these views that no State, upon its own mere motion, can lawfully get out of the Union,—that *resolves* and *ordinances* to that effect are legally void; and that acts of violence, within any State or States, against the authority of the United States, are insurrectionary or revolutionary, according to circumstances.

I therefore consider that, in view of the Constitution and the laws, the Union is unbroken; and, to the extent of my ability, I shall take care, as the Constitution itself expressly enjoins upon me, that the laws of the Union be faithfully executed in all the States. Doing this I deem to be only a simple duty on my part; and I shall perform it, so far as practicable, unless my rightful masters, the American people, shall withhold the requisite means, or, in some authoritative manner, direct the contrary. I trust this will not be regarded as a menace, but only as the declared purpose of the Union that it *will* constitutionally defend, and maintain itself.

In doing this there needs to be no bloodshed or violence; and there shall be none, unless it be forced upon the national authority. The power confided to me, will be used to hold, occupy, and possess the property, and places belonging to the government, and to collect the duties and imposts; but beyond what may be necessary for these objects, there will be no invasion—no using of force against, or among the people anywhere. Where hostility to the United States, in any interior locality, shall be so great and so universal, as to prevent competent resident citizens from holding the Federal offices, there will be no attempt to force obnoxious strangers among the people for that object. While the strict legal right may exist in the government to enforce the exercise of these offices, the attempt to do so would be so irritating, and so nearly impracticable with all, that I deem it better to forego, for the time, the uses of such offices.

The mails, unless repelled, will continue to be furnished in all parts of the Union. So far as possible, the people everywhere shall have that sense of perfect security which is most favorable to calm thought and reflection. The course here indicated will be followed, unless current events, and experience, shall show a modification, or change, to be proper; and in every case and exigency, my best discretion will be exercised, according to circumstances actually existing, and with a view and a hope of a peaceful solution of the national troubles, and the restoration of fraternal sympathies and affections.

That there are persons in one section, or another who seek to destroy the Union at all events, and are glad of any pretext to do it, I will neither affirm or deny; but if there be such, I need address no word to them. To those, however, who really love the Union, may I not speak?

Before entering upon so grave a matter as the destruction of our national fabric, with all its benefits, its memories, and its hopes, would it not be wise to ascertain precisely why we do it? Will you hazard so desperate a step, while there is any possibility that any portion of the ills you fly from, have no real existence? Will you, while the certain ills you fly to, are greater than all the real ones you fly from? Will you risk the commission of so fearful a mistake?

All profess to be content in the Union, if all constitutional rights can be maintained. Is it true, then, that any right, plainly written in the Constitution, has been denied? I think not. Happily the human mind is so constituted, that no party can reach to the audacity of doing this. Think, if you can, of a single instance in which a plainly written provision of the Constitution has ever been denied. If, by the mere force of numbers, a majority should deprive a minority of any clearly written constitutional right, it might, in a moral point of view, justify revolution—certainly would, if such right were a vital one. But such is not our case. All the vital rights of minorities, and of individuals, are so plainly assured to them, by affirmations and negations, guarranties and prohibitions, in the Constitution, that controversies never arise concerning them. But no organic law can ever be framed with a provision specifically applicable to every question which may occur in practical administration. No foresight can anticipate, nor any document of reasonable length contain express provisions for all possible questions. Shall fugitives from labor be surrendered by national or by State authority? The Constitution does not expressly say. *May* Congress prohibit slavery in the territories? The Constitution does not expressly say. *Must* Congress protect slavery in the territories? The Constitution does not expressly say.

From questions of this class spring all our constitutional controversies, and we divide upon them into majorities and minorities. If the minority will not acquiesce, the majority must, or the government must cease. There is no other alternative; for continuing the government, is acquiescence on one side or the other. If a minority, in such case, will secede rather than acquiesce, they make a precedent which, in turn, will divide and ruin them; for a minority of their own will secede from them, whenever a majority refuses to be controlled by such minority. For instance, why may not any portion of a new confederacy, a year or two hence, arbitrarily secede again, precisely as portions of the present Union now claim to secede from it. All who cherish disunion sentiments, are now being educated to the exact temper of doing this. Is there such perfect identity of interests among the States to compose a new Union, as to produce harmony only, and prevent renewed secession?

Plainly, the central idea of secession, is the essence of anarchy. A majority, held in restraint by constitutional checks, and limitations, and always changing easily, with deliberate changes of popular opinions and sentiments, is the only true sovereign of a free people. Whoever rejects it, does, of necessity, fly to anarchy or to despotism. Unanimity is impossible; the rule of a minority, as a permanent arrangement, is wholly inadmissible; so that, rejecting the majority principle, anarchy, or despotism in some form, is all that is left.

I do not forget the position assumed by some, that constitutional questions are to be decided by the Supreme Court; nor do I deny that such decisions must be binding in any case, upon the parties to a suit, as to the object of that suit, while they are also entitled to very high respect and consideration, in all parallel cases, by all other departments of the government. And while it is obviously possible that such decision may be erroneous in any given case, still the evil effect following it, being limited to that particular case, with the chance that it may be over-ruled, and never become a precedent for other cases, can better be borne than could the evils of a different practice. At the same time the candid citizen must confess that if the policy of the government, upon vital questions, affecting the whole people, is to be irrevocably fixed by decisions of the Supreme Court, the instant they are made, in ordinary litigation between parties, in personal actions, the people will have ceased, to be their own rulers, having, to that extent, practically resigned their government, into the hands of that eminent tribunal. Nor is there, in this view, any assault upon the court, or the judges. It is a duty, from which they may not shrink, to decide cases properly brought before them; and it is no fault of theirs, if others seek to turn their decisions to political purposes.

One section of our country believes slavery is *right*, and ought to be extended, while the other believes it is *wrong*, and ought not to be extended. This is the only substantial dispute. The fugitive slave clause of the Constitution, and the law for the suppression of the foreign slave trade, are each as well enforced, perhaps, as any law can ever be in a community where the moral sense of the people imperfectly supports the law itself. The great body of the people abide by the dry legal obligation in both cases, and a few break over in each. This, I think, cannot be perfectly cured; and it would be worse in both cases *after* the separation of the sections, than before. The foreign slave trade, now imperfectly suppressed, would be ultimately revived without restriction, in one section; while fugitive slaves, now only partially surrendered, would not be surrendered at all, by the other.

Physically speaking, we cannot separate. We cannot remove our respective sections from each other, nor build an impassable wall between them. A husband and wife may be divorced, and go out of the presence, and beyond the reach of each other; but the different parts of our country cannot do this. They cannot but remain face to face; and intercourse, either amicable or hostile, must continue between them. Is it possible then to make that intercourse more advantageous, or more satisfactory, *after* separation than *before*? Can aliens make treaties easier than friends can make laws? Can treaties be more faithfully enforced between aliens, than laws can among friends? Suppose you go to war, you cannot fight always; and when, after much loss on both sides, and no gain on either, you cease fighting, the identical old questions, as to terms of intercourse, are again upon you.

This country, with its institutions, belongs to the people who inhabit it. Whenever they shall grow weary of the existing government, they can exercise their *constitutional* right of amending it, or their *revolutionary* right to dismember, or overthrow it. I can not be ignorant of the fact that many worthy, and patriotic citizens are desirous of having the national constitution amended. While I make no recommendation of amendments, I fully recognize the rightful authority of the people over the whole subject, to be exercised in either of the modes prescribed in the instrument itself; and I should, under existing circumstances, favor, rather than oppose, a fair opportunity being afforded the people to act upon it.

I will venture to add that, to me, the convention mode seems preferable, in that it allows amendments to originate with the people themselves, instead of only permitting them to take, or reject, propositions, originated by others, not especially chosen for the purpose, and which might not be precisely such, as they would wish to either accept or refuse. I understand a proposed amendment to the Constitution—which amendment, however, I have not seen, has passed Congress, to the effect that the federal government, shall never interfere with the domestic institutions of the States, including that of persons held to service. To avoid misconstruction of what I have said, I depart from my purpose not to speak of particular amendments, so far as to say that, holding such a provision to now be implied constitutional law, I have no objection to its being made express, and irrevocable.

The Chief Magistrate[2] derives all his authority from the people, and they have conferred none upon him to fix terms for the separation of the States. The people themselves can do this also if they choose; but the executive, as such, has nothing to do with it. His duty is to administer the present government, as it came to his hands, and to transmit it, unimpaired by him, to his successor.

Why should there not be a patient confidence in the ultimate justice of the people? Is there any better, or equal hope, in the world? In our present differences, is either party without faith of being in the right? If the Almighty Ruler of nations, with his eternal truth and justice, be on your side of the North, or on yours of the South, that truth, and that justice, will surely prevail, by the judgment of this great tribunal, the American people.

By the frame of the government under which we live, this same people have wisely given their public servants but little power for mischief; and have, with equal wisdom, provided for the return of that little to their own hands at very short intervals.

While the people retain their virtue, and vigilance, no administration, by any extreme of wickedness or folly, can very seriously injure the government, in the short space of four years.

My countrymen, one and all, think calmly and *well*, upon this whole subject. Nothing valuable can be lost by taking time. If there be an object to *hurry* any of you, in hot haste, to a step which you would never take *deliberately*, that object will be frustrated by taking time; but no good object can be frustrated by it. Such of you as are now dissatisfied, still have the old Constitution unimpaired, and, on the sensitive point, the laws of your own framing under it; while the new administration will have no immediate power, if it would, to change either. If it were admitted that you who are dissatisfied, hold the right side in the dispute, there still is no single good reason for precipitate action. Intelligence, patriotism, Christianity, and a firm reliance on Him, who has never yet forsaken this favored land, are still competent to adjust, in the best way, all our present difficulty.

In *your* hands, my dissatisfied fellow countrymen, and not in *mine*, is the momentous issue of civil war. The government will not assail *you*. You can have no conflict, without being yourselves the aggressors. *You* have no oath registered in Heaven to destroy the government, while *I* shall have the most solemn one to "preserve, protect and defend" it.[3]

I am loth to close. We are not enemies, but friends. We must not be enemies. Though passion may have strained, it must not break our bonds of affection. The mystic chords of memory, stretching from every battle-field, and patriot grave, to every living heart and hearthstone, all over this broad land, will yet swell the chorus of the Union, when again touched, as surely they will be, by the better angels of our nature.

注释：

1. fugitives：逃亡者，此处指逃跑的奴隶。
2. The Chief Magistrate：这里指美国总统。
3. 林肯最初打算用这段话来结束发言，但国务卿威廉·西沃德建议最后说些"慈爱的话——心平气和与满怀信心的话"，并提供了他自己措辞的额外一段话。林肯采纳了这个建议，他把西沃德的句子改成了慷慨激昂、动人心弦的请求，也就是演说的最后一段。

思考题：

1. How did Lincoln defend his claim that the Union was "perpetual" and "unbroken"? Do you think it was convincing? Why or why not?
2. What was Lincoln's position on slavery? Why?

20. The Emancipation Proclamation (1863)[①]

Abraham Lincoln

导读:

亚伯拉罕·林肯奉行人人生而平等的原则，崇尚自由劳动，加之社会底层出身，亲眼看见奴隶主的残暴和黑人奴隶的凄惨境况，对于奴隶制，他是坚决反对的。他始终认为，不能把国家建立在罪恶的奴役制度基础之上，否则就是对先辈们所倡导的自由平等原则的背叛。在奴隶制问题上，随着形势的变化，林肯经历了从限奴[②]到赎奴[③]再到废奴的转变。

到1862年夏秋之际，距离叛军向萨姆特要塞发射第一枚炮弹[④]已有一年多的时间。总的来说，北方进展甚微，损失较大。人民群众的不满情绪不断高涨，对战争正义性的质疑声越来越大，解放奴隶的呼声越来越高。国际上，欧洲列强的统治集团对南部同盟公开表示同情，英国更是公开承认南部同盟为交战国一方，为其提供经济、军事援助，甚至意欲武装干涉。面对国际国内的严峻形势，为了赢得战争，维护联邦统一[⑤]，林肯决定发表解放黑奴的宣言。1862年9月北方在安提塔姆战役中获得胜利，为林肯发布宣言提供了良机[⑥]。9月22日，林肯在内阁会议上

① Abraham Lincoln, *Abraham Lincoln: Selected Speeches and Writings* (Library of America, 2009): 368-369.

② 在1860年总统竞选时，林肯在共和党政纲中提出“不再给奴隶制一寸新的土地”。

③ 1862年3月6日，林肯在致国会咨文中提出逐步有偿地解放奴隶的方针。同年7月，林肯向边境州的奴隶主发出呼吁，要他们同意用赎买方式逐步解放奴隶。

④ 1861年4月12日上午4时30分，叛军向萨姆特要塞发射了内战的第一枚炮弹，揭开了美国内战的序幕。萨姆特是当时南卡罗来纳州内唯一未被叛军占领的联邦要塞。

⑤ 林肯将维护联邦统一作为战争的最高目标。他曾在一封公开信中讲道：“在这场竞争中，我的首要任务不在于拯救奴隶或消灭奴隶制，而在于拯救联邦。如果无须解放奴隶就可以解救联邦，我愿意；如果必须解放一部分奴隶，对另一部分听之任之，我也愿意。我对奴隶制和黑人所做的事情是出于这样一种信念，那就是这样做会有利于联邦……”

⑥ 1862年夏天，林肯一直在等待一次胜利，作为发布《解放奴隶宣言》的最佳契机，以免解放黑奴被看成联邦政府的求助和绝望之举。

宣读了他早已修改多次的预告性《解放奴隶宣言》。1863年1月1日林肯发表了正式的《解放奴隶宣言》。

宣言的发布为四百万黑人解开了奴隶的枷锁。在南方，大量黑奴逃离种植园，瓦解了南方的经济，沉重地打击了奴隶制的统治；在北方，宣言使北方赢得了道义上的巨大优势，大批南方黑人的到来又解决了兵源问题，北方人民斗志昂扬，士气高涨，战斗力不断增强；国际上，宣言得到了世界进步力量尤其是英国工人阶级的支持，英国当局不得不放弃武装干涉的计划。因此，宣言发布不久，战争形势就发生了有利于联邦的根本性变化，美国内战最终以北方的胜利而告结束，美国恢复统一。

今天看来，《解放奴隶宣言》有其自身的历史局限性，如它还不是一个全面解放奴隶的法令，仅对叛乱州有效。又如在预告性宣言发表后的一百天内，如果叛乱分子放下武器，南方奴隶制将得以继续维持。但瑕不掩瑜，宣言伟大的历史意义使它成为联邦政府成立以来美国历史上最重要的文件之一。

Whereas, on the twentysecond day of September, in the year of our Lord one thousand eight hundred and sixty two,[1] a proclamation was issued by the President of the United States, containing, among other things, the following, towit:[2]

"That on the first day of January, in the year of our Lord one thousand eight hundred and sixty-three, all persons held as slaves within any State or designated part of a State, the people whereof shall then be in rebellion against the United States, shall be then, thenceforward, and forever free; and the Executive Government of the United States, including the military and naval authority thereof, will recognize and maintain the freedom of such persons, and will do no act or acts to repress such persons, or any of them, in any efforts they may make for their actual freedom.

"That the Executive will, on the first day of January aforesaid, by proclamation, designate the States and parts of States, if any, in which the people thereof, respectively, shall then be in rebellion against the United States; and the fact that any State, or the people thereof, shall on that day be, in good faith, represented in the Congress of the United States by members chosen thereto at elections wherein a majority of the qualified voters of such State shall have participated, shall, in the absence of strong countervailing testimony, be deemed conclusive evidence that such

State, and the people thereof, are not then in rebellion against the United States."

Now, therefore I, Abraham Lincoln, President of the United States, by virtue of the power in me vested as Commander-in-Chief, of the Army and Navy of the United States[3] in time of actual armed rebellion against authority and government of the United States, and as a fit and necessary war measure for suppressing said rebellion, do, on this first day of January, in the year of our Lord one thousand eight hundred and sixty three, and in accordance with my purpose so to do publicly proclaimed for the full period of one hundred days, from the day first above mentioned, order and designate as the States and parts of States wherein the people thereof respectively, are this day in rebellion against the United States, the following, towit:

Arkansas, Texas, Louisiana, (except the Parishes of St. Bernard, Plaquemines, Jefferson, St. John, St. Charles, St. James, Ascension, Assumption, Terrebonne, Lafourche, St. Mary, St. Martin, and Orleans, including the City of New-Orleans) Mississippi, Alabama, Florida, Georgia, South-Carolina, North-Carolina, and Virginia, (except the fortyeight counties designated as West Virginia, and also the counties of Berkley, Accomac, Northampton, Elizabeth-City, York, Princess Ann, and Norfolk, including the cities of Norfolk & Portsmouth); and which excepted parts are, for the present, left precisely as if this proclamation were not issued.

And by virtue of the power, and for the purpose aforesaid, I do order and declare that all persons held as slaves within said designated States, and parts of States, are, and henceforward shall be free; and that the Executive government of the United States, including the military and naval authorities thereof, will recognize and maintain the freedom of said persons.

And I hereby enjoin upon the people so declared to be free to abstain from all violence, unless in necessary self-defence; and I recommend to them that, in all cases when allowed, they labor faithfully for reasonable wages.

And I further declare and make known, that such persons of suitable condition, will be received into the armed service of the United States to garrison forts, positions, stations, and other places, and to man vessels of all sorts in said service.

And upon this act, sincerely believed to be an act of justice, warranted by the Constitution, upon military necessity,[4] I invoke the considerate judgment of mankind, and the gracious favor of Almighty God.

In witness whereof, I have hereunto set my hand and caused the seal of the United States to be affixed.

Done at the City of Washington, this first day of January, in the year of our Lord one thousand eight hundred and sixty three, and of the Independence of the United States of America the eighty-seventh.

注释：

1. 1862年9月22日，林肯在内阁会议上宣读了预告性《解放奴隶宣言》，规定自1863年1月1日起，凡当时仍在叛乱的任何一个州或地区，其辖区内所有奴隶都应永远获得自由。1863年1月1日，林肯正式颁布这项命令。
2. towit：即，就是。
3. 美国总统同时也是美国陆海空三军总司令。不过在林肯时期还没有空军，因此他只是陆海军总司令。
4. 林肯在1861年第一次就职演说中承诺："对于各蓄奴州内存在的奴隶制度，我无意进行直接或间接的干涉。我认为我既无这样做的权力，也没有这样做的意向。"他还建议，处于公私职位上的一切人都应当遵守和服从所有那些未被明令废除的法令。本着同一原则，林肯在1863年1月1日是以"美利坚合众国总统令"的名义发表《解放奴隶宣言》的，依据的是他作为陆海军总司令的职权和必要的战时措施。1865和1868年，国会分别通过宪法第13、14条修正案，正式废除奴隶制。

思考题：

1. How did "The Emancipation Proclamation" contribute to a Union victory?
2. Why did Lincoln free slaves only in Southern rebel states?
3. What was the relationship between Lincoln's goals of preserving the Union and freeing the slaves?

21. The Gettysburg Address (1863)[①]

Abraham Lincoln

导读：

1863年7月1日至3日，美国内战南北双方在宾夕法尼亚州南部边境的小镇葛底斯堡展开了激战。[②]这是美国内战中规模最大、流血最多的一场战役，双方损失十分惨重。联邦军队伤亡2.3万人，南方同盟军伤亡达到2.8万人。葛底斯堡战役成为美国内战的转折点。经此一役，南方被迫由战略进攻转为战略防御，而北方则取得了决定性的优势，保证了最后的胜利。战役结束后不久，联邦政府决定在葛底斯堡修建国家公墓以纪念在这次战役中英勇献身的烈士们。

1863年11月19日，正值葛底斯堡战役结束后四个半月，林肯在葛底斯堡国家公墓揭幕式上发表了这篇演说。演说开篇高屋建瓴，追念了美国开国元勋的丰功伟绩，继而热情讴歌了阵亡将士们为联邦的正义事业捐躯的崇高精神，呼吁活着的人们继承阵亡将士们的遗志，以更大的决心和献身精神致力他们未竟的事业，以使“民有、民治、民享”的政府永存下去。

林肯的这篇演说立意高远，主题明确，结构缜密，措辞精炼而不失优雅，修辞巧妙而不失庄重，句式得体而错落有致，被认为是美国文学中最漂亮、最富有诗意的篇章之一。林肯在演说中讲道“世人不会注意，更不会长久记住我们此刻所说的话”，不知其能否预见到，他这篇演说会经久不衰，名垂史册，被奉为英语演讲中的最高典范。其演讲手稿藏于美国国会图书馆，其演讲词被铸成金文，长存于牛津大学。葛底斯堡也因他的演说而闻名世界。

---

① Abraham Lincoln, *Abraham Lincoln: Selected Speeches and Writings* (Library of America, 2009): 405.

② 南部联盟总司令罗伯特·爱德华·李（Robert Edward Lee）决定在北部开辟战场，他认为只要在北部打一场决定性的胜仗，欧洲列强就会承认南部独立。1863年6月3日，李率军73 000人进军宾夕法尼亚。林肯委派乔治·戈登·米德（George Gordon Meade）寻敌作战。南北两军互相试探，捕捉战机，于6月30日在葛底斯堡遭遇，双方立即交火，并于翌日正式列阵开战，内战中著名的葛底斯堡大会战由此爆发。

Four score and seven years ago our fathers brought forth on this continent, a new nation,[1] conceived in Liberty, and dedicated to the proposition that all men are created equal.

Now we are engaged in a great civil war, testing whether that nation, or any nation so conceived and so dedicated, can long endure. We are met on a great battle-field of that war. We have come to dedicate a portion of that field, as a final resting place for those who here gave their lives that that nation might live. It is altogether fitting and proper that we should do this.

But, in a larger sense, we can not dedicate—we can not consecrate—we can not hallow—this ground. The brave men, living and dead, who struggled here, have consecrated it, far above our poor power to add or detract. The world will little note, nor long remember what we say here, but it can never forget what they did here. It is for us the living, rather, to be dedicated here to the unfinished work which they who fought here have thus far so nobly advanced. It is rather for us to be here dedicated to the great task remaining before us—that from these honored dead we take increased devotion to that cause for which they gave the last full measure of devotion—that we here highly resolve that these dead shall not have died in vain—that this nation, under God, shall have a new birth of freedom—and that government of the people, by the people, for the people,[2] shall not perish from the earth.

注释：

1. 此句指1776年北美13个殖民地联合发表《独立宣言》，宣布脱离英联邦。
2. 林肯在此提出的“民有、民治、民享”的口号深入人心，成为后人推崇民主政治的纲领。

思考题：

1. Lincoln never mentions the word “union” in his speech, instead, he repeatedly referring to the word “nation.” What is the effect of Lincoln’s wording?
2. Do you think “The Gettysburg Address” is still relevant in today’s society? If yes, how?

22. What Social Classes Owe to Each Other (1883)①

William Graham Sumner

导读：

威廉·格雷厄姆·萨姆纳（William Graham Sumner, 1840—1910）是美国社会学家、政治经济学家，美国社会学奠基人之一。萨姆纳原为牧师，1872年出任耶鲁大学社会与政治科学教授，1875年在美国历史上第一次开设了社会学课程，讲授赫伯特·斯宾塞（Herbert Spencer, 1820—1903）的《社会学研究》（*The Study of Sociology*）一书②。萨姆纳专门研究社会风俗中司空见惯的日常生活的细枝末节，他于1906年出版了《民俗伦》（*Folkways: A Study of the Sociological Importance of Usages, Manners, Customs, Mores, and Morals*）一书，因其对社会生活的真知灼见，被誉为美国社会学第一部成熟的著作和美国社会学经典。1909年萨姆纳任美国社会学学会主席。他除了学术水平高超，还是一位能言善辩的大师，"他的早期著作与课堂演讲的水平堪与那个时代的动乱相匹敌"③。

南北战争为美国资本主义发展扫清了道路，随着工业经济迅猛发展，资本主义经济由自由竞争向垄断过渡，大量财富集中于少数垄断资本家手中，大财团、大富豪逐渐掌控了美国的经济生活。与此形成鲜明对照的是广大中小业主和下层工人农民却日益陷入贫困的深渊。他们开始认识到垄断的危害性，通过组织协会、工会、直接罢工等形式进行反垄断斗争。尖锐的社会矛盾使各种社会政治思潮应运而生，其中以"物

① William Graham Sumner, *What Social Classes Owe to Each Other* (New York and London: Haper & Brothers Publishers, 1911): 13-26.

② 赫伯特·斯宾塞是19世纪后期英国著名社会学家和哲学家，他试图用达尔文生物进化学说去解释人类社会，被称为"社会达尔文主义之父"。1873年斯宾塞出版了历史上首部以社会学为名的书籍《社会学研究》。萨姆纳是斯宾塞思想在美国的忠实继承者，是美国社会达尔文主义的代表人物，他用"物竞天择，适者生存"的大自然法则来解释人类社会现象。

③ W. D. 珀杜等著，贾春增、李强等译，《西方社会学——人物·学派·思想》，石家庄：河北人民出版社，1992年，第74页。

竞天择，适者生存”为思想核心的社会达尔文主义就在19世纪60年代至90年代盛极一时。作为美国社会达尔文主义的积极鼓吹者，萨姆纳1883年出版《社会各阶级之间互欠什么》，该书曾产生广泛影响。

在该书中，萨姆纳宣扬竞争的正当性，推崇极端的自由经营，赞成财产集中，反对国家干预，反对社会改革。下文选自该书第一章。在这一章里，萨姆纳明确地回答了该书题目中的疑问：社会各阶级之间什么也不欠，所以“在一个自由的社会里”，无人有权“要求他人予以帮助，也无人可以被要求来帮助他人”。萨姆纳认为，每个阶级只需要保有自己的自由、安全和奋斗的机会，并能够相互尊重就足够了。因此，他反对社会福利和救济事业，认为政府不应该拿一个阶级的收获去救济另一个阶级。

萨姆纳所宣扬的“充分的自由竞争”和“适者生存”的思想，迎合了美国镀金时代（Gilded Age）[①]流行的冒险投机和无情竞争的精神，为当时的贫富不均和社会不公正名，为强者剥削和压榨弱者辩护。随着社会的发展和进步，萨姆纳的社会政治思想受到越来越多的质疑，其反对国家干预经济的主张也逐渐背离了日益成熟的垄断资本的要求，以萨姆纳为代表的社会达尔文主义最终退出了美国社会主流思想的舞台。

It is commonly asserted that there are in the United States no classes, and any allusion to classes is resented. On the other hand, we constantly read and hear discussions of social topics in which the existence of social classes is assumed as a simple fact. “The poor,” “the weak,” “the laborers,” are expressions which are used as if they had exact and well-understood definition. Discussions are made to bear upon the assumed rights, wrongs, and misfortunes of certain social classes; and all public speaking and writing consists, in a large measure, of the discussion of general plans for meeting the wishes of classes of people who have not been able to satisfy their own desires. These classes are sometimes discontented, and sometimes not. Sometimes they do not know that anything is amiss with them until the “friends of humanity” come to them with offers of aid. Sometimes they are discontented and envious. They do not

① 在美国历史上，从内战结束到19世纪末这一时间段被称为镀金时代。这是近代美国向现代美国转变的历史时期，其主要特征是从农业国向工业国转变，自由资本主义向垄断资本主义过渡。在这两个历史性转变的带动下，美国政治、经济、社会结构和思想文化都发生了重大变化，从而为20世纪现代美国奠定了基础。

take their achievements as a fair measure of their rights. They do not blame themselves or their parents for their lot, as compared with that of other people. Sometimes they claim that they have a right to everything of which they feel the need for their happiness on earth. To make such a claim against God and Nature would, of course, be only to say that we claim a right to live on earth if we can. But God and Nature have ordained the chances and conditions of life on earth once for all. The case cannot be reopened. We cannot get a revision of the laws of human life. We are absolutely shut up to the need and duty, if we would learn how to live happily, of investigating the laws of Nature, and deducing the rules of right living in the world as it is. These are very wearisome and commonplace tasks. They consist in labor and self-denial repeated over and over again in learning and doing. When the people whose claims we are considering are told to apply themselves to these tasks they become irritated and feel almost insulted. They formulate their claims as rights against society—that is, against some other men. In their view they have a right, not only to *pursue* happiness, but to *get* it; and if they fail to get it, they think they have a claim to the aid of other men—that is, to the labor and self-denial of other men—to get it for them. They find orators and poets who tell them that they have grievances, so long as they have unsatisfied desires.

Now, if there are groups of people who have a claim to other people's labor and self-denial, and if there are other people whose labor and self-denial are liable to be claimed by the first groups, then there certainly are "classes," and classes of the oldest and most vicious type. For a man who can command another man's labor and self-denial for the support of his own existence is a privileged person of the highest species conceivable on earth. Princes and paupers meet on this plane, and no other men are on it at all. On the other hand, a man whose labor and self-denial may be diverted from his maintenance to that of some other man is not a free man, and approaches more or less toward the position of a slave. Therefore we shall find that, in all the notions which we are to discuss, this elementary contradiction, that there are classes and that there are not classes, will produce repeated confusion and absurdity. We shall find that, in our efforts to eliminate the old vices of class government, we are impeded and defeated by new products of the worst class theory. We shall find that all the schemes for producing equality and obliterating the organization of society produce a new differentiation based on the worst possible distinction—the right to claim and the duty to give one man's effort for another man's satisfaction. We shall find that every effort to realize equality necessitates a sacrifice of liberty.

It is very popular to pose as a "friend of humanity," or a "friend of the working classes." The character, however, is quite exotic in the United States. It is borrowed from England, where some men, otherwise of small account, have assumed it with great success and advantage. Anything which has a charitable sound and a kind-hearted tone generally passes without investigation, because it is disagreeable to assail it. Sermons, essays, and orations assume a conventional standpoint with regard to the poor, the weak, etc.; and it is allowed to pass as an unquestioned doctrine in regard to social classes that "the rich" ought to "care for the poor"; that Churches especially ought to collect capital from the rich and spend it for the poor; that parishes ought to be clusters of institutions by means of which one social class should perform its duties to another; and that clergymen, economists, and social philosophers have a technical and professional duty to devise schemes for "helping the poor." The preaching in England used all to be done to the poor—that they ought to be contented with their lot and respectful to their betters. Now, the greatest part of the preaching in America consists in injunctions to those who have taken care of themselves to perform their assumed duty to take care of others. Whatever may be one's private sentiments, the fear of appearing cold and hard-hearted causes these conventional theories of social duty and these assumptions of social fact to pass unchallenged.

Let us notice some distinctions which are of prime importance to a correct consideration of the subject which we intend to treat.

Certain ills belong to the hardships of human life. They are natural. They are part of the struggle with Nature for existence. We cannot blame our fellow-men for our share of these. My neighbor and I are both struggling to free ourselves from these ills. The fact that my neighbor has succeeded in this struggle better than I constitutes no grievance for me. Certain other ills are due to the malice of men, and to the imperfections or errors of civil institutions. These ills are an object of agitation, and a subject of discussion. The former class of ills is to be met only by manly effort and energy; the latter may be corrected by associated effort. The former class of ills is constantly grouped and generalized, and made the object of social schemes. We shall see, as we go on, what that means. The second class of ills may fall on certain social classes, and reform will take the form of interference by other classes in favor of that one. The last fact is, no doubt, the reason why people have been led, not noticing distinctions, to believe that the same method was applicable to the other class of ills.

The distinction here made between the ills which belong to the struggle for existence and those which are due to the faults of human institutions is of prime importance.

It will also be important, in order to clear up our ideas about the notions which are in fashion, to note the relation of the economic to the political significance of assumed duties of one class to another. That is to say, we may discuss the question whether one class owes duties to another by reference to the economic effects which will be produced on the classes and society; or we may discuss the political expediency of formulating and enforcing rights and duties respectively between the parties. In the former case we might assume that the givers of aid were willing to give it, and we might discuss the benefit or mischief of their activity. In the other case we must assume that some at least of those who were forced to give aid did so unwillingly. Here, then, there would be a question of rights. The question whether voluntary charity is mischievous or not is one thing; the question whether legislation which forces one man to aid another is right and wise, as well as economically beneficial, is quite another question. Great confusion and consequent error is produced by allowing these two questions to become entangled in the discussion. Especially we shall need to notice the attempts to apply legislative methods of reform to the ills which belong to the order of Nature.

There is no possible definition of "a poor man." A pauper is a person who cannot earn his living; whose producing powers have fallen positively below his necessary consumption; who cannot, therefore, pay his way. A human society needs the active co-operation and productive energy of every person in it. A man who is present as a consumer, yet who does not contribute either by land, labor, or capital to the work of society, is a burden. On no sound political theory ought such a person to share in the political power of the State. He drops out of the ranks of workers and producers. Society must support him. It accepts the burden, but he must be cancelled from the ranks of the rulers likewise. So much for the pauper. About him no more need be said. But he is not the "poor man." The "poor man" is an elastic term, under which any number of social fallacies may be hidden.

Neither is there any possible definition of "the weak." Some are weak in one way, and some in another; and those who are weak in one sense are strong in another. In general, however, it may be said that those whom humanitarians and philanthropists call the weak are the ones through whom the productive and conservative forces of society are wasted. They constantly neutralize and destroy the finest efforts of the wise and industrious, and are a dead-weight on the society in all its struggles to realize any better things. Whether the people who mean no harm, but are weak in the essential powers necessary to the performance of one's duties in life, or those who are malicious and vicious, do the more mischief, is a question not easy to answer.

Under the names of the poor and the weak, the negligent, shiftless, inefficient, silly, and imprudent are fastened upon the industrious and prudent as a responsibility and a duty. On the one side, the terms are extended to cover the idle, intemperate, and vicious, who, by the combination, gain credit which they do not deserve, and which they could not get if they stood alone. On the other hand, the terms are extended to include wage-receivers of the humblest rank, who are degraded by the combination. The reader who desires to guard himself against fallacies should always scrutinize the terms "poor" and "weak" as used, so as to see which or how many of these classes they are made to cover.

The humanitarians, philanthropists, and reformers, looking at the facts of life as they present themselves, find enough which is sad and unpromising in the condition of many members of society. They see wealth and poverty side by side. They note great inequality of social position and social chances. They eagerly set about the attempt to account for what they see, and to devise schemes for remedying what they do not like. In their eagerness to recommend the less fortunate classes to pity and consideration they forget all about the rights of other classes; they gloss over all the faults of the classes in question, and they exaggerate their misfortunes and their virtues. They invent new theories of property, distorting rights and perpetuating injustice, as any one is sure to do who sets about the re-adjustment of social relations with the interests of one group distinctly before his mind, and the interests of all other groups thrown into the background. When I have read certain of these discussions I have thought that it must be quite disreputable to be respectable, quite dishonest to own property, quite unjust to go one's own way and earn one's own living, and that the only really admirable person was the good-for-nothing. The man who by his own effort raises himself above poverty appears, in these discussions, to be of no account. The man who has done nothing to raise himself above poverty finds that the social doctors flock about him, bringing the capital which they have collected from the other class, and promising him the aid of the State to give him what the other had to work for. In all these schemes and projects the organized intervention of society through the State is either planned or hoped for, and the State is thus made to become the protector and guardian of certain classes. The agents who are to direct the State action are, of course, the reformers and philanthropists. Their schemes, therefore, may always be reduced to this type—that A and B decide what C shall do for D. It will be interesting to inquire, at a later period of our discussion, who C is, and what the effect is upon him of all these arrangements. In all the discussions attention is concentrated on A and B, the noble social reformers, and on D, the "poor man." I call C the Forgotten Man, because I have never seen that any notice was taken of him in any of the discussions. When we have disposed of A, B, and D we can better appreciate the case of C, and I think that we shall find that he deserves our attention, for the worth of his character and the magnitude of his unmerited burdens. Here it may suffice to observe that, on the theories of the social philosophers to whom I have referred, we should get a new maxim of judicious living: Poverty is the best policy. If you get wealth, you will have to support other people; if you do not get wealth, it will be the duty of other people to support you.

No doubt one chief reason for the unclear and contradictory theories of class relations lies in the fact that our society, largely controlled in all its organization by one set of doctrines, still contains survivals of old social theories which are totally inconsistent with the former. In the Middle Ages men were united by custom and prescription into associations, ranks, guilds, and communities of various kinds. These ties endured as long as life lasted. Consequently society was dependent, throughout all its details, on status, and the tie, or bond, was sentimental. In our modern state, and in the United States more than anywhere else, the social structure is based on contract, and status is of the least importance. Contract, however, is rational—even rationalistic. It is also realistic, cold, and matter-of-fact. A contract relation is based on a sufficient reason, not on custom or prescription. It is not permanent. It endures only so long as the reason for it endures. In a state based on contract sentiment is out of place in any public or common affairs. It is relegated to the sphere of private and personal relations, where it depends not at all on class types, but on personal acquaintance and personal estimates. The sentimentalists among us always seize upon the survivals of the old order. They want to save them and restore them. Much of the loose thinking also which troubles us in our social discussions arises from the fact that men do not distinguish the elements of status and of contract which may be found in our society.

Whether social philosophers think it desirable or not, it is out of the question to go back to status or to the sentimental relations which once united baron and retainer, master and servant, teacher and pupil, comrade and comrade. That we have lost some grace and elegance is undeniable. That life once held more poetry and romance is true enough. But it seems impossible that any one who has studied the matter should doubt that we have gained immeasurably, and that our farther gains lie in going forward, not in going backward. The feudal ties can never be restored. If they could be restored they would bring back personal caprice, favoritism, sycophancy, and intrigue. A society based on contract is a society of free and independent men, who form ties without favor or obligation, and co-operate without cringing or intrigue. A society based on contract, therefore, gives the utmost room and chance for individual development, and for all the self-reliance and dignity of a free man. That a society of free men, co-operating under contract, is by far the strongest society which has ever yet existed; that no such society has ever yet developed the full measure of strength of which it is capable; and that the only social improvements which are now conceivable lie in the direction of more complete realization of a society of free men united by contract, are points which cannot be controverted. It follows, however, that one man, in a free state, cannot claim help from, and cannot be charged to give help to, another…

思考题：

1. What was the disadvantage of philanthropy and humanitarianism, according to Sumner?
2. Are you convinced by Sumner's thoughts on poverty, social responsibility, and the duties of government, why or why not?

23. The Atlanta Exposition Address (1895)①

Booker T. Washington

导读:

布克·托利弗·华盛顿(Booker Taliaferro Washington, 1856—1915)是美国政治家、教育家和作家。他出生于美国弗吉尼亚州富兰克林县,父亲是白人奴隶主,母亲是黑奴。他通过自学掌握了读写技能,16岁时到弗吉尼亚汉普顿的师范和农业学院(现在的汉普顿大学)接受教师培训。1881年,他被任命为亚拉巴马州塔斯基吉学院的校长。1896年和1901年,华盛顿分别获得哈佛大学和达特茅斯学院授予的名誉文学硕士学位和名誉博士学位。1901年,华盛顿被西奥多·罗斯福总统邀请到白宫,是第一位获邀进白宫做客的美国黑人。从1895年直至逝世,华盛顿被公认为当时最有影响力的美国黑人。

时值美国进步时代②,受自身经历和所受教育的影响,华盛顿认为只要通过职业技术教育,使黑人成为美国社会和经济生活中不可或缺的因素,并努力重塑黑人形象,赢得白人的尊重,黑人就能得到一切应有的政治权力和公民权利。因此,他和白人合作,帮助筹款创建数百个社区学校和高等教育机构。他注重职业教育,认为黑人更重要的是学会生存的本领。华盛顿还大力促进美国各种族之间的友谊和合作。其自传《超越奴役》(*Up from Slavery: An Autobiography*)于1901年出版,至今仍然广为流传。

本文"The Atlanta Exposition Address"是1895年9月18日华盛顿应邀在亚特兰大博览会上以黑人代言人的身份向白人听众发表的演说。州长布洛克是这样介绍华盛顿的:"今天,我们有请黑人企业和黑人文明

① Booker T. Washington, *Up from Slavery: An Autobiography* (New York: Penguin Books, 1986): 218-225.

② 1880年至1920年被称为美国的"进步时代"(The Progressive Era)。在此之前的美国腐败横行,假冒伪劣猖獗,重大灾难屡屡发生,社会矛盾异常尖锐。美国在这个时期进行了一系列深刻的制度建设,奠定了其现代国家的基础。

的代表华盛顿先生……”[①]在演说中，华盛顿劝勉黑人同胞要学会一般的职业技能，发展与白人朋友的睦邻关系，脚踏实地从“最低点”而不是“最高点”开始努力。他呼吁南方白人充分利用南部的黑人劳动力，呼吁白人资助黑人的职业技术教育，呼吁黑人留在南部发展，致力农业、家庭服务业、商业等领域。华盛顿在当时提出的关于发展黑人职业教育的思想，对促进美国黑人教育，尤其是黑人职业教育的发展产生了很大的影响。他向白人听众强调：“在一切纯社会性的事务中，白人和黑人可以像手指那样分开，但在一切对共同进步至关重要的事务中则团结得像一只手。”他的这番言论遭到了当时另一位黑人领袖杜波依斯[②]的强烈反对，谴责他一味强调职业技术培训是以“放弃黑人的政治权力、公民权利和对黑人青年高等教育为代价，是在把黑人置于半奴役的危险之中”[③]。然而，华盛顿的演说却得到了白人社会的喝彩，南北方的白人都给予了他极高的荣誉，他的黑人教育理念在当时的美国社会盛极一时。

Mr. President and Gentlemen of the Board of Directors and Citizens:

One-third of the population of the South is of the Negro race. No enterprise seeking the material, civil, or moral welfare of this section can disregard this element of our population and reach the highest success. I but convey to you, Mr. President and Directors, the sentiment of the masses of my race when I say that in no way have the value and manhood of the American Negro been more fittingly and generously recognized than by the managers of this magnificent Exposition at every stage of its progress. It is a recognition that will do more to cement the friendship of the two races than any occurrence since the dawn of our freedom.

Not only this, but the opportunity here afforded will awaken among us a new

---

① Booker T. Washington, *Up from Slavery: An Autobiography* (New York: Penguin Books, 1986): 217.

② 威廉·爱德华·伯格哈特·杜波依斯（William Edward Burghardt Du Bois, 1868—1963）是20世纪上半叶美国最有影响的黑人知识分子。在1903年发表的《黑人问题》中，杜波伊斯批判了布克·托利弗·华盛顿一味强调黑人职业技术教育的主张。杜波依斯和华盛顿的主要分歧在于他们的教育理念：华盛顿认为非洲裔美国人的学校教育应该局限于农业、机械等职业技术培训；但是杜波依斯认为黑人学校还应该提供更多的文科课程（包括经典文学、艺术、人文学科等），只有如此才能培养新的黑人精英领导者。

③ W. E. B. Du Bois, *Souls of Black Folk* (New York: Penguin Books, 1989): 221−222.

era of industrial progress. Ignorant and inexperienced, it is not strange that in the first years of our new life[1] we began at the top instead of at the bottom; that a seat in Congress or the state legislature was more sought than real estate or industrial skill; that the political convention or stump speaking had more attractions than starting a dairy farm or truck garden.

A ship lost at sea for many days suddenly sighted a friendly vessel. From the mast of the unfortunate vessel was seen a signal, "Water, water; we die of thirst!" The answer from the friendly vessel at once came back, "Cast down your bucket where you are." A second time the signal, "Water, water; send us water!" ran up from the distressed vessel, and was answered, "Cast down your bucket where you are." And a third and fourth signal for water was answered, "Cast down your bucket where you are." The captain of the distressed vessel, at last heeding the injunction, cast down his bucket, and it came up full of fresh, sparkling water from the mouth of the Amazon River. To those of my race who depend on bettering their condition in a foreign land or who underestimate the importance of cultivating friendly relations with the Southern white man, who is their next-door neighbor, I would say: "Cast down your bucket where you are"—cast it down in making friends in every manly way of the people of all races by whom we are surrounded.

Cast it down in agriculture, mechanics, in commerce, in domestic service, and in the professions. And in this connection it is well to bear in mind that whatever other sins the South may be called to bear, when it comes to business, pure and simple, it is in the South that the Negro is given a man's chance in the commercial world, and in nothing is this Exposition more eloquent than in emphasizing this chance. Our greatest danger is that in the great leap from slavery to freedom we may overlook the fact that the masses of us are to live by the productions of our hands, and fail to keep in mind that we shall prosper in proportion as we learn to dignify and glorify common labour and put brains and skill into the common occupations of life; shall prosper in proportion as we learn to draw the line between the superficial and the substantial, the ornamental gewgaws of life and the useful. No race can prosper till it learns that there is as much dignity in tilling a field as in writing a poem. It is at the bottom of life we must begin, and not at the top. Nor should we permit our grievances to overshadow our opportunities.

To those of the white race who look to the incoming of those of foreign birth and strange tongue and habits for the prosperity of the South, were I permitted I would repeat what I say to my own race, "Cast down your bucket where you are." Cast it down among the eight millions of Negroes whose habits you know, whose fidelity and love you have tested in days when to have proved treacherous meant the ruin of your firesides. Cast down your bucket among these people who have, without strikes and labour wars, tilled your fields, cleared your forests, builded your railroads and cities, and brought forth treasures from the bowels of the earth, and helped make possible this magnificent representation of the progress of the South. Casting down your bucket among my people, helping and encouraging them as you are doing on these grounds, and to education of head, hand, and heart, you will find that they will buy your surplus land, make blossom the waste places in your fields, and run your factories. While doing this, you can be sure in the future, as in the past, that you and your families will be surrounded by the most patient, faithful, law-abiding, and unresentful people that the world has seen. As we have proved our loyalty to you in the past, in nursing your children, watching by the sick-bed of your mothers and fathers, and often following them with tear-dimmed eyes to their graves, so in the future, in our humble way, we shall stand by you with a devotion that no foreigner can approach, ready to lay down our lives, if need be, in defense of yours, interlacing our industrial, commercial, civil, and religious life with yours in a way that shall make the interests of both races one. In all things that are purely social we can be as separate as the fingers, yet one as the hand in all things essential to mutual progress.

There is no defense or security for any of us except in the highest intelligence and development of all. If anywhere there are efforts tending to curtail the fullest growth of the Negro, let these efforts be turned into stimulating, encouraging, and making him the most useful and intelligent citizen. Effort or means so invested will pay a thousand per cent interest. These efforts will be twice blessed— "blessing him that gives and him that takes." There is no escape through law of man or God from the inevitable:—

The laws of changeless justice bind
Oppressor with oppressed;
And close as sin and suffering joined
We march to fate abreast.[2]

Nearly sixteen millions of hands will aid you in pulling the load upward, or they will pull against you the load downward. We shall constitute one-third and more of the ignorance and crime of the South, or one-third its intelligence and progress; we shall contribute one-third to the business and industrial prosperity of the South, or we shall prove a veritable body of death, stagnating, depressing, retarding every effort to advance the body politic.

Gentlemen of the Exposition, as we present to you our humble effort at an exhibition of our progress, you must not expect overmuch. Starting thirty years ago with ownership here and there in a few quilts and pumpkins and chickens (gathered from miscellaneous sources), remember the path that has led from these to the inventions and production of agricultural implements, buggies, steam-engines, newspapers, books, statuary, carving, paintings, the management of drug-stores and banks, has not been trodden without contact with thorns and thistles. While we take pride in what we exhibit as a result of our independent efforts, we do not for a moment forget that our part in this exhibition would fall far short of your expectations but for the constant help that has come to our educational life, not only from the Southern states, but especially from Northern philanthropists, who have made their gifts a constant stream of blessing and encouragement.

The wisest among my race understand that the agitation of questions of social equality is the extremest folly, and that progress in the enjoyment of all the privileges that will come to us must be the result of severe and constant struggle rather than of artificial forcing. No race that has anything to contribute to the markets of the world is long in any degree ostracized. It is important and right that all privileges of the law be ours, but it is vastly more important that we be prepared for the exercise of these privileges. The opportunity to earn a dollar in a factory just now is worth infinitely more than the opportunity to spend a dollar in an opera-house.

In conclusion, may I repeat that nothing in thirty years has given us more hope and encouragement, and drawn us so near to you of the white race, as this opportunity offered by the Exposition; and here bending, as it were, over the altar that represents the results of the struggles of your race and mine, both starting practically empty-handed three decades ago, I pledge that in your effort to work out the great and intricate problem which God has laid at the doors of the South, you shall have at all times the patient, sympathetic help of my race; only let this he constantly in mind, that, while from representations in these buildings of the product of field, of forest, of mine, of factory, letters, and art, much good will come, yet far above and beyond material benefits will be that higher good, that, let us pray God, will come, in a blotting out of sectional differences and racial animosities and suspicions, in a determination to administer absolute justice, in a willing obedience among all classes to the mandates of law. This, this, coupled with our material prosperity, will bring into our beloved South a new heaven and a new earth.

注释：

1. 1862年9月，林肯发布了著名的《解放奴隶宣言》（“The Emancipation Proclamation”），宣布废除奴隶制，解放黑奴。1865年4月9日，美国南北战争以北方胜利宣告结束，它标志着奴隶制的彻底崩溃，黑人获得期盼已久的自由。
2. 引自约翰·格林里夫·惠蒂埃（John Greenleaf Whittier, 1807—1893）的诗集《内战时期所作》（*In War Time: And Other Poems*, 1864）中的诗作《在皇家港》（“At Port Royal”）。从1833年起，惠蒂埃在废奴主义者威廉·加里逊的影响下积极投入废奴运动，编辑报纸，撰写社论和小册子，同时写诗号召废除奴隶制。诗集《在废奴问题进展过程中写的诗》（*Poems Written During the Progress of the Abolition Question in the United States*, 1837）和《自由的声音》（*Voices of Freedom*, 1846）揭露了奴隶主的暴行和黑奴的悲惨命运。他的诗歌战斗性强，反映了美国废奴斗争中的重大事件，犹如一部废奴运动的编年史。

思考题：

1. Why had Booker T. Washington been chosen to speak at the Atlanta Exposition?
2. What did Washington mean by “cast down your bucket where you are”? Do you agree or disagree with his idea?
3. Was industrial education the only way out for the blacks in the South in the 1890s?

24. The Significance of the Frontier in American History (1893)[1]

Frederick Jackson Turner

导读：

弗雷德里克·杰克逊·特纳（Frederick Jackson Turner, 1861—1932）是19世纪末20世纪初美国著名的历史学家，是美国“边疆学派”[2]的代表人物。特纳出生于美国威斯康星州，在约翰斯·霍普金斯大学获得历史学博士学位，先后执教于威斯康星大学和哈佛大学，从事边疆史学的教学与研究。在一生中，特纳发表了大量的著作与文章，其中最具影响力的是他在芝加哥美国历史协会年会上宣读的《边疆在美国历史上的重要性》（“The Significance of the Frontier in American History”）一文。在该文中，特纳提出“边疆理论”，强调边疆和西进运动对美国历史发展的重要性。他独特的见解与观点翻开了美国史学研究的新篇章，成为美国史学的转折点。

特纳“边疆理论”的提出与美国第二次工业革命和西进运动结束的历史背景息息相关。[3]南北战争结束后，美国经济体系趋于统一，资本主义经济迅猛发展。19世纪70年代开始的第二次工业革命更使美国的综合国力发生了根本性变化，经济跃居世界首位。民族自豪感的增强使美国人愈加重视自身历史与文化的特性。与此同时，美国人口调查局在1890年发布公告，宣称美国边疆的消失标志着西进运动的结束。这场持续了一个多世纪的运动使美国的边疆从大西洋沿岸扩展到太平洋沿岸。

---

① Frederick Jackson Turner, *Rereading Jackson Turner,* with commentary by John Mack Faragher (New Haven: Yale University Press, 1998): 33–60.

② 边疆学派是19世纪末美国史学中出现的一个流派，又称中西部学派，代表人物是弗雷德里克·杰克逊·特纳。该学派系统阐述了西部边疆在美国历史上的作用，颠覆了美国史学的传统观点（美国起源于欧洲），是美国史学发展的转折点。

③ 在1870到1914年间，由于电动机、内燃机的迅速推广，油田的广泛开采，新炼钢法的兴起，美国率先步入了电气化、石油化和钢铁时代，国内经济高速增长。西进运动是一场美国东部居民向西部地区迁移与开发的群众性运动，始于18世纪末，终于19世纪末20世纪初。它大大促进了美国经济的发展。但是，在此过程中，大批印第安人遭到屠杀，幸存者被强行驱赶到更为荒凉的“保留地”。

那么如何评价西进运动在美国历史中的作用与地位？作为史学家的特纳敏锐地看到西进运动的独特性与重要意义，反对当时盛行的“生源论”（germ theory）①学说，用崭新的边疆理论解释了美国独特文化与传统的起源。

本文节选自特纳最著名的文章《边疆在美国历史上的重要性》。在文章中，特纳认为欧洲对美国的影响仅局限于东部沿海地带。然而，随着边疆的不断西移，美国逐渐抹去了欧洲文明的烙印。首先，西进运动促进了民族大融合，形成了美国自己的文化。在垦殖与开拓的过程中，不同种族的拓荒者聚集在一起。他们的文化相互渗透，相互影响，在新的环境下孕育了独具特色的民族文化。其次，边疆开拓促进了西部农业经济的发展，使美国东南部不再依赖于英国的粮食与其他食品，从而摆脱了前宗主国的经济控制。最后，西进运动塑造了美国人民乐观进取、勇敢冒险的民族性格，强化了个人主义思想。特纳谈道，身处荒原与森林中的移民，不仅要面临恶劣的自然环境，还要克服各种困难。移民们通过开发西部，看到了自己的力量，更加坚信只有依靠自己的奋斗才能获得幸福的生活，实现心中的梦想。而西进运动最大的贡献就是创建了美国式民主。在西部边疆，欧洲复杂的社会体系不见踪影，人与人之间更加平等。在特纳看来，美国的民族性格、民主制度、经济与文化并不是对欧洲文明的继承与发展，而是源于西部边疆的拓殖。他认为，只有把视线从大西洋转向大西部，才能真正了解美国的历史。

The American frontier is sharply distinguished from the European frontier—a fortified boundary line running through dense populations. The most significant thing about the American frontier is that it lies at the hither edge of free land. In the census reports it is treated as the margin of that settlement which has a density of two or more to the square mile. The term is an elastic one, and for our purposes does not need sharp definition. We shall consider the whole frontier belt, including the Indian country and the outer margin of the “settled area” of the census reports. This paper will make no attempt to treat the subject exhaustively; its aim is simply to call attention to the frontier as a fertile field for investigation, and to suggest some of the problems which arise in connection with it.

---

① 美国19世纪制度史学派用“生源论”来解释美国制度和文化的起源，认为美国早期的历史只不过是欧洲文明在美洲环境中的发展而已。

...The frontier is the line of most rapid and effective Americanization. The wilderness masters the colonist. It finds him a European in dress, industries, tools, modes of travel, and thought. It takes him from the railroad car and puts him in the birch canoe. It strips off the garments of civilization and arrays him in the hunting shirt and the moccasin. It puts him in the log cabin of the Cherokee and Iroquois and runs an Indian palisade around him[1]. Before long he has gone to planting Indian corn and plowing with a sharp stick; he shouts the war cry and takes the scalp in orthodox Indian fashion. In short, at the frontier the environment is at first too strong for the man. He must accept the conditions which it furnishes, or perish, and so he fits himself into the Indian clearings and follows the Indian trails. Little by little he transforms the wilderness, but the outcome is not the old Europe, not simply the development of Germanic germs, any more than the first phenomenon was a case of reversion to the Germanic mark. The fact is, that here is a new product that is American. At first, the frontier was the Atlantic coast. It was the frontier of Europe in a very real sense. Moving westward, the frontier became more and more American. As successive terminal moraines result from successive glaciations, so each frontier leaves its traces behind it, and when it becomes a settled area the region still partakes of the frontier characteristics. Thus the advance of the frontier has meant a steady movement away from the influence of Europe, a steady growth of independence on American lines. And to study this advance, the men who grew up under these conditions, and the political, economic, and social results of it, is to study the really American part of our history.

...Chiefly from the point of view of the frontier itself, we may next inquire what were the influence on the East and on the Old World...

First, we note that the frontier promoted the formation of a composite nationality for the American people. The coast was preponderantly English, but the later tides of continental immigration flowed across to the free lands. This was the case from the early colonial days. The Scotch-Irish and the Palatine Germans, or "Pennsylvania Dutch," furnished the dominant element in the stock of the colonial frontier. With these peoples were also the freed indented servants, or redemptioners, who at the expiration of their time of service passed to the frontier...Very generally these redemptioners were of non-English stock. In the crucible of the frontier the immigrants were Americanized, liberated, and fused into a mixed race, English in neither nationality nor characteristics. The process has gone on from the early days to our own. Burke and other writers in the middle of the eighteenth century believed that Pennsylvania as "threatened with the danger of being wholly foreign in language, manners, and perhaps even inclinations." The German and Scotch-Irish elements in the frontier of the South were only less great. In the middle of the present century the German element in Wisconsin was already so considerable that leading publicists looked to the creation of a German state out of the commonwealth by concentrating their colonization. Such examples teach us to beware of misinterpreting the fact that there is a common English speech in America into a belief that the stock is also English.

In another way the advance of the frontier decreased our dependence on England. The coast, particularly of the South, lacked diversified industries, and was dependent on England for the bulk of its supplies. In the South there was even a dependence on the Northern colonies for articles of food… Before long the frontier created a demand for merchants. As it retreated from the coast it became less and less possible for England to bring her supplies directly to the consumer's wharfs, and carry away staple crops, and staple crops began to give way to diversified agriculture for a time. The effect of this phase of the frontier action upon the northern section is perceived when we realize how the advance of the frontier aroused seaboard cities like Boston, New York, and Baltimore, to engage in rivalry for what Washington called "the extensive and valuable trade of a rising empire."

…This is a wrong perspective. The pioneer needed the goods of the coast, and so the grand series of internal improvement and railroad legislation began, with potent nationalizing effects. Over internal improvements occurred great debates, in which grave constitutional questions were discussed. Sectional groupings appear in the votes, profoundly significant for the historian. Loose construction increased as the nation marched westward. But the West was not content with bringing the farm to the factory. Under the lead of Clay—"Harry of the West"—protective tariffs were passed, with the cry of bringing the factory to the farm.[2] The disposition of the public lands was a third important subject of national legislation influenced by the frontier…

It is safe to say that the legislation with regard to land, tariff, and internal improvements—the American system of the nationalizing Whig party—was conditioned on frontier ideas and needs.[3] But it was not merely in legislative action that the frontier worked against the sectionalism of the coast. The economic and social characteristics of the frontier worked against sectionalism. The men of the frontier had closer resemblances to the Middle region than to either of the other sections. Pennsylvania had been the seed plot of frontier emigration, and, although she passed on her settlers along the Great Valley into the west of Virginia and the Carolinas, yet the industrial society of these Southern frontiersmen was always more like that of the Middle region than like that of the tide-water portion of the South, which later came to spread its industrial type throughout the South.

The Middle region, entered by New York harbor, was an open door to all Europe. The tide-water part of the South represented typical Englishmen, modified by a warm climate and servile labor, and living in baronial fashion on great plantations; New England stood for a special English movement—Puritanism. The Middle region was less English than the other sections. It had a wide mixture of nationalities, a varied society, the mixed town and county system of local government, a varied economic life, many religious sects. In short, it was a region mediating between New England and the South, and the East and the West. It represented that composite nationality which the contemporary United States exhibits, that juxtaposition of non-English groups, occupying a valley or a little settlement, and presenting reflections of the map of Europe in their variety. It was democratic and nonsectional, if not national; "easy, tolerant, and contented;" rooted strongly in material prosperity. It was typical of the modern United States. It was least sectional, not only because it lay between North and South, but also because with no barriers to shut out its frontiers from its settled region, and with a system of connecting waterways, the Middle region mediated between East and West as well as between North and South. Thus it became the typically American region. Even the New Englander, who was shut out from the frontier by the Middle region, tarrying in New York or Pennsylvania on his westward march, lost the acuteness of his sectionalism on the way…

But the most important effect of the frontier has been in the promotion of democracy here and in Europe. As has been indicated, the frontier is productive of individualism. Complex society is precipitated by the wilderness into a kind of primitive organization based on the family. The tendency is anti-social. It produces antipathy to control, and particularly to any direct control. The tax-gatherer is viewed as a representative of oppression… The frontier conditions prevalent in the colonies are important factors in the explanation of the American Revolution, where individual liberty was sometimes confused with absence of all effective government. The same conditions aid in explaining the difficulty of instituting a strong government in the period of the confederacy. The frontier individualism has from the beginning promoted democracy.

The frontier States that came into the Union in the first quarter of a century of its existence came in with democratic suffrage provisions, and had reactive effects of the highest importance upon the older States whose peoples were being attracted there. An extension of the franchise became essential. It was *western* New York that forced an extension of suffrage in the constitutional convention of that State in 1821; and it was *western* Virginia that compelled the tide-water region to put a more liberal suffrage provision in the constitution framed in 1830, and to give to the frontier region a more nearly proportionate representation with the tide-water aristocracy. The rise of democracy as an effective force in the nation came in with western preponderance under Jackson and William Henry Harrison, and it meant the triumph of the frontier—with all of its good and with all of its evil elements…

From the conditions of frontier life came intellectual traits of profound importance. The works of travelers along each frontier from colonial days onward describe certain common traits, and these traits have, while softening down, still persisted as survivals in the place of their origin, even when a higher social organization succeeded. The result is that to the frontier the American intellect owes its striking characteristics. That coarseness and strength combined with acuteness and inquisitiveness; that practical, inventive turn of mind, quick to find expedients; that masterful grasp of material things, lacking in the artistic but powerful to effect great ends; that restless, nervous energy; that dominant individualism, working for good and for evil, and withal that buoyancy and exuberance which comes with freedom—these are traits of the frontier, or traits called out elsewhere because of the existence of the frontier. Since the days when the fleet of Columbus sailed into the waters of the New World, America has been another name for opportunity, and the people of the United States have taken their tone from the incessant expansion which has not only been open but has even been forced upon them. He would be a rash prophet who should assert that the expansive character of American life has now entirely ceased. Movement has been its dominant fact, and, unless this training has no effect upon a people, the American energy will continually demand a wider field for its exercise. But never again will such gifts of free land offer themselves. For a moment, at the frontier, the bonds of custom are broken and unrestraint is triumphant. There is not *tabula rasa*.[4] The stubborn American environment is there with its imperious summons to accept its conditions; the inherited ways of doing things are also there; and yet, in spite of environment, and in spite of custom, each frontier did indeed furnish a new field of opportunity, a gate of escape from the bondage of the past; and freshness, and confidence, and scorn of older society, impatience of its restraints and its ideas, and indifference to its lessons, have accompanied the frontier. What the Mediterranean Sea was to the Greeks, breaking the bond of custom, offering new experiences, calling out new institutions and activities, that, and more, the ever retreating frontier has been to the United States directly, and to the nations of Europe more remotely. And now, four centuries from the discovery of America, at the end of a hundred years of life under the Constitution, the frontier has gone, and with its going has closed the first period of American history.

注释：

1. 易洛魁是北美印第安人的一支，原分布在密西西比河以西，后迁到安大略湖和伊利湖一带。切罗基人是易洛魁的部落之一。易洛魁诸部落的生活形态为半定居式，从事农耕，必要时用栅栏围住部落，居住在可容纳多人的长形房舍中。
2. 哈里（Harry）即亨利（Henry）的别称。亨利·克莱（Henry Clay, 1777—1852）是美国政治家，曾出任国务卿，创立了辉格党。针对南北有关奴隶制的纷争，克莱主张通过妥协调解矛盾，提出并促成了《1850年的妥协案》（“Compromise of 1850”）。该法案是美国国会为解决蓄奴问题和防止联邦解体而采取的系列权宜措施之一。它包括批准加利福尼亚作为自由州加入联邦，新墨西哥及犹他地区是否蓄奴由该地居民决定，各州司法机构及地方政府必须协助奴隶主追捕逃亡奴隶，在哥伦比亚特区废除奴隶贸易等内容。妥协案只是暂时缓和了南部脱离联邦的危局，并未从根本上解决纷争。在经济上，克莱提出“美式经济体制”（American System），旨在通过提高关税保护美国工业的发展。他的经济政策受到东岸各州的欢迎，却遭到了以农业与种植园经济为主的南方和西部的反对。
3. 美国辉格党始创于19世纪30年代，反对安德鲁·杰克逊总统及其民主党所订立的政治经济政策。在政治上，辉格党维护国会至上地位，反对总统权力过大；经济上，推崇亨利·克莱提出的“美式经济体制”，主张通过建立银行与工厂来深化经济体系改革，对西部的疆土拓展热情不高。
4. *tabula rasa*：拉丁文，直译为“空白的板”。在这里，特纳指出在美国不会再有像西部边疆这样能带给人们新机遇、新气象的自由土地了。

思考题：

1. In Turner's interpretation, what is the definition of frontier in America?
2. What influences did the Westward Movement have on America?
3. In your understanding, what is the implication of Turner's statement "the American energy will continually demand a wider field for its exercise" as the frontier in America is already closed?

25. Women and Economics (1898)[①]

Charlotte Perkins Gilman

导读：

夏洛特·珀金斯·吉尔曼（Charlotte Perkins Gilman, 1860—1935）是美国著名的女性主义作家与理论家，也是美国第一波妇女运动[②]中最具影响力的女权主义者之一。她一生著述颇丰，创作了大量的小说、诗歌与社会学著作。其短篇小说《黄墙纸》（"The Yellow Wallpaper", 1895）与长篇小说《她乡》（*Herland*, 1915）是女权主义思潮的代表作。这两部作品从不同角度表现了父权制下女性的觉醒与斗争，为女性主义文学的发展奠定了重要基础。1898年，吉尔曼出版了《妇女与经济》（*Women and Economics*），倡导妇女经济独立。除了撰写书籍，吉尔曼还创办了女权主义刊物《先驱》（*Forerunner*, 1909—1916），批判以男性为核心的社会。在当时的男权社会，吉尔曼的思想可谓超越了时代，对女性意识的觉醒、推动美国第一波女权运动的开展做出了巨大贡献。

美国第一波女权运动始于19世纪中期，止于20世纪初，以妇女获得选举权为标志。而女权运动的蓬勃开展与当时的历史背景密不可分。在内战结束后，美国进入了从农业社会向工业社会过渡的转型时期。工业化的高速发展、大规模的生产模式创造了更多的就业机会，为妇女走出家庭、接触社会打开了一扇门。家用电器的发明则使女性摆脱了家务之累，让她们有时间参与社会活动。同时，经济的繁荣促进了教育的发展。越来越多的妇女有机会享受高等教育，提高认知水平。接受教育和参加工作不仅赋予了妇女从事改革活动的能力，也使她们更深刻地意识到男女地位的不平等，女性仍然是社会中的弱势群体。为了提高女性地

① Charlotte Perkins Gilman, *Women and Economics* (New York: Prometheus Books, 1994): 64-72.

② 美国第一波女权运动兴起于19世纪40年代，其标志为1848年在纽约州的塞尼卡福尔斯召开的美国第一次妇女大会，其主要的奋斗目标是解放妇女，获得政治权力。经过长达72年的不懈斗争，关于女性选举权的第19条宪法修正案最终于1920年在国会通过，美国妇女从此获得了投票选举权。

位，改变妇女群体命运，一场大规模的、有组织的女权运动在美国轰轰烈烈地展开。

《妇女与经济》是吉尔曼著名的女性主义理论作品，被誉为女权运动的“圣经”，主要论述女性经济独立的必要性。本文节选自该书第四章。在选文中，吉尔曼指出，男女地位的不平等并不存在于原始社会，而是始于女性在经济上对男性的依附。经济的依赖限制了女性的生活空间，限定了她们的劳动种类，淡化了她们在宗教中的作用。首先，经济依附使妇女终日待在家里，与世隔绝。狭窄的环境迫使女性只能接受有限的知识，丧失了独立思考的能力。其次，经济依附决定女性只能从事单调重复的家务或者简单低级的工作。社会分工的专业化，不仅模糊了妇女在家庭中所创造的经济价值，也使她们无法进入专业的工作领域。最后，女性的经济地位使她们从宗教仪式的参与者变成了教会中的沉默者，甚至被排挤在外。吉尔曼谈道，生活空间、劳动种类以及宗教信仰都在潜移默化地影响着女性的自我认知，使她们长期处于从属地位而不反思，并且将这样的观念与意识传给后代。因此，要提升妇女的地位，争取男女平等，女人必须经济独立。否则，一个女人如果要获得财富、权力、社会地位、名望、家庭、闲情逸趣、油盐酱醋等，就只能接受“那小小的金戒指”。

…The human female has been restricted in range from the earliest beginning. Even among savages, she has a much more restricted knowledge of the land she lives in. She moves with the camp, of course, and follows her primitive industries in its vicinity; but the war-path and the hunt are the man's. He has a far larger habitat. The life of the female savage is freedom itself, however, compared with the increasing constriction of custom closing in upon the woman, as civilization advanced, like the iron torture chamber of romance. Its culmination is expressed in the proverb: "A woman should leave her home but three times, —when she is christened, when she is married, and when she is buried." Or this: "The woman, the cat, and the chimney should never leave the house." The absolutely stationary female and the wide-ranging male are distinctly human institutions…

What we do modifies us more than what is done to us. The freedom of expression has been more restricted in women than the freedom of impression, if that be possible. Something of the world she lived in she has seen from her barred windows. Some air has come through the purdah's folds, some knowledge has filtered to her eager ears from the talk of men. Desdemona learned somewhat of Othello.[1] Had she known more, she might have lived longer. But in the ever-growing human impulse to create, the power and will to make, to do, to express one's spirit in new forms, —here she has been utterly debarred. She might work as she had worked from the beginning, —at the primitive labors of the household; but in the inevitable expansion of even those industries to professional levels we have striven to hold her back. To work with her own hands, for nothing, in direct body-service to her own family,—this has been permitted,—yes, compelled. But to be and do anything further from this she has been forbidden. Her labor has not only been limited in kind, but in degree. Whatever she has been allowed to do must be done in private and alone, the first-hand industries of savage times.

Our growth in industry has been not only in kind, but in class. The baker is not in the same industrial grade with the house-cook, though both make bread. To specialize any form of labor is a step up: to organize it is another step. Specialization and organization are the basis of human progress, the organic methods of social life. They have been forbidden to women almost absolutely. The greatest and most beneficent change of this century is the progress of women in these two lines of advance. The effect of this check in industrial development, accompanied as it was by the constant inheritance of increased racial power, has been to intensify the sensations and emotions of women, and to develope great activity in the lines allowed. The nervous energy that up to present memory has impelled women to labor incessantly at something, be it the veriest folly of fancy work, is one mark of this effect.

In religious development the same dead-line has held back the growth of women through all the races and ages. In dim early times she was sharer in the mysteries and rites; but, as religion developed, her place receded, until Paul commanded her to be silent in the churches.[2] And she has been silent until to-day. Even now, with all the ground gained, we have but the beginnings—the slowly forced and disapproved beginnings—of religious equality for the sexes. In some nations, religion is held to be a masculine attribute exclusively, it being even questioned whether women have souls. An early Christian council settled that important decision by vote, fortunately deciding that they had. In a church whose main strength has always been derived from the adherence of women, it would have been an uncomfortable reflection not to have allowed them souls. Ancient family worship ran in the male line. It was the son who kept the sacred grandfathers in due respect, and poured libations to their shades. When the woman married, she changed her ancestors, and had to worship her husband's progenitors instead of her own. This is why the Hindu and the Chinaman and many others of like stamp must have a son to keep them in countenance,—a deep-seated sex-prejudice, coming to slow extinction as women rise in economic importance.

It is painfully interesting to trace the gradual cumulative effect of these conditions upon women: first, the action of large natural laws, acting on her as they would act on any other animal; then the evolution of social customs and laws (with her position as the active cause), following the direction of mere physical forces, and adding heavily to them; then, with increasing civilization, the unbroken accumulation of precedent, burnt into each generation by the growing force of education, made lovely by art, holy by religion, desirable by habit; and, steadily acting from beneath, the unswerving pressure of economic necessity upon which the whole structure rested. These are strong modifying conditions, indeed.

The process would have been even more effective and far less painful but for one important circumstance. Heredity has no Salic law.[3] Each girl child inherits from her father a certain increasing percentage of human development, human power, human tendency; and each boy as well inherits from his mother the increasing percentage of sex-development, sex-power, sex-tendency. The action of heredity has been to equalize what every tendency of environment and education made to differ. This has saved us from such a female as the gypsy moth.[4] It has held up the woman, and held down the man. It has set iron bounds to our absurd effort to make a race with one sex a million years behind the other. But it has added terribly to the pain and difficulty of human life,—a difficulty and a pain that should have taught us long since that we were living on wrong lines. Each woman born, re-humanized by the current of race activity carried on by her father and re-womanized by her traditional position, has had to live over again in her own person the same process of restriction, repression, denial; the smothering "no" which crushed down all her human desires to create, to discover, to learn, to express, to advance. Each woman has had, on the other hand, the same single avenue of expression and attainment; the same one way in which alone she might do what she could, get what she might. All other doors were shut, and this one always open; and the whole pressure of advancing humanity was upon her…

To the young man confronting life the world lies wide. Such powers as he has he may use, must use. If he chooses wrong at first, he may choose again, and yet again. Not effective or successful in one channel, he may do better in another. The growing, varied needs of all mankind call on him for the varied service in which he finds his growth. What he wants to be, he may strive to be. What he wants to get, he may strive to get. Wealth, power, social distinction, fame, —what he wants he can try for.

To the young woman confronting life there is the same world beyond, there are the same human energies and human desires and ambition within. But all that she may wish to have, all that she may wish to do, must come through a single channel and a single choice. Wealth, power, social distinction, fame,—not only these, but home and happiness, reputation, ease and pleasure, her bread and butter,—all, must come to her through a small gold ring. This is a heavy pressure. It has accumulated behind her through heredity, and continued about her through environment. It has been subtly trained into her through education, till she herself has come to think it a right condition, and pours its influence upon her daughter with increasing impetus. Is it any wonder that women are over-sexed? But for the constant inheritance from the more human male, we should have been queen bees, indeed, long before this. But the daughter of the soldier and the sailor, of the artist, the inventor, the great merchant, has inherited in body and brain her share of his development in each generation, and so stayed somewhat human for all her femininity…

注释：

1. Othello：《奥赛罗》（*Othello*, 1603）是莎士比亚（William Shakespeare, 1564—1616）的四大悲剧之一。故事主要讲述了勇敢诚实的摩尔人统帅奥赛罗（Othello）因听信谗言，误认妻子苔丝德蒙娜（Desdemona）不贞，将她杀害。在真相大白后，奥赛罗追悔莫及，拔剑自刎。事实上，从第三幕开始，苔丝德蒙娜已经明显感受到奥赛罗对她态度的转变。但是，对于丈夫的暴怒行为与羞辱的语言，苔丝德蒙娜只是逆来顺受，直到死前才知道其中缘由。
2. 保罗在《圣经·哥林多前书》第14章第34节中讲道"妇女在会中要闭口不言"。吉尔曼借此经文指出宗教对女性地位与权力的压制。
3. Salic law：萨利克法，起源于法兰克人萨利克部族中通行的各种习惯法。公元6世纪初，法兰克王国国王克洛维一世（Clovis Ⅰ, 466—511）将这些习惯法汇编为法律，取名萨利克法，成为古代西欧通行的法典。萨利克法中的民法法令规定女性后裔不得继承土地。
4. gypsy moth：舞毒蛾，一种飞蛾，原产于东半球。幼虫以树叶为食；雄蛾在日间飞翔；雌蛾不善飞行，常静伏于枝梢、树干或草丛中产卵。吉尔曼在这里说明女性因遗传了父亲的品质，不会像雌蛾一样待在固定的环境中，将繁衍后代作为一生的使命。

思考题：

1. According to Gilman, what factors had crushed down a woman's "desire to create, to discover, to learn to express, to advance"?
2. What is your understanding of Gilman's statement "what we do modifies us more than what is done to us"?

26. Wealth (1889)[①]

Andrew Carnegie

导读：

安德鲁·卡内基（Andrew Carnegie, 1835—1919）是叱咤商海的钢铁大王，与约翰·戴维森·洛克菲勒（John Davison Rockefeller, 1839—1937）、约翰·皮尔庞特·摩根（John Pierpont Morgan, 1837—1913）并称为美国经济界的三巨头[②]。钢铁大王卡内基的一生充满了传奇色彩。他白手起家，靠自己不懈的奋斗，创建了闻名世界的钢铁帝国——卡内基钢铁公司，从一名贫困潦倒的苏格兰移民跃居世界首富之列。更让人惊讶的是，当卡内基事业达到巅峰之时，他毫不犹豫地将赚取的巨额财富全部捐给了社会公益事业。他捐资修建纽约著名的卡内基音乐厅，创办匹兹堡的卡内基大学，兴建三千多间图书馆，其慈善行为引得同时代的富人纷纷效仿。

所谓时势造英雄，卡内基的成功与当时美国正经历的第二次工业革命密不可分。在1870到1914年间，因电动机、内燃机的迅速推广，油田的广泛开采，新炼钢法的实施，美国乃至整个欧洲步入了电气化、石油化和钢铁时代。重工业得到前所未有的发展，并逐步赶超轻工业，占据了美国工业的主导地位。然而，新技术设备的采用与重工业的大规模生产，从客观上都要求生产与资本的高度集中。企业只有通过联合兼并的方式，才能实现资本的快速积累，抢占市场资源。在这一过程中，作为

① Andrew Carnegie, "Wealth" in *American Ground: Vistas, Visions & Revisions*, ed. Robert H. Fossum & John K. Roth (New York: Paragon House Publishers, 1988): 229-238.

② 约翰·戴维森·洛克菲勒，美国名副其实的“石油大王”，美国历史上第一位亿万富豪。他创立的标准石油在全盛期垄断了全美90%的石油市场。约翰·皮尔庞特·摩根，美国银行家，是近代金融史上最著名的金融巨头。他创建通用电气公司，合并卡内基钢铁公司后成立美国钢铁公司。他麾下的摩根财团是一个庞大的金融帝国，统治美国整个金融界。

垄断组织形式的托拉斯相继出现在石油、烟草等行业。[①] 这些垄断组织为了追求高额利润，干预自由竞争，操控商品价格，剥削广大工人的薪资报酬，导致美国的财富分配严重不均。1896年美国国民财富的一半集中在1%的人口手里，而工人每年平均工资只有480美元，还不足以维持一个家庭的最低生活[②]。工人阶级与资产阶级的矛盾进一步激化，美国罢工运动一浪高过一浪，遍及各行各业[③]。

为治理当时美国社会的财富分配不均，卡内基于1889年12月在《北美评论》（*North America Review*）上发表了《财富》（"Wealth", 1889）一文，从两方面系统地阐述了他的财富思想。一方面，他认为财富是社会文明的根本，是一个国家经济发展的必然产物。在自由竞争、适者生存的美国社会，大量财富积聚在少数人手里的现象是无法避免的。另一方面，要解决贫富悬殊所激发的阶级矛盾，维持社会稳定，关键在于富人如何管理财富。在卡内基看来，富人处理财富有三种模式：财产留给后代，遗赠公共事业，生前回馈社会。他指出，传统的财产继承使大多数纨绔子弟做了财富的奴隶，不能抵制任何诱惑，以致陷入堕落的境地。而死后捐赠不仅不能确保捐款用于公共事业，还容易被认为是一种钱财无法带走的无奈之举。卡内基推崇最后一种模式：富人应该在生前对赚取的多余财产进行认真、负责的处理，把巨额财产转化为一种不竭的源泉，为社会谋取长远的福利。卡内基谈道，真正的慈善事业应该坚持受益人自助的原则，不加选择地胡乱捐赠只会使接受者养成怠惰和依赖的习惯。因此，富人要参与捐款的管理，投资如兴建图书馆这样有益于整个社会的项目。只有这样，才能提升人们的尊严与生活品质，真正促进人类文明的发展。卡内基独特的慈善理念为当时的慈善事业开辟了一条新路，奠定了美国现代慈善事业的基础。

The problem of our age is the proper administration of wealth, so that the ties

---

① 1879年，美国第一个典型的垄断组织——美孚石油公司托拉斯出现。它拥有14个公司，并持有26个石油公司的多数股票。1880年，美国的烟草大王杜克（James B. Duke）在兼并一百多家烟草公司后，成立了以杜克家族为主的美国烟草公司，控制国内将近90%的卷烟市场，高额的垄断利润使公司的资本迅速膨胀。

② 在当时的美国，维持一个五口之家的最低生活费用为825美元。

③ 1881年至1900年之间，美国爆发了22 793起工人罢工事件，波及一万多家工商企业，斗争目的以提高工资、缩短工时为主。其中影响较大的是1886年5月1日的芝加哥工人大罢工和1892年的卡内基钢铁公司的工人罢工。

of brotherhood may still bind together the rich and poor in harmonious relationship. The conditions of human life have not only been changed, but revolutionized, within the past few hundred years. In former days there was little difference between the dwelling, dress, food, and environment of the chief and those of his retainers. The Indians are to-day where civilized man then was. When visiting the Sioux,[1] I was led to the wigwam of the chief. It was just like the others in external appearance, and even within the difference was trifling between it and those of the poorest of his braves. The contrast between the palace of the millionaire and the cottage of the laborer with us to-day measures the change which has come with civilization.

This change, however, is not to be deplored, but welcomed as highly beneficial. It is well, nay, essential for the progress of the race, that the houses of some should be homes for all that is highest and best in literature and the arts, and for all the refinements of civilization, rather than that none should be so. Much better this great irregularity than universal squalor. Without wealth there can be no Mæcenas.[2] The "good old times" were not good old times. Neither master nor servant was as well situated then as to-day. A relapse to old conditions would be disastrous to both—not the least so to him who serves—and would sweep away civilization with it. But whether the change be for good or ill, it is upon us, beyond our power to alter, and therefore to be accepted and made the best of. It is a waste of time to criticise the inevitable.

It is easy to see how the change has come. One illustration will serve for almost every phase of the cause. In the manufacture of products we have the whole story. It applies to all combinations of human industry, as stimulated and enlarged by the inventions of this scientific age. Formerly articles were manufactured at the domestic hearth or in small shops which formed part of the household. The master and his apprentices worked side by side, the latter living with the master, and therefore subject to the same conditions. When these apprentices rose to be masters, there was little or no change in their mode of life, and they, in turn, educated in the same routine succeeding apprentices. There was, substantially social equality, and even political equality, for those engaged in industrial pursuits had then little or no political voice in the State.

But the inevitable result of such a mode of manufacture was crude articles at high prices. To-day the world obtains commodities of excellent quality at prices which even the generation preceding this would have deemed incredible. In the commercial world similar causes have produced similar results, and the race is benefited thereby. The poor enjoy what the rich could not before afford. What were the luxuries have become the necessaries of life. The laborer has now more comforts than the landlord had a few generations ago. The farmer has more luxuries than the landlord had, and is more richly clad and better housed. The landlord has books and pictures rarer, and appointments more artistic, than the King could then obtain.

The price we pay for this salutary change is, no doubt, great. We assemble thousands of operatives in the factory, in the mine, and in the counting-house, of whom the employer can know little or nothing, and to whom the employer is little better than a myth. All intercourse between them is at an end. Rigid Castes are formed, and, as usual, mutual ignorance breeds mutual distrust. Each Caste is without sympathy for the other, and ready to credit anything disparaging in regard to it. Under the law of competition, the employer of thousands is forced into the strictest economies, among which the rates paid to labor figure prominently, and often there is friction between the employer and the employed, between capital and labor, between rich and poor. Human society loses homogeneity.

The price which society pays for the law of competition, like the price it pays for cheap comforts and luxuries, is also great; but the advantage of this law are also greater still, for it is to this law that we owe our wonderful material development, which brings improved conditions in its train. But, whether the law be benign or not, we must say of it, as we say of the change in the conditions of men to which we have referred: It is here; we cannot evade it; no substitutes for it have been found; and while the law may be sometimes hard for the individual, it is best for the race, because it insures the survival of the fittest in every department. We accept and welcome therefore, as conditions to which we must accommodate ourselves, great inequality of environment, the concentration of business, industrial and commercial, in the hands of a few, and the law of competition between these, as being not only beneficial, but essential for the future progress of the race. Having accepted these, it follows that there must be great scope for the exercise of special ability in the merchant and in the manufacturer who has to conduct affairs upon a great scale. That this talent for organization and management is rare among men is proved by the fact that it invariably secures for its possessor enormous rewards, no matter where or under what laws or conditions. The experienced in affairs always rate the MAN whose services can be obtained as a partner as not only the first consideration, but such as to render the question of his capital scarcely worth considering, for such men soon create capital; while, without the special talent required, capital soon takes wings. Such men become interested in firms or corporations using millions; and estimating only simple interest to be made upon the capital invested, it is inevitable that their income must exceed their expenditures, and that they must accumulate wealth. Nor is there any middle ground which such men can occupy, because the great manufacturing or commercial concern which does not earn at least interest upon its capital soon becomes bankrupt. It must either go forward or fall behind: to stand still is impossible. It is a condition essential for its successful operation that it should be thus far profitable, and even that, in addition to interest on capital, it should make profit. It is a law, as certain as any of the others named, that men possessed of this peculiar talent for affairs, under the free play of economic forces, must, of necessity, soon be in receipt of more revenue than can be judiciously expended upon themselves; and this law is as beneficial for the race as the others.

Objections to the foundations upon which society is based are not in order, because the condition of the race is better with these than it has been with any others which have been tried. Of the effect of any new substitutes proposed we cannot be sure. The Socialist or Anarchist who seeks to overturn present conditions is to be regarded as attacking the foundation upon which civilization itself rests, for civilization took its start from the day that the capable, industrious workman said to his incompetent and lazy fellow, "If thou dost net sow, thou shalt net reap," and thus ended primitive Communism by separating the drones from the bees. One who studies this subject will soon be brought face to face with the conclusion that upon the sacredness of property civilization itself depends—the right of the laborer to his hundred dollars in the savings bank, and equally the legal right of the millionaire to his millions. To these who propose to substitute Communism for this intense Individualism the answer, therefore, is: The race has tried that. All progress from that barbarous day to the present time has resulted from its displacement. Not evil, but good, has come to the race from the accumulation of wealth by those who have the ability and energy that produce it. But even if we admit for a moment that it might be better for the race to discard its present foundation, Individualism, —that it is a nobler ideal that man should labor, not for himself alone, but in and for a brotherhood of his fellows, and share with them all in common, realizing Swedenborg's[3] idea of Heaven, where, as he says, the angels derive their happiness, not from laboring for self, but for each other, —even admit all this, and a sufficient answer is, This is not evolution, but revolution. It necessitates the changing of human nature itself—a work of æons, even if it were good to change it, which we cannot know. It is not practicable in our day or in our age. Even if desirable theoretically, it belongs to another and long-succeeding sociological stratum. Our duty is with what is practicable now; with the next step possible in our day and generation. It is criminal to waste our energies in endeavoring to uproot, when all we can profitably or possibly accomplish is to bend the universal tree of humanity a little in the direction most favorable to the production of good fruit under existing circumstances. We might as well urge the destruction of the highest existing type of man because he failed to reach our ideal as favor the destruction of Individualism, Private Property, the Law of Accumulation of Wealth, and the Law of Competition; for these are the highest results of human experience, the soil in which society so far has produced the best fruit. Unequally or unjustly, perhaps, as these laws sometimes operate, and imperfect as they appear to the Idealist, they are, nevertheless, like the highest type of man, the best and most valuable of all that humanity has yet accomplished.

We start, then, with a condition of affairs under which the best interests of the race are promoted, but which inevitably gives wealth to the few. Thus far, accepting conditions as they exist, the situation can be surveyed and pronounced good. The question then arises,—and, if the foregoing be correct, it is the only question with which we have to deal,—What is the proper mode of administering wealth after the laws upon which civilization is founded have thrown it into the hands of the few? And it is of this great question that I believe I offer the true solution. It will be understood that *fortunes* are here spoken of, not moderate sums saved by many years of effort, the returns from which are required for the comfortable maintenance and education of families. This is not *wealth,* but only *competence* which it should be the aim of all to acquire.

There are but three modes in which surplus wealth can be disposed of. It can be left to the families of the decedents; or it can be bequeathed for public purposes; or, finally, it can be administered during their lives by its possessors. Under the first and second modes most of the wealth of the world that has reached the few has hitherto been applied. Let us in turn consider each of these modes. The first is the most injudicious. In monarchical countries, the estates and the greatest portion of the wealth are left to the first son, that the vanity of the parent may be gratified by the thought that his name and title are to descend to succeeding generations unimpaired. The condition of this class in Europe to-day teaches the futility of such hopes or ambitions. The successors have become impoverished through their follies or from the fall in the value of land. Even in Great Britain the strict law of entail has been found inadequate to maintain the status of an hereditary class. Its soil is rapidly passing into the hands of the stranger. Under republican institutions the division of property among the children is much fairer, but the question which forces itself upon thoughtful men in all lands is: Why should men leave great fortunes to their children? If this is done from affection, is it not misguided affection? Observation teaches that, generally speaking, it is not well for the children that they should be so burdened. Neither is it well for the state. Beyond providing for the wife and daughters moderate sources of income, and very moderate allowances indeed, if any, for the sons, men may well hesitate, for it is no longer questionable that great sums bequeathed oftener work more for the injury than for the good of the recipients. Wise men will soon conclude that, for the best interests of the members of their families and of the state, such bequests are an improper use of their means.

It is not suggested that men who have failed to educate their sons to earn a livelihood shall cast them adrift in poverty. If any man has seen fit to rear his sons with a view to their living idle lives, or, what is highly commendable, has instilled in them the sentiment that they are in a position to labor for public ends without reference to pecuniary considerations, then, of course, the duty of the parent is to see that such are provided for *in moderation.* There are instances of millionaires' sons unspoiled by wealth, who, being rich, still perform great services in the community. Such are the very salt of the earth, as valuable as, unfortunately, they are rare; still it is not the exception, but the rule, that men must regard, and, looking at the usual result of enormous sums conferred upon legatees, the thoughtful man must shortly say, "I would as soon leave to my son a curse as the almighty dollar," and admit to himself that it is not the welfare of the children, but family pride, which inspires these enormous legacies.

As to the second mode, that of leaving wealth at death for public uses, it may be said that this is only a means for the disposal of wealth, provided a man is content to wait until he is dead before it becomes of much good in the world. Knowledge of the results of legacies bequeathed is not calculated to inspire the brightest hopes of much posthumous good being accomplished. The cases are not few in which the real object sought by the testator is not attained, nor are they few in which his real wishes are thwarted. In many cases the bequests are so used as to become only monuments of his folly. It is well to remember that it requires the exercise of not less ability than that which acquired the wealth to use it so as to be really beneficial to the community. Besides this, it may fairly be said that no man is to be extolled for doing what he cannot help doing, nor is he to be thanked by the community to which he only leaves wealth at death. Men who leave vast sums in this way may fairly be thought men who would not have left it at all, had they been able to take it with them. The memories of such cannot be held in grateful remembrance, for there is no grace in their gifts. It is not to be wondered at that such bequests seem so generally to lack the blessing.

The growing disposition to tax more and more heavily large estates left at death is a cheering indication of the growth of a salutary change in public opinion. The State of Pennsylvania now takes—subject to some exceptions—one-tenth of the property left by its citizens. The budget presented in the British Parliament the other day proposes to increase the death-duties; and, most significant of all, the new tax is to be a graduated one. Of all forms of taxation, this seems the wisest. Men who continue hoarding great sums all their lives, the proper use of which for public ends would work good to the community, should be made to feel that the community, in the form of the state, cannot thus be deprived of its proper share. By taxing estates heavily at death the state marks its condemnation of the selfish millionaire's unworthy life.

It is desirable that nations should go much further in this direction. Indeed, it is difficult to set bounds to the share of a rich man's estate which should go at his death to the public through the agency of the state, and by all means such taxes should be graduated, beginning at nothing upon moderate sums to dependents, and increasing rapidly as the amounts swell, until of the millionaire's hoard, as of Shylock's, at least

> "—The other half
> Comes to the privy coffer of the state." [4]

This policy would work powerfully to induce the rich man to attend to the administration of wealth during his life, which is the end that society should always have in view, as being that by far most fruitful for the people. Nor need it be feared that this policy would sap the root of enterprise and render men less anxious to accumulate, for to the class whose ambition it is to leave great fortunes and be talked about after their death, it will attract even more attention, and, indeed, be a somewhat nobler ambition to have enormous sums paid over to the state from their fortunes.

There remains, then, only one mode of using great fortunes; but in this we have the true antidote for the temporary unequal distribution of wealth, the reconciliation of the rich and the poor [...] It is founded upon the present most intense individualism, and the race is projected to put it in practice by degree whenever it pleases. Under its sway we shall have an ideal state, in which the surplus wealth of the few will become, in the best sense, the property of the many, because administered for the common good, and this wealth, passing through the hands of the few, can be made a much more potent force for the elevation of our race than if it had been distributed in small sums to the people themselves. Even the poorest can be made to see this, and to agree that great sums gathered by some of their fellow-citizens and spent for public purposes, from which the masses reap the principal benefit, are more valuable to them than if scattered among them through the course of many years in trifling amounts.

If we consider what results flow from the Cooper Institute, for instance, to the best portion of the race in New York not possessed of means, and compare these with those which would have arisen for the good of the masses from an equal sum distributed by Mr. Cooper in his lifetime in the form of wages, which is the highest form of distribution, being for work done and not for charity, we can form some estimate of the possibilities for the improvement of the race which lie embedded in the present law of the accumulation of wealth. Much of this sum, if distributed in small quantities among the people, would have been wasted in the indulgence of appetite, some of it in excess, and it may be doubted whether even the part put to the best use, that of adding to the comforts of the home, would have yielded results for the race, as a race, at all comparable to those which are flowing and are to flow from the Cooper Institute from generation to generation. Let the advocate of violent or radical change ponder well this thought.

We might even go so far as to take another instance, that of Mr. Tilden's bequest of five millions of dollars for a free library in the city of New York, but in referring to this one cannot help saying involuntarily, How much better if Mr. Tilden had devoted the last years of his own life to the proper administration of this immense sum; in which case neither legal contest nor any other cause of delay could have interfered with his aims. But let us assume that Mr. Tilden's millions finally become the means of giving to this city a noble public library, where the treasures of the world contained in books will be open to all forever, without money and without price. Considering the good of that part of the race which congregates in and around Manhattan Island, would its permanent benefit have been better promoted had these millions been allowed to circulate in small sums through the hands of the masses? Even the most strenuous advocate of Communism must entertain a doubt upon this subject. Most of those who think will probably entertain no doubt whatever.

Poor and restricted are our opportunities in this life; narrow our horizon; our best work most imperfect; but rich men should be thankful for one inestimable boon. They have it in their power during their lives to busy themselves in organizing benefactions from which the masses of their fellows will derive lasting advantage, and thus dignify their own lives. The highest life is probably to be reached, not by such imitation of the life of Christ as Count Tolstoï[5] gives us, but, while animated by Christ's spirit, by recognizing the changed conditions of this age, and adopting modes of expressing this spirit suitable to the changed conditions under which we live; still laboring for the good of our fellows, which was the essence of his life and teaching, but laboring in a different manner. This, then, is held to be the duty of the man of Wealth: First, to set an example of modest, unostentatious living, shunning display or extravagance; to provide moderately for the legitimate wants of those dependent upon him; and after doing so to consider all surplus revenues which come to him simply as trust funds, which he is called upon to administer, and strictly bound as a matter of duty to administer in the manner which, in his judgment, is best calculated to produce the most beneficial results for the community—the man of wealth thus becoming the mere agent and trustee for his poorer brethren, bringing to their service his superior wisdom, experience and ability to administer, doing for them better than they would or could do for themselves.

We are met here with the difficulty of determining what are moderate sums to leave to members of the family; what is modest, unostentatious living; what is the test of extravagance. There must be different standards for different conditions. The answer is that it is as impossible to name exact amounts or actions as it is to define good manners, good taste, or the rules of propriety; but, nevertheless, these are verities, well known although undefinable. Public sentiment is quick to know and to feel what offends these. So in the case of wealth. The rule in regard to good taste in the dress of men or women applies here. Whatever makes one conspicuous offends the canon. If any family be chiefly known for display, for extravagance in home, table, equipage, for enormous sums ostentatiously spent in any form upon itself, —if these be its chief distinctions, we have no difficulty in estimating its nature or culture. So likewise in regard to the use or abuse of its surplus wealth, or to generous, freehanded cooperation in good public uses, or to unabated efforts to accumulate and hoard to the last, whether they administer or bequeath. The verdict rests with the best and most enlightened public sentiment. The community will surely judge and its judgments will not often be wrong.

The best uses to which surplus wealth can be put have already been indicated. These who would administer wisely must, indeed, be wise, for one of the serious obstacles to the improvement of our race is indiscriminate charity. It were better for mankind that the millions of the rich were thrown in to the sea than so spent as to encourage the slothful, the drunken, the unworthy. Of every thousand dollars spent in so called charity to-day, it is probable that $950 is unwisely spent; so spent, indeed as to produce the very evils which it proposes to mitigate or cure. A well-known writer of philosophic books admitted the other day that he had given a quarter of a dollar to a man who approached him as he was coming to visit the house of his friend. He knew nothing of the habits of this beggar; knew not the use that would be made of this money, although he had every reason to suspect that it would be spent improperly. This man professed to be a disciple of Herbert Spencer[6]; yet the quarter-dollar given that night will probably work more injury than all the money which its thoughtless donor will ever be able to give in true charity will do good. He only gratified his own feelings, saved himself from annoyance,—and this was probably one of the most selfish and very worst actions of his life, for in all respects he is most worthy.

In bestowing charity, the main consideration should be to help those who will help themselves; to provide part of the means by which those who desire to improve may do so; to give those who desire to use the aids by which they may rise; to assist, but rarely or never to do all. Neither the individual nor the race is improved by alms-giving. Those worthy of assistance, except in rare cases, seldom require assistance. The really valuable men of the race never do, except in cases of accident or sudden change. Every one has, of course, cases of individuals brought to his own knowledge where temporary assistance can do genuine good, and these he will not overlook. But the amount which can be wisely given by the individual for individuals is necessarily limited by his lack of knowledge of the circumstances connected with each. He is the only true reformer who is as careful and as anxious not to aid the unworthy as he is to aid the worthy, and, perhaps, even more so, for in alms-giving more injury is probably done by rewarding vice than by relieving virtue.

The rich man is thus almost restricted to following the examples of Peter Cooper, Enoch Pratt of Baltimore, Mr. Pratt of Brooklyn, Senator Stanford, and others, who know that the best means of benefiting the community is to place within its reach the ladders upon which the aspiring can rise—parks, and means of recreation, by which men are helped in body and mind; works of art, certain to give pleasure and improve the public taste, and public institutions of various kinds, which will improve the general condition of the people; —in this manner returning their surplus wealth to the mass of their fellows in the forms best calculated to do them lasting good.

Thus is the problem of Rich and Poor to be solved. The laws of accumulation will be left free; the laws of distribution free. Individualism will continue, but the millionaire will be but a trustee for the poor; intrusted for a season with a great part of the increased wealth of the community, but administering it for the community far better than it could or would have done for itself. The best minds will thus have reached a stage in the development of the race in which it is clearly seen that there is no mode of disposing of surplus wealth creditable to thoughtful and earnest men into whose hands it flows save by using it year by year for the general good. This day already dawns. But a little while, and although, without incurring the pity of their fellows, men may die sharers in great business enterprises from which their capital cannot be or has not been withdrawn, and is left chiefly at death for public uses, yet the man who dies leaving behind many millions of available wealth, which was his to administer during life, will pass away "unwept, unhonored, and unsung," no matter to what uses he leaves the dross which he cannot take with him. Of such as these the public verdict will then be: "The man who dies thus rich dies disgraced."

Such, in my opinion, is the true Gospel concerning Wealth, obedience to which is destined some day to solve the problem of the Rich and the Poor, and to bring "Peace on earth, among men Good-Will."

注释：

1. Sioux：苏族，北美印第安人中的一个民族，原居于北美五大湖以东地区，以种植玉米为生。19世纪初以来，由于殖民者与白人的压迫和屠杀，部分苏族人西迁到大草原，后来又被迫迁徙到南达科他、北达科他等州的印第安人保留地。
2. Mæcenas：盖乌斯·梅塞纳斯（Gaius Cilnius Mæcenas, 公元前70—公元前8），罗马皇帝奥古斯都的谋臣，不仅是著名的外交家，而且还资助并提携当时颇具才华的诗人及艺术家，其慷慨不仅让受惠者们感激不尽，也引起后世文人的敬佩。因此，他的名字被认为是文学艺术赞助者的代名词。

3. Swedenborg：伊曼纽尔·斯韦登伯格（Emanuel Swedenborg, 1688—1772），瑞典著名的科学家、哲学家和神学家。他早年致力自然科学和工程学，晚年主要研究神学，著有《天堂与地狱》（*Heaven and Hell*, 1758）。在斯韦登伯格看来，所有良善的灵魂聚集起来的地方就是天堂，与是否信仰上帝无关；而所有心怀恶意，想奴役他人的灵魂聚集在一起就成了地狱。他的神学观点不同于传统神学的“审判论”“拣选论”。
4. 此句出自莎士比亚的《威尼斯商人》第四幕。当夏洛克无法按约割肉决定放弃控诉时，鲍西娅说道，作为犹太人的夏洛克企图间接谋害基督徒安东尼奥，根据威尼斯法律，其财产的一半归受害人，“另一半没入公库”。在《财富》一文中，卡内基认为富翁的遗产税应提高到其财产的一半。
5. Count Tolstoï：列夫·尼古拉耶维奇·托尔斯泰（Lev Nikolayevich Tolstoy, 1828—1910），俄国小说家、评论家、剧作家，著有《战争与和平》（*War and Peace*, 1869）、《安娜·卡列尼娜》（*Anna Karenina*, 1877）、《复活》（*Resurrection*, 1899）等经典作品，被认为是世界最伟大的作家之一。托尔斯泰曾逐字解释耶稣对世人道德的教诲，特别是登山宝训的经文。对耶稣教义的理解也使托尔斯泰成为基督教无政府主义者，主张不以暴力抵抗压迫。
6. Herbert Spencer：赫伯特·斯宾塞（Herbert Spencer, 1820—1903），英国哲学家，支持自由意志论，即在不侵犯别人权利的前提下，每个人都有自由做自己想做的事情的权利。

思考题：

1. In the article, Carnegie states that “this wealth, passing through the hands of the few, can be made a much more potent force for the elevation of our race.” Do you think that Carnegie is trying to justify capitalists' exploitation of workers? What's your opinion about it?
2. What is your understanding of Carnegie's “surplus wealth”?

27. Of Mr. Booker T. Washington and Others (1903)[①]

W. E. B. Du Bois

导读：

W. E. B. 杜波依斯（William Edward Burghardt Du Bois, 1868—1963）是美国社会学家、历史学家、民权运动者、泛非主义者、作家和编辑。杜波依斯出生于马萨诸塞州大巴灵顿，曾就读于美国费斯克大学、哈佛大学和德国柏林大学。1895年他获得哈佛大学哲学博士学位，是该校第一个取得博士学位的非裔美国人。毕业之后，他任职于亚特兰大大学，教授历史学、社会学和经济学。他是1909年美国全国有色人种协进会（NAACP[②]）的创建者之一。他在20世纪初到60年代初的美国黑人政治中发挥了重要的作用，其政治思想的核心是黑人民族主义和融入主义。

1895年9月18日，黑人领袖布克·T. 华盛顿应邀在亚特兰大国际博览会开幕式上发言。华盛顿在讲话中呼吁黑人以普通劳动为荣，把希望放到农业、手工业、商业、家庭服务业以及其他行业之中。他认为，在一切纯社会性的事务中，白人和黑人可以像手指那样分开，但在一切对共同进步至关重要的事务中则应团结得像一只手。在美国历史上，华盛顿的这次演说被视为他与白人领袖达成的“亚特兰大妥协案”（“Atlanta Compromise”），即以黑人放弃对政治权力和社会权利的追求来换取白人对黑人经济建设的支持。

针对华盛顿的主张，杜波依斯于1903年撰写了题为《关于布克·T. 华盛顿先生及其他人》（“Of Mr. Booker T. Washington and Others”）的文章，该文后来收录于他里程碑式的著作《黑人的灵魂》（*The Souls*

---

① W. E. B. Du Bois, *Souls of Black Folk*, http://www.bartleby.com/114/3.html. (accessed Oct. 4, 2021).

② NAACP，全国有色人种协进会（National Association for the Advancement of Colored People），是一个由美国白人和黑人组成的旨在促进黑人民权的全国性组织，总部设在纽约。协进会的目标是通过改良的道路，让黑人享有完全的公民权、法庭公平裁判权以及经济、社会、教育、政治等方面的平等权利。协进会采用的主要手段是法庭诉讼、争取民主立法和宣传教育。

of Black Folk）。杜波依斯在该文中指出，尽管取得了诸多成就，但是华盛顿实际上接受了种族隔离，而这种隔离必定导致黑人处于劣等地位，尤其是在教育方面。他认为，华盛顿一味强调职业技术培训是以“放弃黑人的政治权力、公民权利和对黑人青年高等教育为代价，是在把黑人置于半奴役的危险之中”。他指出，在种族主义统治下，美国黑人应该奋力反抗，主动为争取平等权利而斗争，而不是被动地服从华盛顿的“亚特兰大妥协案”，这样才能实现社会变革并获得平等的权利。

关于黑人教育的模式及其发展，杜波依斯和华盛顿有许多分歧，其中之一便是教育理念：华盛顿认为美国黑人的学校教育应该局限于农业、机械等职业技术教育；但杜波依斯认为黑人学校还应该提供更多的人文知识方面的教育，即推广以知识的传承、人文素质的培养为目标的博雅教育（liberal arts education），只有如此才能培养出新的黑人精英领导者，民族崛起靠的是精英而不是民众的力量。杜波依斯对美国黑人教育有自己独特的教育理论和理念，“有天赋的十分之一”是他最著名的一种教育理论。其核心思想是：美国黑人教育应首先实现对黑人中最优秀人才的培养，让他们受到最好的教育，使他们成为民众的领袖，担负起振兴民族的重任。杜波依斯敢于挑战盛极一时的布克·T. 华盛顿的教育观点，在当时的美国社会引起了强烈反响。作为20世纪上半叶美国黑人的精神领袖，杜波依斯的教育观及其教育思想对美国黑人的教育影响巨大。

> From birth till death enslaved; in word, in deed, unmanned!
> ……
> Hereditary bondsmen! Know ye not
> Who would be free themselves must strike the blow?
>
> —BYRON[1]

Easily the most striking thing in the history of the American Negro since 1876 is the ascendancy of Mr. Booker T. Washington.… Mr. Washington came, with a single definite programme, at the psychological moment when the nation was a little ashamed of having bestowed so much sentiment on Negroes, and was concentrating its energies on Dollars. His programme of industrial education, conciliation of the South, and submission and silence as to civil and political rights, was not wholly original; the

Free Negroes from 1830 up to wartime had striven to build industrial schools, and the American Missionary Association[2] had from the first taught various trades; and Price and others had sought a way of honorable alliance with the best of the Southerners. But Mr. Washington first indissolubly linked these things; he put enthusiasm, unlimited energy, and perfect faith into this programme, and changed it from a by-path into a veritable Way of Life....

To gain the sympathy and coöperation of the various elements comprising the white South was Mr. Washington's first task; ... ten years later it was done in the word spoken at Atlanta: "In all things purely social we can be as separate as the five fingers, and yet one as the hand in all things essential to mutual progress." This "Atlanta Compromise" is by all odds the most notable thing in Mr. Washington's career. The South interpreted it in different ways: the radicals received it as a complete surrender of the demand for civil and political equality; the conservatives, as a generously conceived working basis for mutual understanding. So both approved it, and to-day its author is certainly the most distinguished Southerner since Jefferson Davis,[3] and the one with the largest personal following.

Next to this achievement comes Mr. Washington's work in gaining place and consideration in the North. Others less shrewd and tactful had formerly essayed to sit on these two stools and had fallen between them; but as Mr. Washington knew the heart of the South from birth and training, so by singular insight he intuitively grasped the spirit of the age which was dominating the North....

Among his own people, however, Mr. Washington has encountered the strongest and most lasting opposition...there is among educated and thoughtful colored men in all parts of the land a feeling of deep regret, sorrow, and apprehension at the wide currency and ascendancy which some of Mr. Washington's theories have gained....

Nearly all the former ones had become leaders by the silent suffrage of their fellows, had sought to lead their own people alone, and were usually, save Douglass, little known outside their race. But Booker T. Washington arose as essentially the leader not of one race but of two,—a compromiser between the South, the North, and the Negro. Naturally the Negroes resented, at first bitterly, signs of compromise which surrendered their civil and political rights, even though this was to be exchanged for larger chances of economic development. The rich and dominating North, however, was not only weary of the race problem, but was investing largely in Southern enterprises, and welcomed any method of peaceful coöperation. Thus, by national opinion, the Negroes began to recognize Mr. Washington's leadership; and the voice of criticism was hushed.

Mr. Washington represents in Negro thought the old attitude of adjustment and submission; but adjustment at such a peculiar time as to make his programme unique. This is an age of unusual economic development, and Mr. Washington's programme naturally takes an economic cast, becoming a gospel of Work and Money to such an extent as apparently almost completely to overshadow the higher aims of life. Moreover, this is an age when the more advanced races are coming in closer contact with the less developed races, and the race-feeling is therefore intensified; and Mr. Washington's programme practically accepts the alleged inferiority of the Negro races. Again, in our own land, the reaction from the sentiment of war time has given impetus to race-prejudice against Negroes, and Mr. Washington withdraws many of the high demands of Negroes as men and American citizens. In other periods of intensified prejudice all the Negro's tendency to self-assertion has been called forth; at this period a policy of submission is advocated. In the history of nearly all other races and peoples the doctrine preached at such crises has been that manly self-respect is worth more than lands and houses, and that a people who voluntarily surrender such respect, or cease striving for it, are not worth civilizing.

In answer to this, it has been claimed that the Negro can survive only through submission. Mr. Washington distinctly asks that black people give up, at least for the present, three things, —

First, political power,

Second, insistence on civil rights,

Third, higher education of Negro youth,

—and concentrate all their energies on industrial education, the accumulation of wealth, and the conciliation of the South. This policy has been courageously and insistently advocated for over fifteen years, and has been triumphant for perhaps ten years. As a result of this tender of the palm-branch, what has been the return? In these years there have occurred:

1. The disfranchisement of the Negro.

2. The legal creation of a distinct status of civil inferiority for the Negro.

3. The steady withdrawal of aid from institutions for the higher training of the Negro.

These movements are not, to be sure, direct results of Mr. Washington's teachings; but his propaganda has, without a shadow of doubt, helped their speedier accomplishment. The question then comes: Is it possible, and probable, that nine millions of men can make effective progress in economic lines if they are deprived of political rights, made a servile caste, and allowed only the most meagre chance for developing their exceptional men? If history and reason give any distinct answer to these questions, it is an emphatic No. And Mr. Washington thus faces the triple paradox of his career:

1. He is striving nobly to make Negro artisans business men and property-owners; but it is utterly impossible, under modern competitive methods, for workingmen and property-owners to defend their rights and exist without the right of suffrage.

2. He insists on thrift and self-respect, but at the same time counsels a silent submission to civic inferiority such as is bound to sap the manhood of any race in the long run.

3. He advocates common-school and industrial training, and depreciates institutions of higher learning; but neither the Negro common-schools, nor Tuskegee itself, could remain open a day were it not for teachers trained in Negro colleges, or trained by their graduates….

Nevertheless, the questions involved are so fundamental and serious that it is difficult to see how men like the Grimkes, Kelly Miller, J. W. E. Bowen, and other representatives of this group, can much longer be silent. Such men feel in conscience bound to ask of this nation three things.

1. The right to vote.
2. Civic equality.
3. The education of youth according to ability….

They advocate, with Mr. Washington, a broad system of Negro common schools supplemented by thorough industrial training; but they are surprised that a man of Mr. Washington's insight cannot see that no such educational system ever has rested or can rest on any other basis than that of the well-equipped college and university, and they insist that there is a demand for a few such institutions throughout the South to train the best of the Negro youth as teachers, professional men, and leaders.

This group of men honor Mr. Washington for his attitude of conciliation toward the white South; they accept the "Atlanta Compromise" in its broadest interpretation… They do not expect that the free right to vote, to enjoy civic rights, and to be educated, will come in a moment; they do not expect to see the bias and prejudices of years disappear at the blast of a trumpet; but they are absolutely certain that the way for a people to gain their reasonable rights is not by voluntarily throwing them away and insisting that they do not want them; that the way for a people to gain respect is not by continually belittling and ridiculing themselves; that, on the contrary, Negroes must insist continually, in season and out of season, that voting is necessary to modern manhood, that color discrimination is barbarism, and that black boys need education as well as white boys.

...then those black men, if they are really men, are called upon by every consideration of patriotism and loyalty to oppose such a course by all civilized methods, even though such opposition involves disagreement with Mr. Booker T. Washington....

It would be unjust to Mr. Washington not to acknowledge that in several instances he has opposed movements in the South which were unjust to the Negro; he sent memorials to the Louisiana and Alabama constitutional conventions, he has spoken against lynching, and in other ways has openly or silently set his influence against sinister schemes and unfortunate happenings. Notwithstanding this, it is equally true to assert that on the whole the distinct impression left by Mr. Washington's propaganda is, first, that the South is justified in its present attitude toward the Negro because of the Negro's degradation; secondly, that the prime cause of the Negro's failure to rise more quickly is his wrong education in the past; and, thirdly, that his future rise depends primarily on his own efforts. Each of these propositions is a dangerous half-truth. The supplementary truths must never be lost sight of: first, slavery and race-prejudice are potent if not sufficient causes of the Negro's position; second, industrial and common-school training were necessarily slow in planting because they had to await the black teachers trained by higher institutions,—it being extremely doubtful if any essentially different development was possible, and certainly a Tuskegee was unthinkable before 1880; and, third, while it is a great truth to say that the Negro must strive and strive mightily to help himself, it is equally true that unless his striving be not simply seconded, but rather aroused and encouraged, by the initiative of the richer and wiser environing group, he cannot hope for great success.

In his failure to realize and impress this last point, Mr. Washington is especially to be criticised. His doctrine has tended to make the whites, North and South, shift the burden of the Negro problem to the Negro's shoulders and stand aside as critical and rather pessimistic spectators; when in fact the burden belongs to the nation, and the hands of none of us are clean if we bend not our energies to righting these great wrongs.

The South ought to be led, by candid and honest criticism, to assert her better self and do her full duty to the race she has cruelly wronged and is still wronging. The North—her co-partner in guilt—cannot salve her conscience by plastering it with gold. We cannot settle this problem by diplomacy and suaveness, by "policy" alone. If worse comes to worst, can the moral fibre of this country survive the slow throttling and murder of nine millions of men?

The black men of America have a duty to perform, a duty stern and delicate,—a forward movement to oppose a part of the work of their greatest leader. So far as Mr. Washington preaches Thrift, Patience, and Industrial Training for the masses, we must hold up his hands and strive with him, rejoicing in his honors and glorying in the strength of this Joshua[4] called of God and of man to lead the headless host. But so far as Mr. Washington apologizes for injustice, North or South, does not rightly value the privilege and duty of voting, belittles the emasculating effects of caste distinctions, and opposes the higher training and ambition of our brighter minds,—so far as he, the South, or the Nation, does this,—we must unceasingly and firmly oppose them. By every civilized and peaceful method we must strive for the rights which the world accords to men, clinging unwaveringly to those great words which the sons of the Fathers would fain forget: "We hold these truths to be self-evident: That all men are created equal; that they are endowed by their Creator with certain unalienable rights; that among these are life, liberty, and the pursuit of happiness."[5]

注释：

1. 引自英国诗人乔治·戈登·拜伦（George Gordon Byron, 1788—1824）的长篇诗作《唐璜》（*Don Juan*）。《唐璜》是拜伦最重要的一组诗，讲述了西班牙贵族子弟唐璜的游历、恋爱、冒险等浪漫故事，揭露了社会中黑暗、丑恶、虚伪的一面，奏响了为自由、幸福和解放而斗争的战歌。杜波依斯在开篇引用了《唐璜》第二章第74至76行的内容，讲述主人公渴望打破奴役的枷锁，追寻自由。
2. American Missionary Association：美国传教协会。1866年，一些传教士和慈善机构也加入了改善黑人教育状况的行列。美国传教协会就曾发挥积极的作用，在美国南部建立了11所黑人学院。
3. Jefferson Davis：杰斐逊·戴维斯（Jefferson Davis, 1808—1889），美国军人、政治家，美国历史上最有影响力的政治人物之一，于美国内战期间担任美利坚邦联国

（The Confederate Sates of America）首任也是唯一一任总统。戴维斯毕业于西点军校，内战前曾任职于密西西比议会、合众国众议院及参议院。他于1889年10月完成《美利坚邦联国简史》（*A Short History of the Confederate States of America*）一书。杰斐逊·戴维斯以81岁高龄逝于路易斯安那的新奥尔良。其葬礼乃当时南方所举行过的规模最大的葬礼。

4. Joshua：约书亚，圣经中的人物，是继摩西后以色列人的首领。其主要事迹记载于旧约《申命记》《约书亚记》等章节中。此处杜波依斯把布克·T. 华盛顿比作约书亚，认为他是美国黑人的领袖。
5. 此处引自美国《独立宣言》。

思考题：

1. Why did W. E. B. Du Bois quote Lord Byron's poem at the very beginning of his essay? What did he want to convey to African Americans through those lines?
2. In Du Bois's eyes, what were the rights that Booker T. Washington asked African Americans to give up in his "Atlanta Compromise"?
3. What was the basic conflict between W. E. B. Du Bois and Booker T. Washington in their understanding of African Americans' education and development?

28. The Meaning of Democracy (1912)[①]

Woodrow Wilson

导读：

伍德罗·威尔逊（Woodrow Wilson, 1856—1924），美国第28任总统，杰出的资本主义政治家与进步主义改革领袖，也是美国历史上学术成就最高的一位总统。他不仅获得了霍普金斯大学哲学博士学位，还发表了对美国政治发展和行政体制影响深远的专著与论文。如《国会政体：美国政治研究》（“Congressional Government: A Study in American Politics”，1885）、《美国人民史》（“A History of the American People”，1903）、《美国的立宪政体》（*Constitutional Government of the United States*, 1908）。同时，威尔逊也是一名开明且具改革精神的校长。在普林斯顿大学担任校长期间，他改革学科建制与行政管理体系，设立并推行“导修课”[②]，成为当时美国高校的榜样。1912年美国大选中，曾出任新泽西州州长的威尔逊以给人民“新自由”[③]的口号赢得了胜利。

威尔逊上台之时正值美国进步主义改革时期（1890—1920），这次改革浪潮是美国工业化的必然产物。工业化虽然推动了美国经济的快速发展，但是也衍生了严重的社会问题：政府官员贪污腐败，大企业经济垄断，财富分配不公，贫富悬殊，社会冲突与阶级矛盾日益加剧。不满垄断经济的农民与工人运动开展得如火如荼，美国社会主义运动也在

① Woodrow Wilson. “The Meaning of Democracy”, http://teachingamericanhistory.org/document/campaign-address-in-scranton-penn/ (accessed Oct. 4, 2021).

② 威尔逊引进的导修课（preceptorial），是指教授每周带领10至15名学生对所学课程进行研究与讨论，从而给学生们更大的空间去理解课堂所学的理论，弥补了大班授课的不足。

③ 威尔逊提出的“新自由”是指把普通民众从大企业、大商家的剥削中解放出来。

1912年前后达到历史顶点。[①]面临社会经济的动荡不安与革命情绪的蔓延，威尔逊总统以他敏锐深邃的学者眼光和政治家的气魄胆识，重新定位美国政府的行政职能与执政方向，旨在通过渐进改革的方式缓解社会矛盾。任期内，他调低商品关税，扩大对外开放，实行累进所得税制，限制暴富，进行银行体制改革，建立联邦储备银行体系，签署了《克莱顿反托拉斯法案》（"Clayton Antitrust Act"，1914）与《联邦贸易委员会法》（"Federal Trade Commission Act"，1914），完善了《谢尔曼反托拉斯法》（"Sherman Antitrust Act"，1890），打击了垄断财团。[②]

本选文是1912年威尔逊作为民主党候选人发表的竞选演讲。在这篇演讲中，威尔逊在继承美国传统自由主义思想的基础上，重新阐释了民主的意义：美国的发展不是依赖某个家族、某个阶级或者某个州，而是依靠为国家共同利益奋斗的每一个美国人，所以政府的职责应该是反对并遏制某个团体对特殊利益的追求，更好地维护国家利益与国民的共同利益。威尔逊提到，杰斐逊总统主张的自由放任思想只适用于美国传统经济模式，即以农业为基础、个体经营分散、大众均能参与整个社会的经济管理。但是，随着工业化的不断深入，兴起的大公司、大财团利用政府提高关税，垄断国内市场，操控整个国家经济生活。在这种情况下，如果政府依然恪守杰斐逊时代的自由放任理念，"人民做主，大众参与"的美国民主必将败坏，美国的经济也必将凋零。因此，威尔逊强调，对于大型的工业企业，尤其是钢铁、煤矿等具有公共事务性质的公司，美国政府必须监管其经济运作是否存在欺诈与违规行为，确保行业内的公平竞争，保障工人的薪酬待遇

① 19世纪末以来，由于对垄断弊端的不满，农民发起了一系列的改革运动。其中规模最大的当属19世纪80年代的农民运动，也被称为"人民党"运动。这是美国历史上第一个名副其实的"第三党"，其纲领主要关心运输，以及对土地投机公司与铁路垄断公司的税收问题。为了改善工作条件、缩短工时、增加工资，美国工人在1893至1898年间发起了7000多次大罢工。1905年，"世界产业工人联合会"成立，其斗争纲领仍以经济为主。1901年，尤金·维克托·德布斯（Eugene Victor Debs, 1855—1926）领导的美国社会党传播共产主义，公开倡导推翻资本主义制度，旨在"改变现存的生产和分配工具的私有制为全民集体所有制"。德布斯作为社会党的总统候选人，参加了1901到1912年间的四次竞选，获得的选票从1901年的逾9万张增加到1912年的逾89.9万张，占投票总数的6%。1912年，社会党的党员也从创立之初的1万名增加到12万名。在德布斯的领导下，社会主义的力量不断增长，社会主义的思想在美国群众中产生了广泛的影响。

② 1896年制定的《谢尔曼反托拉斯法》没有清晰界定何为垄断行为，以及应何时限制贸易活动，导致反托分寸难以把握。《克莱顿反托拉斯法》则明确规定了各项反托拉斯法的意图，成立了全联邦的商务委员会，对违法的个人进行刑事处罚。

以及工作环境的安全。威尔逊宣称，只有反抗凌驾于美国人民头上的“垄断”权势，维护美国的自由民主，才能更好地促进个人与企业的发展，实现美国经济在资本主义制度下持久、稳定、有序的增长。威尔逊在演讲中宣扬的这些观念听起来不错。他上任后通过的一系列反托拉斯议案也在一定程度上打击了垄断财团，抑制了大公司的垄断趋势，缓解了当时的社会矛盾，不过并没有从根本上消除自由主义经济的顽疾，即贫富差距越来越大，社会财富越来越集中在少数人手中，垄断财团不仅资本雄厚，而且左右政府为之服务。威尔逊于1913年3月4日至1921年3月4日任美国总统。在其卸任8年之后，即1929年，美国就爆发了后来波及整个资本主义世界的经济大萧条。这次经济大萧条与托拉斯垄断主义在美国的泛滥不无关系：资本垄断导致财富分配不均，财富分配不均导致资方的生产能力与普通劳动者的购买能力不匹配，从而引发所谓的生产过剩，最终导致经济失控。

…I know that the Government of the United States is not a free instrument and that it is our duty to set it free. Very well, set it free from whom? And how set it free? Because I have always been impatient of the discussion of abstract propositions. That may seem a strange statement to be made by a man whose opponents, whenever they can't answer his arguments, call him academic. But I have always been opposed to the mere presentation to audiences of the abstract conceptions of government.

Of course this was intended to be a government of free citizens and of equal opportunity, but how are we going to make it such—that is the question. Because I realize that while we are followers of Jefferson, there is one principle of Jefferson's which no longer can obtain in the practical politics of America. You know that it was Jefferson who said that the best government is that which does as little governing as possible, which exercises its power as little as possible. And that was said in a day when the opportunities of America were so obvious to every man, when every individual was so free to use his powers without let or hindrance, that all that was necessary was that the government should withhold its hand and see to it that every man got an opportunity to act if he would. But that time is past. America is not now and cannot in the future be a place for unrestricted individual enterprise. It is true that we have come upon an age of great cooperative industry. It is true that we must act absolutely upon that principle.

Let me illustrate what I mean. You know that it used to be true in our cities that every family occupied a separate house of its own, that every family had its own little premises, that every family was separated in its life from every other family. But you know that that is no longer the case, and that it cannot be the case in our great cities. Families live in layers. They live in tenements, the live in flats, they live on floors, they are piled layer upon layer in the great tenement houses of our crowded districts. And not only are they piled layer upon layer, but they are associated room by room so that there is in each room, sometimes in our congested districts, a separate family.

Now, what has happened in foreign countries, in some of which they have made much more progress than we in handling these things, is this: In the city of Glasgow, for example, which is one of the model cities of the world, they have made up their minds that the entries, that hallways, of great tenements are public streets. Therefore the policeman goes up the stairway and patrols the corridors. The lighting department of the city sees to it that the corridors are abundantly lighted, and the staircases. And the city does not deceive itself into supposing that that great building is a unit from which the police are to keep out and the city authority to be excluded, but it says: "These are the high-ways of human movement, and wherever light is needed, wherever order is needed, there we will carry the authority of the city."

And I have likened that to our modern industrial enterprises. You know that a great many corporations, like the Steel Corporation, for example, are very like a great tenement house. It isn't the premises of a single commercial family. It is just as much a public business as a great tenement house is a public highway. When you offer the securities of a great corporation to anybody who wishes to purchase them, you must open that corporation to the inspection of everybody who wants to purchase. There must, to follow out the figure of the tenement house, be lights along the corridor; there must be police patrolling the openings; there must be inspection wherever it is known that men may be deceived with regard to the contents of the premises. If we believe that fraud lies in wait for us, we must have the means of determining whether fraud lies there or not.

Similarly, treatment of labor by the great corporations is not now what it was in Jefferson's time. Who in this great audience knows his employer? I mean among those who go down into the mines, or go into the mills and factories, and who never see, who practically never deal with, the president of the corporation. You probably don't know the directors of the corporation by sight. The only thing you know is that by the score, by the hundred, by the thousand, you are employed with your fellow workmen by some agent of an invisible employer. Therefore, whenever bodies of men employ bodies of men it ceases to be a private relationship. So that when a court, when a court in my own state, held that workmen could not peaceably dissuade other workingmen from taking employment, and based the decision upon the analogy of domestic servants, they simply showed that their minds and understandings were lingering in an age which had passed away two or three generations ago. This dealing of great bodies of men with other bodies of men is a matter of public scrutiny and should be a matter of public regulation.

Similarly, it was no business of the law in the time of Jefferson to come into the house and see how I kept the house. But when my house, when my property, when my so-called private property, became a great mine, and men went along dark corridors amid every kind of danger to dig out of the bowels of the earth things necessary for the industries of a whole nation, and when it was known that no individual owned these mines, that they were owned by great stock companies, that their partnership was as wide as great communities, then all the old analogies absolutely collapsed, and it became the right of the government to go down in those mines and see whether accidents were properly safeguarded against, to see whether the modern methods of using these inestimable riches of the world were followed or were not followed. And so you know that, by the action of a Democratic House only two years ago, the Bureau of Mines and Mining was first equipped to act as foster father of the miners of the United States, and to go into these so-called private properties and see that the life of human beings was just as much safeguarded there as it could be in the circumstances, just as much safeguarded as it would be upon the streets of Scranton; because there are dangers on the streets of Scranton.[1] If somebody puts a derrick improperly erected and secured on top of a building or overtopping the street upon any kind of structure, then the government of the city has the right to see that the derrick is so secured that you and I can walk under it and not be afraid that the heavens are going to fall on us. And, similarly, in these great beehives, wherein every corridor swarm men of flesh and blood, it is similarly the privilege of the government, whether of the state or of the United States, as the case may be, to see that human life is properly cared for and that the human lungs have something to breathe.

What I am illustrating for you is this, and it is something that our Republican opponents don't seem to credit us with intelligence enough to comprehend. Because we won't take the dictum of a leader who thinks he knows exactly what ought to be done for everybody, we are accused of wishing to minimize the powers of the Government of the United States. I am not afraid of the utmost exercise of the powers of the government of Pennsylvania, or of the Union, provided they are exercised with patriotism and intelligence and really in the interest of the people who are living under them. But when it is proposed to set up guardians over those people to take care of them by a process of tutelage and supervision, in which they play no active part, I utter my absolute objection. Because the proposal of the third party, for example, is not to take you out of the hands of the men who have corrupted the Government of the United States, but to see to it that you remain in their hands and that the government guarantees to you that it will be humane to you.[2]

The most corrupting thing in this country has been this self-same tariff...The workingmen of America are not going to allow themselves to be deceived by a colossal bluff any longer. One of the corporations in the United States which has succeeded in mastering the laborer and saying to him, "You shall not organize; you shall not exercise your liberty of cooperation, though we who employ you are using the power of organization to the outmost point of absolute control," namely, the United States Steel Corporation, paid enormous dividends and still more enormous bonuses to those who promoted its organization at the same time that it was making men work twelve hours, seven days a week, at wages which in the 365 days of the year would now allow enough to support a family. If they have millions to divide among themselves and get those millions, as they profess to get them, from the opportunities created by the tariff, where does the workingman come in?

Mr. Roosevelt himself has spoken of the profits which they get as "prize money," and his objection is just the objection that I am raising. He says that not enough of the "prize money" gets into the pay envelope. And I quite agree with him. But I want to know how he proposes to get it there. I search his program from top to bottom, and the only proposal I can find is this: that there shall be an industrial commission charged with the supervision of the great monopolistic combinations which have been formed under the protection of the tariff, and that the Government of the United States shall see to it that these gentlemen who have conquered labor shall be kind to labor. And I find then the proposition is this: that there shall be two masters, the great corporation and, over it, the Government of the United States, and I ask, "Who is going to be the master of the Government of the United States?" It has a master now, those who in combination control these monopolies. And if the government controlled by the monopolies in its turn controls the monopolies, the partnership is finally consummated.

I don't care how benevolent the master is going to be, I will not live under a master. That is not what America was created for. America was created in order that every man should have the same chance with every other man to exercise mastery over his own fortunes. Now, what I want to do is to follow the example of the authorities of the city of Glasgow. I want to light and patrol the corridors of these great organizations in order to see that nobody who tries to traverse them is waylaid and maltreated. If you will but hold them off, if you will but see to it that the weak are protected, I will venture a wager with you that there are some men in the United States now weak, economically weak, who have brains enough to compete with these gentlemen. If you will but protect them, they will presently come into the market and put these gentlemen on their mettle. And the minute they come into the market, there will be a bigger market for labor and a different wage scale for labor. Because it is susceptible of absolute proof that the high-paid labor of America—where it is high paid—is cheaper than the low-paid labor of the continent of Europe.

Do you know that about 90 per cent, I am told, of those who are employed in labor in this country are not employed in the protected industries, and that their wages are almost without exception higher than the wages of those who are employed in the protected industries? There is no corner on carpenters, there is no corner on bricklayers, there is no corner on scores of individual instances of classes of skilled laborers. But there is a corner on the poolers in the furnaces, there is a corner on the men who dive down into the mines. They are in the grip of a controlling power which determines the market rates of wages in the United States, and only where labor is free is labor highly paid in America.

So that when I am fighting against monopolistic control, I am fighting for the liberty of every man in America, and I am fighting for the liberty of American industry. These gentlemen say that this commission which they wish to set up should not be bound too much by laws, but that they should be allowed to indulge in what they call constructive regulation, which amounts to administration. And they intimate, though they do not say, that it will be perfectly feasible for this commission to regulate prices and also to regulate, I dare say, in the long run, though they do not now propose it, the rates of wages. How are they going to regulate them? Suppose that they take the net profits of a great concern…and suppose they say these net profits are too large. How are they going to tell how much of those profits came from efficiency of administration and how much from excessive prices? Now, if you tax efficiency, you discourage industry. If you tax excessive profits, you destroy your monopoly without increasing its efficiency. Because without competition there isn't going to be efficiency.

Do you know that railway rates in the United States came down and came steadily down during the period which preceded the regulation of the Interstate Commerce Commission, and that since the regulation of the Interstate Commerce Commission the rates have steadily, though not rapidly, gone up? That means that the cost of operation of the railways in the competitive period under the stimulation of competition went down, and that the cost of operation since the period of competition was closed has not gone down. I am not going to explain it, but I suspect that nobody brings his operation costs down unless he has to, and that he doesn't have to unless somebody more intelligent and more efficient than himself gets in the field against him.

…We believe that the power of America resides not in the men who have made good and gained a great supremacy in the field of business, but in the men who are to make good. Where is the power, where is the distinction of the great office of President of the United States? Is America going to be saved because George Washington was great? Because Lincoln was great? Because men of devoted characters have served in that great office? Don't you know that America is safe only because we do not know who the future Presidents of the United States are going to be? If we had depended upon the lineage of these gentlemen, they might have failed to have sons like themselves. But we are not depending on anybody except the great American people, and we know that when the time comes some figure, it may be hitherto unknown, from some family whose name and fame the country has never heard, will come a man fated for the great task by the gift of God and by virtue of his own indomitable character.

I say this with a certain degree of embarrassment because I am a candidate for that great office. And I am not going to pretend to any body of my fellow citizens that I have any sort of confidence that I am a big enough man for the place. But I do feel proud of this, that no law, no rule of blood, no privilege of money, picked me out to be a candidate even. It may be a mistake, but you can't blame your system for it, because it is a fine system where some remote, severe academic schoolmaster may become President of the United States. He is not connected at least with the powers that have been, and he has even upon occasion set himself against the powers that are. Men speculate as to what he might be ignorant or audacious enough to do. But all of that is the excitement of the democratic game. We are sports. We aren't going to tie up to a particular family. We aren't going to tie up to a particular class. We are going to say, "We have played this game long enough now to be perfectly serene about it, and we are going to take the chances of the game." That is the beauty of democracy. Democracy means that instead of depending for the fertility of your genius upon a little acre long tilled, you are going to depend upon all the wide prairies and the hillsides and the forested mountains, and that you don't care whether a man comes from Maine or from Texas, or from Washington or from Florida, or anywhere in between, provided when he comes and you look at him you like him.

And your confidence of the future is in this, that some man of some kind, probably from an uncalculated quarter, is going to come. You see, therefore, that I am simply going about to illustrate a single thing. I am simply trying to hold your attention to one theme, namely this, that America must be fertile, or she cannot be great, that if you confine the processes of your industry or the processes of you politics to these lines where there may be or has been monopoly, you impoverish the great country which we would enrich. That to my mind is the whole lesson of history.

Men have always, sooner or later, kicked over the traces after they had for a little while lived upon the theory that some of them ought to take care of the rest of them. There is no man, there is no group of men, there is no class of men, big enough or wise enough to take care of a free people. If the free people can't take care of itself, then it isn't free. It hasn't grown up. That is the very definition of freedom. If you are afraid to trust any and every man to put forth his powers as he pleases, then you are afraid of liberty itself. I am willing to risk liberty to the utmost, and I am not willing to risk anything else. So that, for my part, having once got blood in my eye and felt the zest of the active quest for the scalps of the men who don't know any better than to resist the liberties of a great people, it doesn't make any difference to me whether I am elected President or not. I'll find some means somewhere of making it infinitely uncomfortable for them.

…For the vision of America will never change. America once, when she was a little people, sat upon a hill of privilege and had a vision of the future. She saw men happy because they were free. She saw them free because they were equal. She saw them banded together because they had the spirit of brothers. She saw them safe because they did not wish to impose upon one another. The multitude has grown—that welcome multitude that comes from all parts of the world to seek a safe place of life and of hope in America.

And so America will move forward, if she moves forward at all, only with her face to that same sun of promise. Just so soon as she forgets the sun in the heavens, just so soon as she looks so intently upon the road before her and around her that she does not know where it leads, then will she forget what America was created for; her light will go out, the nations will grope again in darkness and they will say, "Where are those who prophesied a day of freedom for us? Where are the lights that we followed? Where is the torch that the runners bore? Where are those who bade us hope? Where came in these whispers of dull despair? Has America turned back? Has America forgotten her mission? Has America forgotten that her politics are part of her life and that only as the red blood of her people flows in the veins of her polity shall she occupy that point of vantage which has made her the beacon and the leader of mankind?"

注释：

1. 1907年，西弗吉尼亚州发生了美国历史上最大的一次矿难，造成362名矿工死亡。同年，宾夕法尼亚州达尔煤矿爆炸，239人遇难。矿难的频繁发生促使美国国会通过了《1910法案》（"Organic Act of Nineteen Ten"），成立了美国矿务局，负责为矿工提供建议与培训。不足的是，该法案并没有赋予矿务局检查煤矿与调查矿难的权利。斯克兰顿（Scranton）是美国宾夕法尼亚州东北部的工矿业城市。在19世纪后半期至20世纪初，斯克兰顿的煤矿大量开采，成为美国钢铁生产的中心与铁路运输的枢纽，实现了工业与商业的繁荣。同时，斯克兰顿的经济发展促进了城市建设，高楼大厦平地而起。但是，无论是城市建设，还是煤矿开采，都应该保障施工的安全，避免事故的发生。
2. 1912年，曾连任美国总统的西奥多·罗斯福（Theodore Roosevelt, 1858—1919）因不满威廉·霍华德·塔夫脱（William Howard Taft, 1857—1930）政府与共和党人的保守政策，临时成立进步党，以第三党候选人的身份参加总统竞选。罗斯福的参选分散了通常投给共和党人的选票，间接使民主党候选人威尔逊在竞选中获胜。

思考题：

1. Wilson stated that he agreed with Theodore Roosevelt on the fact that workers did not get fair payment. Their propositions to tackle the issue, however, were different. Can you illustrate the differences according to the speech?
2. Wilson claimed that he was "willing to risk liberty to the utmost" to set every American individual free from "monopolistic control." In your opinion, can his proposal be interpreted as a way to strengthen government power?

29. Principles and Ideals of the United States Government (1928)①

Herbert Clark Hoover

导读：

赫伯特·克拉克·胡佛（Herbert Clark Hoover, 1874—1964），美国第31任总统，共和党籍，毕业于斯坦福大学，曾是一名出色的采矿工程师。第一次世界大战爆发后，胡佛担任美国救济委员会主席，在战争与饥饿救济中表现杰出。胡佛曾出任沃伦·加梅利尔·哈丁（Warren Gamaliel Harding, 1865—1923）和约翰·卡尔文·柯立芝（John Calvin Coolidge, 1872—1933）两届总统的商务部部长，将消除政府及企业浪费、提升效率奉为圭臬。1928年，他在国内一片欣欣向荣的乐观气氛中当选总统。

当选八个月后，华尔街金融恐慌暴发。胡佛宣传干预有害论，试图通过市场的自由运作来战胜随之而来的经济大萧条。在经济急剧衰退的初期，胡佛拒绝通过立法给予援助。他坚信自救论，认为立法会使民众变得依赖联邦政府。胡佛主张救济由地方政府、社区和私人慈善团体来进行，联邦政府少管为好。然而，在一片萧条面前，经济自由放任主义和私人慈善事业已无法满足贫民的需要，臭名昭著的"胡佛村"②随处可见。直到任期快结束时，胡佛才开始支持一系列的立法解决方案，但是对抑制经济的下滑为时已晚。

本文是胡佛参加总统竞选时在纽约州发表的演讲。在演讲中，胡佛大肆宣扬美国制度是"个人奋斗的自由放任主义"：政府不干涉个人在社会、经济领域的自由竞争活动，使个人独创性得到充分发挥，从而实现美国人的个人主义理想。其中，他强调联邦政府在经济领域应该扮演监管商业竞争的"公断人"，而不是干预或操控商业贸易的角色。他坚信，只有坚持自由放任的经济体制，才能激发个人与企业的能动性与创

① Herbert Clark Hoover, "Principles and Ideals of the United States Government," http://www.speeches-usa.com/Transcripts/herbert_hoover-campaign.html (accessed Oct. 5, 2021).

② 由于美国经济不断恶化，数以万计的美国贫民因无家可归而聚居在帐篷搭建的城市营地中。这些营地被称为"胡佛村"，意在讽刺胡佛政府面对金融危机时的束手无策。

造力，促进经济的繁荣发展。政府对经济的干预与操控势必会破坏美国制度，阻碍经济发展，使自由主义逐渐枯竭。他指出：首先，联邦政府对经济的干预会导致中央集权，瓦解地方分权自治原则，加剧政府的权力滥用与腐败；其次，经济干预会扰乱市场自由竞争，剥夺企业的个性与独立，致使其丧失经济活力；最后，经济干预会限制个人自由和公民公平竞争的机会，削弱个体的主观能动性。胡佛没有看到自由放任主义的弊端，也没有意识到在重大经济危机面前，政府的适当干预并不是对个人自由的否定，而是对社会经济的宏观调节与控制，可以有效应对经济波动和经济危机。

During one hundred and fifty years we have builded up a form of self-government and a social system which is peculiarly our own. It differs essentially from all others in the world. It is the American system. It is just as definite and positive a political and social system as has ever been developed on earth. It is founded upon a particular conception of self-government in which decentralized local responsibility is the very base…It is founded upon the conception that only through ordered liberty, freedom and equal opportunity to the individual will his initiative and enterprise spur on the march of progress. And in our insistence upon equality of opportunity has our system advanced beyond all the world.

During the war we necessarily turned to the government to solve every difficult economic problem. The government having absorbed every energy of our people for war, there was no other solution. For the preservation of the State, the Federal Government became a centralized despotism which undertook unprecedented responsibilities, assumed autocratic powers, and took over the business of citizens. To a large degree we regimented our whole people temporarily into a socialistic state. However justified in time of war, if continued in peace-time it would destroy not only our American system, but with it our progress and freedom.

When the War closed, the most vital of all issues both in our own country and throughout the world was whether governments should continue their wartime ownership and operation of many instrumentalities of production and distribution. We were challenged with a peace-time choice between the American system of rugged individualism and a European philosophy of diametrically opposed doctrines—doctrines of paternalism and state socialism. The acceptance of these ideas would have meant the destruction of self-government through centralization of government. It would have meant the undermining of the individual initiative and enterprise through which our people have grown to unparalleled greatness.

The Republican Party from the beginning resolutely turned its face away from these ideas and these war practices. A Republican Congress co-operated with the Democratic administration to demobilize many of our war activities. At that time the two parties were in accord upon that point. When the Republican Party came into full power, it went at once resolutely back to our fundamental conception of the state and the rights and responsibilities of the individual. Thereby it restored confidence and hope in the American people, it freed and stimulated enterprise, it restored the government to its position as an umpire instead of a player in the economic game. For these reasons the American people have gone forward in progress while the rest of the world has halted, and some countries have even gone backward. If anyone will study the causes of retarded recuperation in Europe, he will find much of it due to the stifling of private initiative on one hand, and overloading of the government with business on the other.

There has been revived in this campaign, however, a series of proposals which, if adopted, would be a long step toward the abandonment of our American system and a surrender to the destructive operation of governmental conduct of commercial business. Because the country is faced with difficulty and doubt over certain national problems—that is, prohibition, farm relief, and electrical power—our opponents propose that we must thrust government a long way into the businesses which give rise to these problems. In effect, they abandon the tenets of their own party and turn to state socialism as a solution for the difficulties presented by all three. It is proposed that we shall change from prohibition to the state purchase and sale of liquor. If their agricultural relief program means anything, it means that the government shall directly or indirectly buy and sell and fix prices of agricultural products. And we are to go into the hydroelectric power business. In other words, we are confronted with a huge program of government in business.

The effect would reach to the daily life of every man and woman. It would impair the very basis of liberty and freedom not only for those left outside the fold of expanded bureaucray but for those embraced within it. Let us first see the effect upon self-government. When the Federal Government undertakes to go into commerical business, it must at once set up the organization and administration of that business, and it immediately finds itself in a labyrinth, every alley of which leads to the destruction of self-government.

The first problem of the government about to adventure in commercial business is to determine a method of administration. It must secure leadership and direction. Shall this leadership be chosen by political agencies or shall we make it elective? The hard practical fact is that leadership in business must come through the sheer rise in ability and character. That rise can only take place in a free atmosphere of competition. Competition is closed in a bureaucracy. Political agencies are feeble channels through which to select able leaders to conduct commercial business.

Government, in order to avoid the possible incompetence, corruption, and tyranny of too great authority in individuals entrusted with commercial business, inevitably turns to boards and commissions. To make sure that there are checks and balances, each member of such boards and commissions must have equal authority. Each has his separate responsibility to the public, and at once we have the conflict of ideas and the lack of decision which would ruin any commercial business. It has contributed greatly to the demoralization of our shipping business. Moreover, these commissions must be representative of different sections and different political parties, so that at once we have an entire blight upon coordinated action within their ranks which destroys any possibility of effective administration.

Thus every time the Federal Government goes into a commercial business, five hundred and thirty-one Senators and Congressmen become the actual board of directors of that business. Every time a state government goes into business, one or two hundred state senators and legislators become the actual directors of that business. Even if they were supermen and if there were no politics in the United States, no body of such numbers could competently direct commercial activities; for that requires initiative, instant decision, and action. It took Congress six years of constant discussion to even decide what the method of administration Muscle Shoals should be.

During the war the government found it necessary to operate the railways. That operation continued after the war. In the year before being freed from government operation they were not able to meet the demands for transportation. Eight years later, we find them under private enterprise transporting fifteen percent more goods and meeting every demand for service. Rates have been reduced by fifteen percent and net earnings increased from less than one percent on their valuation to about five percent. Wages of employees have improved by thirteen percent. The wages of railway employees are to day one hundred and twenty-one percent above pre-war, while the wages of government employees are today only sixty-five percent above pre-war. That should be a sufficient commentary upon the efficiency of government operation.

The government in commercial business does not tolerate among its customers the freedom of competitive reprisals to which private business is subject. Bureaucracy does not tolerate the spirit of independence; it spreads the spirit of submission into our daily life and penetrates the temper of our people not with the habit of powerful resistance to wrong but with the habit of timid acceptance of irresistible might.

Bureaucracy is ever desirous of spreading its influence and its power. You cannot extend the mastery of the government over the daily working life of a people without at the same time making it the master of the people's souls and thoughts. Every expansion of government in business means that government, in order to protect itself from the political consequences of its errors and wrongs, is driven irresistibly without peace to greater and greater control of the nations' press and platform. Free speech does not live many hours after free industry and free commerce die.

It is a false liberalism that interprets itself into the government operation of commercial business. Every step of bureaucratizing of the business of our country poisons the very roots of liberalism—that is, political equality, free speech, free assembly, free press, and equality of opportunity.

True liberalism is a force truly of the spirit, a force proceeding from the deep realization that economic freedom cannot be sacrificed if political freedom is to be preserved. Even if governmental conduct of business could give us more efficiency instead of less efficiency, the fundamental objection to it would remain unaltered and unabated. It would destroy political equality. It would increase rather than decrease abuse and corruption. It would stifle initiative and invention. It would undermine the development of leadership. It would cramp and cripple the mental and spiritual energies of our people. It would extinguish equality and opportunity. It would dry up the spirit of liberty and progress. For these reasons primarily it must be resisted.

I feel deeply on this subject because during the War I had some practical experience with governmental operation and control. I have witnessed, not only at home but abroad, the many failures of government in business. I have seen its tyrannies, its injustices, its destructions of self-government, its undermining of the very instincts which carry our people forward to progress. I have witnessed the lack of advance, the lowered standards of living, the depressed spirits of people working under such a system. My objection is based not upon theory or upon a failure to recognize wrong or abuse, but I know the adoption of such methods would strike at the very roots of American life and would destroy the very basis of American progress.

In the last fifty years we have discovered that mass production will produce articles for us at half the cost they required previously. We have seen the resultant growth of large units of production and distribution. This is big business. Many businesses must be bigger, for our tools are bigger, our country is bigger.

The American people, from bitter experience, have a rightful fear that great business units might be used to dominate our industrial life and by illegal and unethical practices destroy equality of opportunity.

Years ago the Republican administration established the principle that such evils could be corrected by regulation. It developed methods by which abuses could be prevented while the full value of industrial progress could be retained for the public. It insisted upon the principle that when great public utilities were clothed with the security of partial monopoly, whether it be railways, power plants, telephones, or what not, then there must be the fullest and most complete control of rates, services, and finances by government or local agencies. It declared that these businesses must be conducted with glass pockets.

As to our great manufacturing and distributing industries, the Republican Party insisted upon the enactment of laws that not only would maintain competition but would destroy conspiracies to destroy the smaller units, or dominate and limit the equality of opportunity amongst our people.

And what have been the results of our American system? Our country has become the land of opportunity to those born without inheritance, not merely because of the wealth of its resources and industry, but because of this freedom of initiative and enterprise.

Russia has natural resources equal to ours. Her people are equally industrious, but she has not had the blessings of one hundred and fifty years of our form of government and of our social system.

By adherence to the principles of decentralized self-government, ordered liberty, equal opportunity and freedom to the individual, our American experiment in human welfare has yielded a degree of well-being unparalleled in all the world. It has come nearer to the abolition of poverty, to the abolition of fear of want, than humanity has ever reached before. Progress of the past seven years is the proof of it. This alone furnishes the answer to our opponents, who ask us to introduce destructive elements into the system by which this has been accomplished.

Let us see what this system has done for us in our recent years of difficult and trying reconstruction and then solemnly ask ourselves if we now wish to abandon it…

I do not need to recite more figures and more evidence. I cannot believe that the American people wish to abandon, or in any way to weaken, the principles of economic freedom and self-government which have been maintained by the Republican Party, and which have produced results so amazing and so stimulating to the spiritual as well as to the material advance of the nation.

Your city has been an outstanding beneficiary of this great progress and of these safeguarded principles. With its suburbs it has, during the last seven and one-half years, grown by over a million and a half of people until it has become the largest metropolitan district of all the world. Here you have made abundant opportunity, not only for the youth of the land, but for the immigrant from foreign shores. This city is the commercial center of the United States. It is the commercial agent of the American people. It is a great organism of specialized skill and leadership in finance, industry and commerce, which reaches every spot in our country. Its progress and its beauty are the pride of the whole American people. It leads our nation in its benevolences to charity, to education, and to scientific research. It is the center of art, music, literature, and drama. It has come to have a more potent voice than any other city in the United States.

But when all is said and done, the very life, progress, and prosperity of this city is wholly dependent on the prosperity of the 115,000,000 people who dwell in our mountains and valleys across the three-thousand miles to the Pacific Ocean. Every activity of this city is sensitive to every evil and every favorable tide that sweeps this great nation of ours. Be there a slackening of industry in any place, it affects New York far more than any other part of the country. In a time of depression, one-quarter of all the unemployed in the United States can be numbered in this city. In a time of prosperity, the citizens of the great interior of our country pour into your city for business and entertainment at the rate of one hundred and fifty thousand a day. In fact, so much is this city the reflex of the varied interests of our country, that the concern of every one of your citizens for national stability, for national prosperity, for national progress, for preservation of our American system is far greater than that of any other single part of our country.

We still have great problems if we would achieve the full economic advancement of our country. In these past few years, some groups in our country have lagged behind others in the march of progress. I refer more particularly to those engaged in the textile, coal, and agricultural industries. To the agricultural industry we shall need to advance initial capital to assist them to stabilize their industry. But this proposal implies that they shall conduct it themselves, and not the government. It is in the interest of our cities that we shall bring agriculture and all industries into full stability and prosperity. I know you will gladly cooperate in the faith that in the common prosperity of our country lies its future.

In bringing this address to a conclusion, I should like to restate to you some of the fundamental things I have endeavored to bring out. The foundations of progress and prosperity are dependent as never before upon the wise policies of government, for government now touches at a thousand points the intricate web of economic and social life. Under administration by the Republican Party, in the last seven and one-half years, our country as a whole has made unparalleled progress, and this has been in generous part reflected to this great city. Prosperity is no idle expression. It is a job for every worker; it is the safety and the safeguard of every business and every home. A continuation of the policies of the Republican Party is fundamentally necessary to the further advancement of this progress and to the further building up of this prosperity.

I have dwelt at some length on the principles of relationship between the government and business. I make no apologies for dealing with this subject. The first necessity of any nation is the smooth functioning of the vast business machinery for employment, feeding, clothing, housing, and providing luxuries and comforts to a people. Unless these basic elements are properly organized and function, there can be no progress in business, in education, literature, music, or art. There can be no advance in the fundamental ideals of a people. A people cannot make progress in poverty.

I have endeavored to present to you that the greatness of America has grown out of a political and social system and a method of control of economic forces distinctly its own—our American system—which has carried this great experiment in human welfare farther than ever before in all history. We are nearer today to the ideal of the abolition of poverty and fear from the lives of men and women than ever before in any land. And I again repeat that the departure from our American system by injecting principles destructive to it, which our opponents propose, will jeopardize the very liberty and freedom of our people will destroy equality of opportunity, not alone to ourselves but to our children.

My conception of America is a land where men and women may walk in ordered freedom in the independent conduct of their occupations; where they may enjoy the advantages of wealth, not concentrated in the hands of the few, but spread through the lives of all; where they build and safeguard their homes, and give to their children the fullest advantages and opportunities of American life; where every man shall be respected in the faith that his conscience and his heart direct him to follow; where a contented and happy people, secure in their liberties, free from poverty and fear, shall have the leisure and impulse to seek a fuller life.

Some may ask where all this may lead, beyond mere material progress. It leads to a release of the energies of men and women from the dull drudgery of life to a wider vision and a higher hope. It leads to the opportunity for greater and greater service, not alone from man to man in our own land, but from our country to the whole world. It leads to an America, healthy in body, healthy in spirit, unfettered, youthful, eager—with a vision searching beyond the farthest horizons, with an open mind, sympathetic and generous. It is to these higher ideals and for these purposes that I pledge myself and the Republican Party.

思考题：

1. Herbert Hoover stated that United States was not "free-for-all and devil-take-the-hindmost.... It is no system of laissez faire." At the same time, he insisted that the government should not interfere with commercial business. Do you think these two statements are contradictory? What is your interpretation of these two points of views?
2. In your opinion, to what extent should the government regulate and control commerce and industry?

30. The Four Freedoms (1941)[①]

Franklin D. Roosevelt

导读：

富兰克林·德拉诺·罗斯福（Franklin D. Roosevelt, 1882—1945）是美国第32任总统，也是美国历史上唯一连任四届的总统。他“带领美国走过经济大萧条和第二次世界大战，迈入繁荣的未来”[②]。

罗斯福出生在纽约州哈德逊河谷中的海德帕克。其父亲老詹姆斯·罗斯福和母亲萨拉·罗斯福分别来自纽约州富裕的荷兰裔和法裔大家族。他中学时期就读于马萨诸塞州的格罗顿学校。当时该校的校长恩迪科特·皮博迪（Endicott Peabody, 1857—1944）主张道德教育，重视培养学生的慈善意识，罗斯福深受影响。进入哈佛大学后，罗斯福曾担任《哈佛深红报》（*The Harvard Crimson*）总编。在校期间，罗斯福的远房堂兄西奥多·罗斯福（Theodore Roosevelt, 1857—1919）就任美国第26任总统，西奥多精力旺盛，其领导作风和改革热情感染了他，他以西奥多为英雄榜样。

罗斯福执政的20世纪30年代的美国可谓是内忧外患。当时，美国正处于有史以来最大经济萧条的谷底：银行倒闭，失业问题严峻，农产品价格降至最低点，200万人无家可归。国际上，世界大战一触即发。1933年罗斯福总统上任后，面对国内严重的经济衰退，他积极推行3R新政——救济（relief）、复兴（recovery）、改革（reform）——以促进经济复苏。在新政期间，罗斯福政府通过国会制定了《紧急银行法令》《国家产业复兴法》《农业调整法》《社会保障法案》等法案，以政府干预经济的方式大大缓解了大萧条所带来的经济危机与社会矛盾。第二次世界大战爆发后，罗斯福打破孤立主义，带领美国加入反法西斯阵营，为战争的最终胜利做出了不可磨灭的贡献。战争后期，他提出建立联合国的构想，勾勒了一幅维护世界和平与秩序的蓝图。

---

① Franklin D. Roosevelt, “The Four Freedoms,” http://voicesofdemocracy.umd.edu/fdr-the-four-freedoms-speech-text/ (accessed Oct. 5, 2021).

② Edward Smith, FDR (Random House, 2007): ix.

本文《四大自由》选自富兰克林·罗斯福于1941年1月6日致国会的咨文，是他对第二次世界大战后世界秩序的设想。在该咨文中，罗斯福谈到第二次世界大战给美国的安全与民主带来的威胁，提出美国应为战争中的同盟国以租借方式提供武器。他的这番讲话打破了美国外交政策上的孤立主义。在咨文的前半部分，罗斯福总结了民主的价值，警示人们在独裁统治下不可能有真正的世界和平、国家独立，以及言论与宗教自由。在咨文的后半部分，他列举了民主给经济、就业、社会安全等方面带来的益处，提出了构建未来世界的基础——四大自由，即言论自由、宗教信仰自由、免除匮乏的自由、免于恐惧的自由。其中，免除匮乏的自由被认为是一种新的自由。政府不仅要关注人们争取工作机会的自由，而且要主动承担起保障公民基本生活的责任和义务，因为基本经济保障是获得工作自由的前提。免于恐惧的自由，旨在建立一个安全的世界，使各国人民免于对侵略、死亡的恐惧。几年以后，在"四大自由"的基础上，联合国成立了，并相继制定了符合"四大自由"精神的《联合国宪章》与《世界人权宣言》。

第二次世界大战时期，罗斯福提出的"四大自由"极大地调动了美国乃至世界各国人民参与反法西斯战争的积极性，起到了非常正面的作用。但在第二次世界大战之后，这"四大自由"却渐渐违背了其初衷，日益成为美国打着自由的旗号称霸世界、长臂干预他国内政外交、在世界各地煽风点火甚至发动战争的借口。事实上，美国今日的行径已完全有悖于这"四大自由"：首先，在国际关系上，它动辄就把与其体制、观念或信仰不同的国家和人民树为敌国或敌人；其次，罗斯福所谓"免于恐惧的自由"是指"从全球意义上说，进行世界范围内的彻底裁军，从而使得任何一个国家都不会向其邻国采取武力侵略行动"，可美国天天叫嚷他国裁军，自己却年年增加军费，成了世界上军事实力独大、军事存在几乎遍及全球的国家，且频繁向他国发起战争，给世界各国人民造成了极大的恐惧；第三，在国际上，因其发动战争和长臂干预他国内政外交而产生的难民不计其数。在国内，非洲裔、拉美裔和原住民的贫困率居高不下，种族歧视甚至种族仇恨事件此起彼伏，接连不断。

…Even when the World War broke out in 1914, it seemed to contain only small threat of danger to our own American future. But, as time went on, as we remember, the American people began to visualize what the downfall of democratic nations might mean to our own democracy.

We need not overemphasize imperfections in the peace of Versailles. We need not harp on failure of the democracies to deal with problems of world reconstruction. We should remember that the peace of 1919 was far less unjust than the kind of "pacification" which began even before Munich, and which is being carried on under the new order of tyranny that seeks to spread over every continent today. The American people have unalterably set their faces against that tyranny.

I suppose that every realist knows that the democratic way of life is at this moment being directly assailed in every part of the world—assailed either by arms, or by secret spreading of poisonous propaganda by those who seek to destroy unity and promote discord in nations that are still at peace.

During sixteen long months this assault has blotted out the whole pattern of democratic life in an appalling number of independent nations, great and small. And the assailants are still on the march, threatening other nations, great and small.

Therefore, as your President, performing my constitutional duty to "give to the Congress information of the state of the Union," I find it, unhappily, necessary to report that the future and the safety of our country and of our democracy are overwhelmingly involved in events far beyond our borders.

Armed defense of democratic existence is now being gallantly waged in four continents. If that defense fails, all the population and all the resources of Europe, and Asia, and Africa and Australasia will be dominated by conquerors. And let us remember that the total of those populations in those four continents, the total of those populations and their resources greatly exceed the sum total of the population and the resources of the whole of the Western Hemisphere—yes, many times over.

In times like these it is immature—and incidentally, untrue—for anybody to brag that an unprepared America, single-handed and with one hand tied behind its back, can hold off the whole world.

No realistic American can expect from a dictator's peace international generosity, or return of true independence, or world disarmament, or freedom of expression, or freedom of religion—or even good business.

Such a peace would bring no security for us or for our neighbors. "Those, who would give up essential liberty to purchase a little temporary safety, deserve neither liberty nor safety."

As a nation, we may take pride in the fact that we are softhearted; but we cannot afford to be softheaded.

We must always be wary of those who with sounding brass and a tinkling cymbal preach the "ism" of appeasement.

We must especially beware of that small group of selfish men who would clip the wings of the American eagle in order to feather their own nests.

I have recently pointed out how quickly the tempo of modern warfare could bring into our very midst the physical attack which we must eventually expect if the dictator nations win this war.

There is much loose talk of our immunity from immediate and direct invasion from across the seas. Obviously, as long as the British Navy retains its power, no such danger exists. Even if there were no British Navy, it is not probable that any enemy would be stupid enough to attack us by landing troops in the United States from across thousands of miles of ocean, until it had acquired strategic bases from which to operate.

But we learn much from the lessons of the past years in Europe—particularly the lesson of Norway, whose essential seaports were captured by treachery and surprise built up over a series of years.[1]

The first phase of the invasion of this hemisphere would not be the landing of regular troops. The necessary strategic points would be occupied by secret agents and by their dupes—and great numbers of them are already here, and in Latin America.

As long as the aggressor nations maintain the offensive, they—not we—will choose the time and the place and the method of their attack.

And that is why the future of all the American Republics is today in serious danger.

That is why this Annual Message to the Congress is unique in our history.

That is why every member of the Executive Branch of the Government and every member of the Congress face great responsibility and great accountability.

The need of the moment is that our actions and our policy should be devoted primarily—almost exclusively—to meeting this foreign peril. For all our domestic problems are now a part of the great emergency.

Just as our national policy in internal affairs has been based upon a decent respect for the rights and the dignity of all our fellow men within our gates, so our national policy in foreign affairs has been based on a decent respect for the rights and the dignity of all nations, large and small. And the justice of morality must and will win in the end.

Our national policy is this:

First, by an impressive expression of the public will and without regard to partisanship, we are committed to all-inclusive national defense.

Second, by an impressive expression of the public will and without regard to partisanship, we are committed to full support of all those resolute people everywhere who are resisting aggression and are thereby keeping war away from our Hemisphere. By this support, we express our determination that the democratic cause shall prevail; and we strengthen the defense and the security of our own nation.

Third, by an impressive expression of the public will and without regard to partisanship, we are committed to the proposition that principles of morality and considerations for our own security will never permit us to acquiesce in a peace dictated by aggressors and sponsored by appeasers. We know that enduring peace cannot be bought at the cost of other people's freedom.

In the recent national election there was no substantial difference between the two great parties in respect to that national policy. No issue was fought out on this line before the American electorate. And today it is abundantly evident that American citizens everywhere are demanding and supporting speedy and complete action in recognition of obvious danger.

Therefore, the immediate need is a swift and driving increase in our armament production.

Leaders of industry and labor have responded to our summons. Goals of speed have been set. In some cases these goals are being reached ahead of time; in some cases we are on schedule; in other cases there are slight but not serious delays; and in some cases—and, I am sorry to say very important cases—we are all concerned by the slowness of the accomplishment of our plans.

The Army and Navy, however, have made substantial progress during the past year. Actual experience is improving and speeding up our methods of production with every passing day. And today's best is not good enough for tomorrow.

I am not satisfied with the progress thus far made. The men in charge of the program represent the best in training, in ability, and in patriotism. They are not satisfied with the progress thus far made. None of us will be satisfied until the job is done.

No matter whether the original goal was set too high or too low, our objective is quicker and better results.

We are behind schedule in turning out finished airplanes; we are working day and night to solve the innumerable problems and to catch up.

We are ahead of schedule in building warships but we are working to get even further ahead of that schedule.

To change a whole nation from a basis of peacetime production of implements of peace to a basis of wartime production of implements of war is no small task. And the greatest difficulty comes at the beginning of the program, when new tools, new plant facilities, new assembly lines, new ship ways must first be constructed before the actual material begins to flow steadily and speedily from them.

The Congress, of course, must rightly keep itself informed at all times of the progress of the program. However, there is certain information, as the Congress itself will readily recognize, which, in the interests of our own security and those of the nations that we are supporting, must of needs be kept in confidence.

New circumstances are constantly begetting new needs for our safety. I shall ask this Congress for greatly increased new appropriations and authorizations to carry on what we have begun.

I also ask this Congress for authority and for funds sufficient to manufacture additional munitions and war supplies of many kinds, to be turned over to those nations which are now in actual war with aggressor nations.

Our most useful and immediate role is to act as an arsenal for them as well as for ourselves. They do not need man power, but they do need billions of dollars worth of the weapons of defense.

The time is near when they will not be able to pay for them all in ready cash. We cannot, and we will not, tell them that they must surrender, merely because of present inability to pay for the weapons which we know they must have.

I do not recommend that we make them a loan of dollars with which to pay for these weapons—a loan to be repaid in dollars.

I recommend that we make it possible for those nations to continue to obtain war materials in the United States, fitting their orders into our own program.[2] And nearly all of their material would, if the time ever came, be useful in our own defense.

Taking counsel of expert military and naval authorities, considering what is best for our own security, we are free to decide how much should be kept here and how much should be sent abroad to our friends who by their determined and heroic resistance are giving us time in which to make ready our own defense.

For what we send abroad, we shall be repaid, repaid within a reasonable time following the close of hostilities, repaid in similar materials, or at our option, in other goods of many kinds, which they can produce and which we need.

Let us say to the democracies: "We Americans are vitally concerned in your defense of freedom. We are putting forth our energies, our resources and our organizing powers to give you the strength to regain and maintain a free world. We shall send you, in ever-increasing numbers, ships, planes, tanks, guns. That is our purpose and our pledge."

In fulfillment of this purpose we will not be intimidated by the threats of dictators that they will regard as a breach of international law or as an act of war our aid to the democracies which dare to resist their aggression. Such aid…such aid is not an act of war, even if a dictator should unilaterally proclaim it so to be.

And when the dictators, if the dictators, are ready to make war upon us, they will not wait for an act of war on our part. They did not wait for Norway or Belgium or the Netherlands to commit an act of war.

Their only interest is in a new one-way international law, which lacks mutuality in its observance, and, therefore, becomes an instrument of oppression.

The happiness of future generations of Americans may well depend on how effective and how immediate we can make our aid felt. No one can tell the exact character of the emergency situations that we may be called upon to meet. The Nation's hands must not be tied when the Nation's life is in danger.

Yes, and we must prepare—all of us prepare—to make the sacrifices that the emergency—almost as serious as war itself—demands. Whatever stands in the way of speed and efficiency in defense—in defense preparations of any kind—must give way to the national need.

A free nation has the right to expect full cooperation from all groups. A free nation has the right to look to the leaders of business, of labor, and of agriculture to take the lead in stimulating effort, not among other groups but within their own group.

The best way of dealing with the few slackers or trouble makers in our midst is, first, to shame them by patriotic example, and if that fails, to use the sovereignty of government to save government.

As men do not live by bread alone, they do not fight by armaments alone. Those who man our defenses, and those behind them who build our defenses, must have the stamina and the courage which come from unshakable belief in the manner of life which they are defending. The mighty action that we are calling for cannot be based on a disregard of all the things worth fighting for.

The Nation takes great satisfaction and much strength from the things which have been done to make its people conscious of their individual stake in the preservation of democratic life in America. Those things have toughened the fiber of our people, have renewed their faith and strengthened their devotion to the institutions we make ready to protect.

Certainly this is no time for any of us to stop thinking about the social and economic problems which are the root cause of the social revolution which is today a supreme factor in the world.

For there is nothing mysterious about the foundations of a healthy and strong democracy. The basic things expected by our people of their political and economic systems are simple. They are:

Equality of opportunity for youth and for others.

Jobs for those who can work.

Security for those who need it.

The ending of special privilege for the few.

The preservation of civil liberties for all.

The enjoyment…the enjoyment of the fruits of scientific progress in a wider and constantly rising standard of living.

These are the simple, the basic things that must never be lost sight of in the turmoil and unbelievable complexity of our modern world. The inner and abiding strength of our economic and political systems is dependent upon the degree to which they fulfill these expectations.

Many subjects connected with our social economy call for immediate improvement.

As examples:

We should bring more citizens under the coverage of old-age pensions and unemployment insurance.

We should widen the opportunities for adequate medical care.

We should plan a better system by which persons deserving or needing gainful employment may obtain it.

I have called for personal sacrifice. And I am assured of the willingness of almost all Americans to respond to that call.

A part of the sacrifice means the payment of more money in taxes. In my Budget Message I will recommend that a greater portion of this great defense program be paid for from taxation than we are paying for today. No person should try, or be allowed, to get rich out of the program; and the principle of tax payments in accordance with ability to pay should be constantly before our eyes to guide our legislation.

If the Congress maintains these principles, the voters, putting patriotism ahead pocketbooks, will give you their applause.

In the future days, which we seek to make secure, we look forward to a world founded upon four essential human freedoms.

The first is freedom of speech and expression—everywhere in the world.

The second is freedom of every person to worship God in his own way—everywhere in the world.

The third is freedom from want—which, translated into world terms, means economic understandings which will secure to every nation a healthy peacetime life for its inhabitants—everywhere in the world.

The fourth is freedom from fear—which, translated into world terms, means a world-wide reduction of armaments to such a point and in such a thorough fashion that no nation will be in a position to commit an act of physical aggression against any neighbor—anywhere in the world.

That is no vision of a distant millennium. It is a definite basis for a kind of world attainable in our own time and generation. That kind of world is the very antithesis of the so-called new order of tyranny which the dictators seek to create with the crash of a bomb.

To that new order we oppose the greater conception—the moral order. A good society is able to face schemes of world domination and foreign revolutions alike without fear.

Since the beginning of our American history, we have been engaged in change—in a perpetual peaceful revolution—a revolution which goes on steadily, quietly adjusting itself to changing conditions—without the concentration camp or the quick-lime in the ditch. The world order which we seek is the cooperation of free countries, working together in a friendly, civilized society.

This nation has placed its destiny in the hands and heads and hearts of its millions of free men and women; and its faith in freedom under the guidance of God. Freedom means the supremacy of human rights everywhere. Our support goes to those who struggle to gain those rights and keep them. Our strength is our unity of purpose.

To that high concept there can be no end save victory.

注释：

1. 1940年，德国进攻挪威时，挪威军人政治家维德孔·吉斯林（Vidkun Quisling, 1887—1945）与纳粹德国“合作”。在挪威被德军攻占后，吉斯林出任挪威新政权的总理。第二次世界大战结束后，吉斯林以叛国罪被枪决，而吉斯林的名字成为英文里“卖国贼”或“叛国者”的代名词。
2. 罗斯福总统提到的武器租借方式经美国国会批准于1941年3月11日生效，名为《租借法案》（“Lend-Lease Act”）。其目的是美国在不卷入战争的情况下为同盟国提供战争物资，使美国成为“民主国家的兵工厂”。

思考题：

1. Has the U.S. clamped down too broadly on civil liberties in response to security threats? How can advocates of security and human rights work together more effectively?
2. Freedom from fear, as President Roosevelt stated, “means a world-wide reduction of armaments” so that national aggression could be infeasible. What is your understanding of freedom from fear nowadays?

31. Atoms for Peace (1953)[①]

Dwight D. Eisenhower

导读：

德怀特·大卫·艾森豪威尔（Dwight David Eisenhower, 1890—1969）是美国陆军五星上将、第34任总统。第二次世界大战期间，他任盟军在欧洲的最高指挥官。战争结束后，他以“维护世界和平”为竞选宣言，以压倒性优势战胜持“不干涉”外交政策[②]的罗伯特·塔夫特（Robert Taft, 1889—1953），成为美国第34任总统。

艾森豪威尔执政后，提出要让美国人民过得更加幸福。20世纪50年代初期，美国人生活在对核战和社会主义的恐惧中。当时的流行文学大部分都与“惧核”“恐社”有关。[③]学校里，老师向学生讲授遭遇核袭击的应对措施；生活中，人们忙于修缮地下室和囤积粮食，以应对核战的到来；社会上，麦卡锡主义力求肃清共产党，人们在监视和被监视中神经紧绷。艾森豪威尔上台后，废除麦卡锡主义，让社会重心回到经济发展的正轨上。他对和平的追求极大程度地安抚了民众的“惧核”情绪。另外，他反对种族隔离，为后来的民权运动奠定了良好基础。

本文是1953年艾森豪威尔在联合国大会上的演讲——《和平利用原子能》（“Atoms for Peace”）。此演讲是一篇精明的政治辞令，旨在树立美国的正面形象，同时抨击对手苏联。艾森豪威尔暗指掌握核技术的苏联是“侵略者”（aggressor）和“恐怖的暗室”（the dark chamber of horrors），而把美国喻为“光明”（the light）。他声称美国及其盟

① Dwight D. Eisenhower, “Atoms for Peace,” *Speech Presented by Eisenhower on December 8, 1953*. Last edited by Martin J. Medhurst and Belinda Stillion Southard in 2005. http://voicesofdemocracy.umd.edu/eisenhower-atoms-for-peace-speech-text/ (accessed Oct. 6, 2021).

② “不干涉”外交政策反对美国与其他国家结盟，不支持美国参与国际纷争。第二次世界大战后，世界格局表现为资本主义和社会主义两大敌对阵营间的较量。

③ 如要研究当时的流行文化，可参见以下作品：Philip Wylie, “Deliverance or Doom?” *Collier’s*, Sept. 29, 1945; “H-Bomb Odds: 1 Million to 1,” *Newsweek*, Apr. 5, 1954; Maryland Civil Defense Agency, *The H-Bomb and You*, distributed to Washington DC/Maryland area residents, 1954.

国在核能方面的优势可为人类科技进步服务，而苏联的核能优势则是对世界和平的潜在威胁。总之，他认为只有在美国及其盟国的领导下，发展核能才会对人类有益。具有讽刺意味的是，美国是迄今唯一一个在战争中使用过核武器的国家。

艾森豪威尔的演讲巧妙地掩饰了美国军事和外交政策的逻辑矛盾：美国一方面裁减军队数量，另一方面增强军队实际战斗力；一方面寻求美苏合作，另一方面希望彻底挫败社会主义。在演讲的最后，艾森豪威尔强调美国发展核能和军队是为了维护世界和平。但实际上，这样的军队发展反而让美苏军备竞赛愈演愈烈。自此以后，艾森豪威尔的这种“遏制对手、发展军队、维护和平”的逻辑为美国发起国际战争提供了借口，也成为其他很多国家发展核武器的托词。

…I feel impelled to speak today in a language that, in a sense, is new—one, which I, who have spent so much of my life in the military profession, would have preferred never to use.

That new language is the language of atomic warfare.[1]

The atomic age has moved forward at such a pace that every citizen of the world should have some comprehension, at least in comparative terms, of the extent of this development, of the utmost significance to every one of us. Clearly, if the peoples of the world are to conduct an intelligent search for peace, they must be armed with the significant facts of today's existence.

My recital of atomic danger and power is necessarily stated in United States terms, for these are the only incontrovertible facts that I know. I need hardly point out to this Assembly, however, that this subject is global, not merely national in character.

On July 16th, 1945, the United States set off the world's first atomic explosion. Since that date in 1945, the United States of America has conducted 42 test explosions.

Atomic bombs today are more than 25 times as powerful as the weapons with which the atomic age dawned, while hydrogen weapons are in the ranges of millions of tons of TNT equivalent.

Today, the United States' stockpile of atomic weapons, which, of course, increases daily, exceeds by many times the total equivalent of the total of all bombs and all shells that came from every plane and every gun in every theatre of war in all the years of World War Ⅱ.[2]

A single air group, whether afloat or land-based, can now deliver to any reachable target a destructive cargo exceeding in power all the bombs that fell on Britain in all of World War Ⅱ.

In size and variety the development of atomic weapons has been no less remarkable. The development has been such that atomic weapons have virtually achieved conventional status within our armed services. In the United States, the Army, the Navy, the Air Force and the Marine Corps are all capable of putting this weapon to military use.

But the dread secret, and the fearful engines of atomic might, are not ours alone.

In the first place, the secret is possessed by our friends and allies, Great Britain and Canada, whose scientific genius made a tremendous contribution to our original discoveries and the designs of atomic bombs.

The secret is also known by the Soviet Union.

The Soviet Union has informed us that, over recent years, it has devoted extensive resources to atomic weapons. During this period, the Soviet Union has exploded a series of atomic devices, including at least one involving thermo-nuclear reactions.

If at one time the United States possessed what might have been called a monopoly of atomic power, that monopoly ceased to exist several years ago. Therefore, although our earlier start has permitted us to accumulate what is today a great quantitative advantage, the atomic realities of today comprehend two facts of even greater significance.

First, the knowledge now possessed by several nations will eventually be shared by others, possibly all others.

Second, even a vast superiority in numbers of weapons, and a consequent capability of devastating retaliation, is no preventive, of itself, against the fearful material damage and toll of human lives that would be inflicted by surprise aggression.

The free world, at least dimly aware of these facts, has naturally embarked on a large program of warning and defense systems. That program will be accelerated and expanded.

But let no one think that the expenditure of vast sums for weapons and systems of defense can guarantee absolute safety for the cities and citizens of any nation. The awful arithmetic of the atomic bomb does not permit of any such easy solution. Even against the most powerful defense, an aggressor in possession of the effective minimum number of atomic bombs for a surprise attack could probably place a sufficient number of his bombs on the chosen targets to cause hideous damage.

Should such an atomic attack be launched against the United States, our reactions would be swift and resolute. But for me to say that the defense capabilities of the United States are such that they could inflict terrible losses upon an aggressor—for me to say that the retaliation capabilities of the United States are so great that such an aggressor's land would be laid waste—all this, while fact, is not the true expression of the purpose and the hope of the United States.

To pause there would be to confirm the hopeless finality of a belief that two atomic colossi are doomed malevolently to eye each other indefinitely across a trembling world. To stop there would be to accept helplessly the probability of civilization destroyed—the annihilation of the irreplaceable heritage of mankind handed down to us generation from generation—and the condemnation of mankind to begin all over again the age-old struggle upward from savagery toward decency, and right, and justice.

Surely no sane member of the human race could discover victory in such desolation. Could anyone wish his name to be coupled by history with such human degradation and destruction?

Occasional pages of history do record the faces of the "Great Destroyers" but the whole book of history reveals mankind's never-ending quest for peace and mankind's God-given capacity to build.

It is with the book of history, and not with isolated pages, that the United States will ever wish to be identified. My country wants to be constructive, not destructive. It wants agreements, not wars, among nations. It wants itself to live in freedom, and in the confidence that the people of every other nation enjoy equally the right of choosing their own way of life.

So my country's purpose is to help us move out of the dark chamber of horrors into the light, to find a way by which the minds of men, the hopes of men, the souls of men everywhere, can move forward toward peace and happiness and well-being.

In this quest, I know that we must not lack patience.

I know that in a world divided, such as ours today, salvation cannot be attained by one dramatic act.

I know that many steps will have to be taken over many months before the world can look at itself one day and truly realize that a new climate of mutually peaceful confidence is abroad in the world.

But I know, above all else, that we must start to take these steps—now….[3]

In its resolution of November 18th, 1953, this General Assembly suggested—and I quote—"that the Disarmament Commission study the desirability of establishing a sub-committee consisting of representatives of the Powers principally involved, which should seek in private an acceptable solution…and report such a solution to the General Assembly and to the Security Council not later than September 1, 1954."

The United States, heeding the suggestion of the General Assembly of the United Nations, is instantly prepared to meet privately with such other countries as may be "principally involved," to seek "an acceptable solution" to the atomic armaments race which overshadows not only the peace, but the very life, of the world.

We shall carry into these private or diplomatic talks a new conception.

The United States would seek more than the mere reduction or elimination of atomic materials for military purposes.

It is not enough to take this weapon out of the hands of the soldiers. It must be put into the hands of those who will know how to strip its military casing and adapt it to the arts of peace.

The United States knows that if the fearful trend of atomic military build-up can be reversed, this greatest of destructive forces can be developed into a great boon, for the benefit of all mankind.

The United States knows that peaceful power from atomic energy is no dream of the future. That capability, already proved, is here—now—today. Who can doubt, if the entire body of the world's scientists and engineers had adequate amounts of fissionable material with which to test and develop their ideas, that this capability would rapidly be transformed into universal, efficient, and economic usage?

To hasten the day when fear of the atom will begin to disappear from the minds of people, and the governments of the East and West, there are certain steps that can be taken now.

I therefore make the following proposal:

The Governments principally involved, to the extent permitted by elementary prudence, to begin now and continue to make joint contributions from their stockpiles of normal uranium and fissionable materials to an International Atomic Energy Agency. We would expect that such an agency would be set up under the aegis of the

United Nations.

The ratios of contributions, the procedures and other details would properly be within the scope of the "private conversations" I have referred to earlier.

The United States is prepared to undertake these explorations in good faith. Any partner of the United States acting in the same good faith will find the United States a not unreasonable or ungenerous associate.

Undoubtedly initial and early contributions to this plan would be small in quantity. However, the proposal has the great virtue that it can be undertaken without the irritations and mutual suspicions incident to any attempt to set up a completely acceptable system of world-wide inspection and control.

The Atomic Energy Agency could be made responsible for the impounding, storage, and protection of the contributed fissionable and other materials. The ingenuity of our scientists will provide special safe conditions under which such a bank of fissionable material can be made essentially immune to surprise seizure.

The more important responsibility of this Atomic Energy Agency would be to devise methods whereby this fissionable material would be allocated to serve the peaceful pursuits of mankind. Experts would be mobilized to apply atomic energy to the needs of agriculture, medicine, and other peaceful activities. A special purpose would be to provide abundant electrical energy in the power-starved areas of the world. Thus the contributing powers would be dedicating some of their strength to serve the needs rather than the fears of mankind.

The United States would be more than willing—it would be proud to take up with others "principally involved" the development of plans whereby such peaceful use of atomic energy would be expedited.

Of those "principally involved" the Soviet Union must, of course, be one.

I would be prepared to submit to the Congress of the United States, and with every expectation of approval, any such plan that would:

First, encourage world-wide investigation into the most effective peacetime uses of fissionable material, and with the certainty that they had all the material needed for the conduct of all experiments that were appropriate;

Second, begin to diminish the potential destructive power of the world's atomic stockpiles;

Third, allow all peoples of all nations to see that, in this enlightened age, the great powers of the earth, both of the East and of the West, are interested in human aspirations first, rather than in building up the armaments of war;

Fourth, open up a new channel for peaceful discussion, and initiate at least a new approach to the many difficult problems that must be solved in both private and public conversations, if the world is to shake off the inertia imposed by fear, and is to make positive progress toward peace.

Against the dark background of the atomic bomb, the United States does not wish merely to present strength, but also the desire and the hope for peace.

The coming months will be fraught with fateful decisions. In this Assembly; in the capitals and military headquarters of the world; in the hearts of men everywhere, be they governed or governors, may they be the decisions which will lead this world out of fear and into peace.

To the making of these fateful decisions, the United States pledges before you—and therefore before the world—its determination to help solve the fearful atomic dilemma—to devote its entire heart and mind to find the way by which the miraculous inventiveness of man shall not be dedicated to his death, but consecrated to his life.

I again thank the delegates for the great honor they have done me, in inviting me to appear before them, and in listening to me so courteously. Thank you.

注释：

1. 演讲开篇提到美国及其盟国为争取世界和平所做的努力。因篇幅限制，选文省略了开篇部分。这句话承上启下，开始论述原子能对和平的威胁。
2. 演讲中像这样提及美国核能储备和军事力量的地方还有很多。可见艾森豪威尔一方面宣扬和平，另一方面绝不允许美国在军备竞赛中处于劣势。
3. 省略部分是艾森豪威尔重述美国在维护和平方面所做的努力，并且重申美国并不想与苏联为敌，希望美苏以维护和平为目的进行合作。

思考题：

1. What rhetoric devices does Eisenhower use in the speech in framing the images of both America and USSR?
2. Do you think the speech is paradoxical that Eisenhower calls for peaceful cooperation while demonstrating the military strength of the United States?

32. Inaugural Address (1961)①

John F. Kennedy

导读：

约翰·菲茨杰拉德·肯尼迪（John Fitzgerald Kennedy, 1917—1963）是美国第35任总统，也是美国首位爱尔兰裔、首位信奉罗马天主教的总统。他在美苏冷战期间临危受命。②

肯尼迪出身于马萨诸塞州布鲁克莱恩的一个政治世家。在父亲和兄长的影响下，他对欧洲政治和国际关系产生了浓厚的兴趣，并显示出优异的政治天赋。肯尼迪执政的20世纪60年代，美国社会面临前所未有的剧变和挑战：在内政外交方面，战后重建迫在眉睫，民权运动如火如荼，冷战危机四伏，核战一触即发；在社会文化方面，R. G. 沃尔德克（R. G. Waldeck, 1898—1982）的《同性恋国际》（"Homosexual International"，1961）、贝蒂·弗里丹（Betty Friedan, 1921—2006）的《女性的奥秘》（*The Feminine Mystique*, 1963）和雷切尔·卡森（Rachel Carson, 1907—1964）的《寂静的春天》（*Silent Spring*, 1962）引发了民众热烈的讨论。民众开始关心同性恋、女权、环境等人文主义问题，同时电视通信技术的发展也积极引导民众讨论和参与公共事务。

1961年当选总统后，肯尼迪对内刺激经济，消除贫困，争取人权平等，缓和种族矛盾；对外倡导国际合作，建立国际新秩序，并鼓励美国青年参加维和部队（Peace Corps），把民主和自由推向全世界。面对严峻的冷战格局，肯尼迪向往和平，但仍然不遗余力确保美国在军备和太空竞赛中的领先地位。他冷静化解古巴导弹危机，并同苏联签署了《部分禁止核试验条约》（"Partial Nuclear Test Ban Treaty"，1963）。此

① John F. Kennedy, "Inaugural Address," *Speech by Kennedy on January 20, 1961*. Edited by Gerhard Peters and John T. Woolley. http://www.presidency.ucsb.edu/documents/inaugural-address-2 (accessed Oct. 6, 2021).

② 肯尼迪执政时期美苏矛盾尖锐，美国在越南战场愈陷愈深。与此同时，国内民权运动方兴未艾，"新左派"运动如火如荼。经济上，直至肯尼迪上台的1961年，美国已面临七个月的衰退、三年半的停滞、七年的经济增长速度降低和九年的农场收入下降。因此，肯尼迪的上任可以说是"临危受命"。

外，肯尼迪对美国文化艺术的繁荣也做出了很大贡献。肯尼迪一家邀请学术界、艺术界名流到白宫做客，第一夫人杰奎琳甚至把白宫内部重装一新，让历史、艺术渗透到生活的各个层面。肯尼迪对生活和文化的倡导对后来美国人的生活态度和家庭观念都影响深远。

本文是肯尼迪1961年的总统就职演说。这篇著名的就职演说集中体现了肯尼迪的政治理想和他对美国及世界局势的看法。在短短的一篇演讲里，肯尼迪阐述了美国面临的一系列挑战：人权问题、冷战局势、核战危机、经济发展和国际合作。他倡议全世界人民协力应对共同的敌人，那就是“暴政、贫穷、疾病和战争”。肯尼迪提出，此时美国已然站在一个新前线上，新一代的美国人要明确自己作为美国公民的责任：“不要问国家为你做了什么，要问你自己能为你的国家奉献什么。”这篇演讲不仅是一篇有力的政治辞令，更是一剂强心针，把肯尼迪对未来的乐观态度传播给每个美国人。

January 20, 1961

Vice President Johnson, Mr. Speaker, Mr. Chief Justice, President Eisenhower, Vice President Nixon, President Truman, Reverend Clergy, fellow citizens:

We observe today not a victory of party but a celebration of freedom—symbolizing an end as well as a beginning—signifying renewal as well as change. For I have sworn before you and Almighty God the same solemn oath our forebears prescribed nearly a century and three quarters ago.

The world is very different now. For man holds in his mortal hands the power to abolish all forms of human poverty and all forms of human life. And yet the same revolutionary beliefs for which our forebears fought are still at issue around the globe—the belief that the rights of man come not from the generosity of the state but from the hand of God.

We dare not forget today that we are the heirs of that first revolution. Let the word go forth from this time and place, to friend and foe alike, that the torch has been passed to a new generation of Americans—born in this century, tempered by war, disciplined by a hard and bitter peace, proud of our ancient heritage—and unwilling to witness or permit the slow undoing of those human rights to which this nation has always been committed, and to which we are committed today at home and around the world.

Let every nation know, whether it wishes us well or ill, that we shall pay any price, bear any burden, meet any hardship, support any friend, oppose any foe to assure the survival and the success of liberty.

This much we pledge—and more.

To those old allies whose cultural and spiritual origins we share, we pledge the loyalty of faithful friends. United, there is little we cannot do in a host of cooperative ventures. Divided, there is little we can do—for we dare not meet a powerful challenge at odds and split asunder.

To those new states whom we welcome to the ranks of the free, we pledge our word that one form of colonial control shall not have passed away merely to be replaced by a far more iron tyranny. We shall not always expect to find them supporting our view. But we shall always hope to find them strongly supporting their own freedom—and to remember that, in the past, those who foolishly sought power by riding the back of the tiger ended up inside.

To those peoples in the huts and villages of half the globe struggling to break the bonds of mass misery, we pledge our best efforts to help them help themselves, for whatever period is required—not because the communists may be doing it, not because we seek their votes, but because it is right. If a free society cannot help the many who are poor, it cannot save the few who are rich.

To our sister republics south of our border, we offer a special pledge—to convert our good words into good deeds—in a new alliance for progress—to assist free men and free governments in casting off the chains of poverty. But this peaceful revolution of hope cannot become the prey of hostile powers. Let all our neighbors know that we shall join with them to oppose aggression or subversion anywhere in the Americas. And let every other power know that this Hemisphere intends to remain the master of its own house.

To that world assembly of sovereign states, the United Nations, our last best hope in an age where the instruments of war have far outpaced the instruments of peace, we renew our pledge of support—to prevent it from becoming merely a forum for invective—to strengthen its shield of the new and the weak—and to enlarge the area in which its writ may run.

Finally, to those nations who would make themselves our adversary, we offer not a pledge but a request: that both sides begin anew the quest for peace, before the dark powers of destruction unleashed by science engulf all humanity in planned or accidental self-destruction.

We dare not tempt them with weakness. For only when our arms are sufficient beyond doubt can we be certain beyond doubt that they will never be employed.

But neither can two great and powerful groups of nations take comfort from our present course—both sides overburdened by the cost of modern weapons, both rightly alarmed by the steady spread of the deadly atom, yet both racing to alter that uncertain balance of terror that stays the hand of mankind's final war.

So let us begin anew—remembering on both sides that civility is not a sign of weakness, and sincerity is always subject to proof. Let us never negotiate out of fear. But let us never fear to negotiate.

Let both sides explore what problems unite us instead of belaboring those problems which divide us.

Let both sides, for the first time, formulate serious and precise proposals for the inspection and control of arms—and bring the absolute power to destroy other nations under the absolute control of all nations.

Let both sides seek to invoke the wonders of science instead of its terrors. Together let us explore the stars, conquer the deserts, eradicate disease, tap the ocean depths and encourage the arts and commerce.

Let both sides unite to heed in all corners of the earth the command of Isaiah—to "undo the heavy burdens... (and) let the oppressed go free."

And if a beach-head of cooperation may push back the jungle of suspicion, let both sides join in creating a new endeavor, not a new balance of power, but a new world of law, where the strong are just and the weak secure and the peace preserved.

All this will not be finished in the first one hundred days. Nor will it be finished in the first one thousand days, nor in the life of this Administration, nor even perhaps in our lifetime on this planet. But let us begin.

In your hands, my fellow citizens, more than mine, will rest the final success or failure of our course. Since this country was founded, each generation of Americans has been summoned to give testimony to its national loyalty. The graves of young Americans who answered the call to service surround the globe.

Now the trumpet summons us again—not as a call to bear arms, though arms we need—not as a call to battle, though embattled we are—but a call to bear the burden of a long twilight struggle, year in and year out, "rejoicing in hope, patient in tribulation"—a struggle against the common enemies of man: tyranny, poverty, disease and war itself.

Can we forge against these enemies a grand and global alliance, North and South, East and West, that can assure a more fruitful life for all mankind? Will you join in that historic effort?

In the long history of the world, only a few generations have been granted the role of defending freedom in its hour of maximum danger. I do not shrink from this responsibility—I welcome it. I do not believe that any of us would exchange places with any other people or any other generation. The energy, the faith, the devotion which we bring to this endeavor will light our country and all who serve it—and the glow from that fire can truly light the world.[1]

And so, my fellow Americans: ask not what your country can do for you—ask what you can do for your country.

My fellow citizens of the world: ask not what America will do for you, but what together we can do for the freedom of man.

Finally, whether you are citizens of America or citizens of the world, ask of us here the same high standards of strength and sacrifice which we ask of you. With a good conscience our only sure reward, with history the final judge of our deeds, let us go forth to lead the land we love, asking His blessing and His help, but knowing that here on earth God's work must truly be our own.

注释：

1. 1963年11月21日，肯尼迪在达拉斯遇刺身亡。为缅怀他的政治理想，人们在他位于华盛顿阿灵顿公墓的墓碑前点了一盏长明灯，誉为"Eternal Flame"，以纪念他在演讲中提到的"the glow from that fire can truly light the world"。

思考题:

1. On which issues did this speech address, and what attitude/policy would be applied to those issues?
2. Do you think this speech is an embodiment of the so called American Manifest Destiny? Why or why not?
3. From what point can you see this speech influences the later domestic and international events?

33. Letter from a Birmingham Jail (1963)[①]

Martin Luther King, Jr.

导读：

马丁·路德·金（Martin Luther King, Jr., 1929—1968），美国牧师，民权运动领袖。1955至1968年间，民权运动在金“非暴力抵抗”（nonviolent direct action）理念的领导下取得了前所未有的成就。金本人也因其在民权运动中的卓越贡献，获得1964年诺贝尔和平奖。

非裔美国人在争取平等权利的道路上，既付出了惨痛的代价，又取得了许多里程碑式的进步：1863年林肯签署《解放奴隶宣言》（“The Emancipation Proclamation”，1863），1865年宪法第13条修正案正式废除奴隶制，1868年宪法第14条修正案赋予非裔美国人公民权，1870年宪法第15条修正案赋予非裔美国人选举权。然而，直至金生活的20世纪中期，非裔美国人仍没有在真正意义上走出种族歧视的阴霾。在宣称“人人生而平等”的美国，非裔美国人竟然不能与白人在同一家餐馆里用餐，在同一家汽车旅馆住宿，在同一所学校上学[②]，在同一个游乐场游玩，而且大多数非裔美国人的选举权并没有得到落实[③]，更糟糕的是，非裔美国人还受到白人至上的种族主义者的迫害。非裔美国人被白人社会视作“二等公民”，公民权利乃至人身安全完全得不到保障，以至他们在绝望中惶惶不可终日。

美国社会深陷种族问题的泥沼，宪法和人性的神圣性岌岌可危。在其撰写的《来自伯明翰监狱的公开信》中，金回应了伯明翰当地几位白

① Martin Luther King, Jr., “Letter from a Birmingham Jail,” http://www.africa.upenn.edu/Articles_Gen/Letter_Birmingham.html (accessed Oct. 7, 2021).

② 何顺果：《美国史通论》，上海：学林出版社，2001年，第308页。据此书统计，“在1954年之前，有17个州及哥伦比亚特区在教育方面存在种族隔离的制度”。即使在联邦最高法院宣布初等和中等学校的种族隔离违宪以后，“到1955年这些州的6001个学区中仍只有741个允许黑白同校”。

③ 美国法律对选民有诸多约束条件，例如公民必须达到一定文化水平并缴纳相应税收，才能够登记成为选民。因此，即使宪法第15条修正案赋予公民选举权，这些关于选举的法律实质上使非裔美国人的选举权名存实亡。

人牧师对民权运动的曲解，呼吁非裔美国人奋起反抗，同时呼吁整个美国社会反思民权和人权问题。这封公开信主要回答了两个问题：种族斗争为什么必须采取直接反抗行为而不是寄望于谈判？为什么非裔美国人无法遵守现有的关于种族隔离、选举制度和集会结社的法律？此信中，金运用娴熟的修辞技巧和缜密的逻辑思维，既援引基督教及林肯、杰斐逊等的经典话语，又罗列身边发生的具体案例，让读者为非裔美国人的遭遇动容。同时，金全面系统地阐述了他对公正、法律和社会运动的理解。在他看来，非暴力抵抗不是旨在制造事端，而是力求在事态一发不可收拾之前找到解决途径；非正义的法律需要先驱者去倡导变革，而他甘愿为此流血牺牲；非裔美国人不能坐以待毙，而应该主动去推动历史的车轮；民权运动不只影响到非裔美国人的命运，更是和整个美国社会的命运息息相关。本文节选自该公开信。时至今日，金的这些见解对社会运动仍然具有一定的启示作用。

You may well ask: "Why direct action? Why sit ins, marches and so forth? Isn't negotiation a better path?"[1] You are quite right in calling for negotiation. Indeed, this is the very purpose of direct action. Nonviolent direct action seeks to create such a crisis and foster such a tension that a community which has constantly refused to negotiate is forced to confront the issue. It seeks so to dramatize the issue that it can no longer be ignored.[2] My citing the creation of tension as part of the work of the nonviolent resister may sound rather shocking. But I must confess that I am not afraid of the word "tension." I have earnestly opposed violent tension, but there is a type of constructive, nonviolent tension which is necessary for growth. Just as Socrates felt that it was necessary to create a tension in the mind so that individuals could rise from the bondage of myths and half truths to the unfettered realm of creative analysis and objective appraisal, so must we see the need for nonviolent gadflies to create the kind of tension in society that will help men rise from the dark depths of prejudice and racism to the majestic heights of understanding and brotherhood. The purpose of our direct action program is to create a situation so crisis packed that it will inevitably open the door to negotiation. I therefore concur with you in your call for negotiation. Too long has our beloved Southland been bogged down in a tragic effort to live in monologue rather than dialogue.

One of the basic points in your statement is that the action that I and my associates have taken in Birmingham is untimely. Some have asked: "Why didn't you give the new city administration time to act?" The only answer that I can give to this query is that the new Birmingham administration must be prodded about as much as the outgoing one, before it will act. We are sadly mistaken if we feel that the election of Albert Boutwell as mayor will bring the millennium to Birmingham. While Mr. Boutwell is a much more gentle person than Mr. Connor, they are both segregationists, dedicated to maintenance of the status quo. I have hope that Mr. Boutwell will be reasonable enough to see the futility of massive resistance to desegregation. But he will not see this without pressure from devotees of civil rights. My friends, I must say to you that we have not made a single gain in civil rights without determined legal and nonviolent pressure. Lamentably, it is an historical fact that privileged groups seldom give up their privileges voluntarily. Individuals may see the moral light and voluntarily give up their unjust posture; but, as Reinhold Niebuhr has reminded us, groups tend to be more immoral than individuals.

We know through painful experience that freedom is never voluntarily given by the oppressor; it must be demanded by the oppressed. Frankly, I have yet to engage in a direct action campaign that was "well timed" in the view of those who have not suffered unduly from the disease of segregation. For years now I have heard the word "Wait!" It rings in the ear of every Negro with piercing familiarity. This "Wait" has almost always meant "Never." We must come to see, with one of our distinguished jurists, that "justice too long delayed is justice denied."

We have waited for more than 340 years for our constitutional and God given rights. The nations of Asia and Africa are moving with jetlike speed toward gaining political independence, but we still creep at horse and buggy pace toward gaining a cup of coffee at a lunch counter. Perhaps it is easy for those who have never felt the stinging darts of segregation to say, "Wait." But when you have seen vicious mobs lynch your mothers and fathers at will and drown your sisters and brothers at whim; when you have seen hate filled policemen curse, kick and even kill your black brothers and sisters; when you see the vast majority of your twenty million Negro brothers smothering in an airtight cage of poverty in the midst of an affluent society; when you suddenly find your tongue twisted and your speech stammering as you seek to explain to your six year old daughter why she can't go to the public amusement park that has just been advertised on television, and see tears welling up in her eyes when she is told that Funtown is closed to colored children, and see ominous clouds of inferiority beginning to form in her little mental sky, and see her beginning to distort her personality by developing an unconscious bitterness toward white people; when you have to concoct an answer for a five year old son who is asking: "Daddy, why do white people treat colored people so mean?"; when you take a cross county drive and find it necessary to sleep night after night in the uncomfortable corners of your automobile because no motel will accept you; when you are humiliated day in and day out by nagging signs reading "white" and "colored"; when your first name becomes "nigger," your middle name becomes "boy" (however old you are) and your last name becomes "John," and your wife and mother are never given the respected title "Mrs."; when you are harried by day and haunted by night by the fact that you are a Negro, living constantly at tiptoe stance, never quite knowing what to expect next, and are plagued with inner fears and outer resentments; when you are forever fighting a degenerating sense of "nobodiness"—then you will understand why we find it difficult to wait. There comes a time when the cup of endurance runs over, and men are no longer willing to be plunged into the abyss of despair. I hope, sirs, you can understand our legitimate and unavoidable impatience. You express a great deal of anxiety over our willingness to break laws. This is certainly a legitimate concern. Since we so diligently urge people to obey the Supreme Court's decision of 1954[3] outlawing segregation in the public schools, at first glance it may seem rather paradoxical for us consciously to break laws. One may well ask: "How can you advocate breaking some laws and obeying others?" The answer lies in the fact that there are two types of laws: just and unjust. I would be the first to advocate obeying just laws. One has not only a legal but a moral responsibility to obey just laws. Conversely, one has a moral responsibility to disobey unjust laws. I would agree with St. Augustine that "an unjust law is no law at all."

Now, what is the difference between the two? How does one determine whether a law is just or unjust? A just law is a man made code that squares with the moral law or the law of God. An unjust law is a code that is out of harmony with the moral law. To put it in the terms of St. Thomas Aquinas: An unjust law is a human law that is not rooted in eternal law and natural law. Any law that uplifts human personality is just. Any law that degrades human personality is unjust. All segregation statutes are unjust because segregation distorts the soul and damages the personality. It gives the segregator a false sense of superiority and the segregated a false sense of inferiority. Segregation, to use the terminology of the Jewish philosopher Martin Buber, substitutes an "I it" relationship for an "I thou" relationship and ends up relegating persons to the status of things. Hence segregation is not only politically, economically and sociologically unsound, it is morally wrong and sinful. Paul Tillich has said that sin is separation. Is not segregation an existential expression of man's tragic separation, his awful estrangement, his terrible sinfulness? Thus it is that I can urge men to obey the 1954 decision of the Supreme Court, for it is morally right; and I can urge them to disobey segregation ordinances, for they are morally wrong.

Let us consider a more concrete example of just and unjust laws. An unjust law is a code that a numerical or power majority group compels a minority group to obey but does not make binding on itself. This is difference made legal. By the same token, a just law is a code that a majority compels a minority to follow and that it is willing to follow itself. This is sameness made legal. Let me give another explanation. A law is unjust if it is inflicted on a minority that, as a result of being denied the right to vote, had no part in enacting or devising the law. Who can say that the legislature of Alabama which set up that state's segregation laws was democratically elected? Throughout Alabama all sorts of devious methods are used to prevent Negroes from becoming registered voters, and there are some counties in which, even though Negroes constitute a majority of the population, not a single Negro is registered.[4] Can any law enacted under such circumstances be considered democratically structured?

Sometimes a law is just on its face and unjust in its application. For instance, I have been arrested on a charge of parading without a permit. Now, there is nothing wrong in having an ordinance which requires a permit for a parade. But such an ordinance becomes unjust when it is used to maintain segregation and to deny citizens the First-Amendment privilege of peaceful assembly and protest.

I hope you are able to see the distinction I am trying to point out. In no sense do I advocate evading or defying the law, as would the rabid segregationist. That would lead to anarchy. One who breaks an unjust law must do so openly, lovingly, and with a willingness to accept the penalty. I submit that an individual who breaks a law that conscience tells him is unjust, and who willingly accepts the penalty of imprisonment in order to arouse the conscience of the community over its injustice, is in reality expressing the highest respect for law.

Of course, there is nothing new about this kind of civil disobedience. It was evidenced sublimely in the refusal of Shadrach, Meshach and Abednego to obey the laws of Nebuchadnezzar, on the ground that a higher moral law was at stake. It was practiced superbly by the early Christians, who were willing to face hungry lions and the excruciating pain of chopping blocks rather than submit to certain unjust laws of the Roman Empire. To a degree, academic freedom is a reality today because Socrates practiced civil disobedience. In our own nation, the Boston Tea Party represented a massive act of civil disobedience.

We should never forget that everything Adolf Hitler did in Germany was "legal" and everything the Hungarian freedom fighters did in Hungary was "illegal." It was "illegal" to aid and comfort a Jew in Hitler's Germany. Even so, I am sure that, had I lived in Germany at the time, I would have aided and comforted my Jewish brothers. If today I lived in a Communist country where certain principles dear to the Christian faith are suppressed, I would openly advocate disobeying that country's antireligious laws.

I must make two honest confessions to you, my Christian and Jewish brothers. First, I must confess that over the past few years I have been gravely disappointed with the white moderate. I have almost reached the regrettable conclusion that the Negro's great stumbling block in his stride toward freedom is not the White Citizen's Counciler or the Ku Klux Klanner,[5] but the white moderate, who is more devoted to "order" than to justice; who prefers a negative peace which is the absence of tension to a positive peace which is the presence of justice; who constantly says: "I agree with you in the goal you seek, but I cannot agree with your methods of direct action"; who paternalistically believes he can set the timetable for another man's freedom; who lives by a mythical concept of time and who constantly advises the Negro to wait for a "more convenient season." Shallow understanding from people of good will is more frustrating than absolute misunderstanding from people of ill will. Lukewarm acceptance is much more bewildering than outright rejection.

I had hoped that the white moderate would understand that law and order exist for the purpose of establishing justice and that when they fail in this purpose they become the dangerously structured dams that block the flow of social progress. I had hoped that the white moderate would understand that the present tension in the South is a necessary phase of the transition from an obnoxious negative peace, in which the Negro passively accepted his unjust plight, to a substantive and positive peace, in which all men will respect the dignity and worth of human personality. Actually, we who engage in nonviolent direct action are not the creators of tension. We merely bring to the surface the hidden tension that is already alive. We bring it out in the open, where it can be seen and dealt with. Like a boil that can never be cured so long as it is covered up but must be opened with all its ugliness to the natural medicines of air and light, injustice must be exposed, with all the tension its exposure creates, to the light of human conscience and the air of national opinion before it can be cured.

In your statement you assert that our actions, even though peaceful, must be condemned because they precipitate violence. But is this a logical assertion? Isn't this like condemning a robbed man because his possession of money precipitated the evil act of robbery? Isn't this like condemning Socrates because his unswerving commitment to truth and his philosophical inquiries precipitated the act by the misguided populace in which they made him drink hemlock? Isn't this like condemning Jesus because his unique God consciousness and never ceasing devotion to God's will precipitated the evil act of crucifixion? We must come to see that, as the federal courts have consistently affirmed, it is wrong to urge an individual to cease his efforts to gain his basic constitutional rights because the quest may precipitate violence. Society must protect the robbed and punish the robber. I had also hoped that the white moderate would reject the myth concerning time in relation to the struggle for freedom. I have just received a letter from a white brother in Texas. He writes: "All Christians know that the colored people will receive equal rights eventually, but it is possible that you are in too great a religious hurry. It has taken Christianity almost two thousand years to accomplish what it has. The teachings of Christ take time to come to earth." Such an attitude stems from a tragic misconception of time, from the strangely irrational notion that there is something in the very flow of time that will inevitably cure all ills. Actually, time itself is neutral; it can be used either destructively or constructively. More and more I feel that the people of ill will have used time much more effectively than have the people of good will. We will have to repent in this generation not merely for the hateful words and actions of the bad people but for the appalling silence of the good people. Human progress never rolls in on wheels of inevitability; it comes through the tireless efforts of men willing to be co workers with God, and without this hard work, time itself becomes an ally of the forces of social stagnation. We must use time creatively, in the knowledge that the time is always ripe to do right. Now is the time to make real the promise of democracy and transform our pending national elegy into a creative psalm of brotherhood. Now is the time to lift our national policy from the quicksand of racial injustice to the solid rock of human dignity.

You speak of our activity in Birmingham as extreme. At first I was rather disappointed that fellow clergymen would see my nonviolent efforts as those of an extremist. I began thinking about the fact that I stand in the middle of two opposing forces in the Negro community. One is a force of complacency, made up in part of Negroes who, as a result of long years of oppression, are so drained of self respect and a sense of "somebodiness" that they have adjusted to segregation; and in part of a few middle-class Negroes who, because of a degree of academic and economic security and because in some ways they profit by segregation, have become insensitive to the problems of the masses. The other force is one of bitterness and hatred, and it comes perilously close to advocating violence. It is expressed in the various black nationalist groups that are springing up across the nation, the largest and best known being Elijah Muhammad's Muslim movement. Nourished by the Negro's frustration over the continued existence of racial discrimination, this movement is made up of people who have lost faith in America, who have absolutely repudiated Christianity, and who have concluded that the white man is an incorrigible "devil."

I have tried to stand between these two forces, saying that we need emulate neither the "do nothingism" of the complacent nor the hatred and despair of the black nationalist. For there is the more excellent way of love and nonviolent protest. I am grateful to God that, through the influence of the Negro church, the way of nonviolence became an integral part of our struggle. If this philosophy had not emerged, by now many streets of the South would, I am convinced, be flowing with blood. And I am further convinced that if our white brothers dismiss as "rabble rousers" and "outside agitators" those of us who employ nonviolent direct action, and if they refuse to support our nonviolent efforts, millions of Negroes will, out of frustration and despair, seek solace and security in black nationalist ideologies—a development that would inevitably lead to a frightening racial nightmare.

Oppressed people cannot remain oppressed forever. The yearning for freedom eventually manifests itself, and that is what has happened to the American Negro. Something within has reminded him of his birthright of freedom, and something without has reminded him that it can be gained. Consciously or unconsciously, he has been caught up by the Zeitgeist, and with his black brothers of Africa and his brown and yellow brothers of Asia, South America and the Caribbean, the United States Negro is moving with a sense of great urgency toward the promised land of racial justice. If one recognizes this vital urge that has engulfed the Negro community, one should readily understand why public demonstrations are taking place. The Negro has many pent up resentments and latent frustrations, and he must release them. So let him march; let him make prayer pilgrimages to the city hall; let him go on freedom rides—and try to understand why he must do so. If his repressed emotions are not released in nonviolent ways, they will seek expression through violence; this is not a threat but a fact of history. So I have not said to my people: "Get rid of your discontent." Rather, I have tried to say that this normal and healthy discontent can be channeled into the creative outlet of nonviolent direct action. And now this approach is being termed extremist. But though I was initially disappointed at being categorized as an extremist, as I continued to think about the matter I gradually gained a measure of satisfaction from the label. Was not Jesus an extremist for love: "Love your enemies, bless them that curse you, do good to them that hate you, and pray for them which despitefully use you, and persecute you." Was not Amos an extremist for justice: "Let justice roll down like waters and righteousness like an ever flowing stream." Was not Paul an extremist for the Christian gospel: "I bear in my body the marks of the Lord Jesus." Was not Martin Luther an extremist: "Here I stand; I cannot do otherwise, so help me God." And John Bunyan: "I will stay in jail to the end of my days before I make a butchery of my conscience." And Abraham Lincoln: "This nation cannot survive half slave and half free." And Thomas Jefferson: "We hold these truths to be self evident, that all men are created equal…" So the question is not whether we will be extremists, but what kind of extremists we will be. Will we be extremists for hate or for love? Will we be extremists for the preservation of injustice or for the extension of justice? In that dramatic scene on Calvary's hill three men were crucified. We must never forget that all three were crucified for the same crime—the crime of extremism. Two were extremists for immorality, and thus fell below their environment. The other, Jesus Christ, was an extremist for love, truth and goodness, and thereby rose above his environment. Perhaps the South, the nation and the world are in dire need of creative extremists….[6]

It is true that the police have exercised a degree of discipline in handling the demonstrators. In this sense they have conducted themselves rather "nonviolently" in public. But for what purpose? To preserve the evil system of segregation. Over the past few years I have consistently preached that nonviolence demands that the means we use must be as pure as the ends we seek. I have tried to make clear that it is wrong to use immoral means to attain moral ends. But now I must affirm that it is just as wrong, or perhaps even more so, to use moral means to preserve immoral ends. Perhaps Mr. Connor and his policemen have been rather nonviolent in public, as was Chief Pritchett in Albany, Georgia, but they have used the moral means of nonviolence to maintain the immoral end of racial injustice. As T. S. Eliot has said: "The last temptation is the greatest treason: To do the right deed for the wrong reason."

I wish you had commended the Negro sit inners and demonstrators of Birmingham for their sublime courage, their willingness to suffer and their amazing discipline in the midst of great provocation. One day the South will recognize its real heroes. They will be the James Merediths, with the noble sense of purpose that enables them to face jeering and hostile mobs, and with the agonizing loneliness that characterizes the life of the pioneer. They will be old, oppressed, battered Negro women, symbolized in a seventy two year old woman in Montgomery, Alabama, who rose up with a sense of dignity and with her people decided not to ride segregated buses, and who responded with ungrammatical profundity to one who inquired about her weariness: "My feets is tired, but my soul is at rest." They will be the young high school and college students, the young ministers of the gospel and a host of their elders, courageously and nonviolently sitting in at lunch counters and willingly going to jail for conscience' sake. One day the South will know that when these disinherited children of God sat down at lunch counters, they were in reality standing up for what is best in the American dream and for the most sacred values in our Judaeo Christian heritage, thereby bringing our nation back to those great wells of democracy which were dug deep by the founding fathers in their formulation of the Constitution and the Declaration of Independence…

注释：

1. 由于篇幅限制，选文省略了该公开信的开头。金开篇提到此公开信是针对伯明翰当地数位牧师的联名文章《白人牧师呼吁当地黑人退出示威游行》（"White Clergymen Urge Local Negroes to Withdraw from Demonstration"，1963）的回应。白人牧师指出：第一，伯明翰的种族问题应该由伯明翰当地人解决，外人（金所属的民权运动组织来自亚特兰大）不应参与；第二，种族问题应该诉诸法律协商途径，而不是通过"不合时宜的"和"极端的"示威游行来解决。所以，金这句话里的"you"，既可理解为撰写该文的白人牧师，也可引申理解为所有对民权运动持怀疑态度的人。

2. 金强调“非暴力抵抗”的目的是揭露社会矛盾，并最终寻求解决问题的途径。
3. The Supreme Court’s decision of 1954：1951年，在全国有色人种协进会（NAACP）的支持下，以奥里夫·布朗（Oliver Brown, 1918—1961）为代表的13位非裔美国人联名诉讼托皮卡教育局，指责公立学校的种族隔离制度违宪。这就是美国历史上著名的“布朗诉托皮卡教育局案”(Brown vs. Board of Education of Topeka）。1954年，以大法官厄尔·沃伦为首的美国最高法院对该案做出最终判决，认为公立学校的种族隔离制度违背了宪法第14条修正案。该判决从法律上保障黑人儿童在入学公立学校时不再受种族隔离的限制，但法律的实施却仍旧遭到种族主义者的阻碍，因此金不断呼吁民众遵守这些尊重民权的法律。
4. 虽然1870年的宪法第15条修正案赋予非裔美国人选举权，但在内战后的重建时期，白人为稳固自己的政权，相继通过一系列有关选举的法律。自1877年起，佐治亚、密西西比、田纳西、阿拉巴马等南方各州相继实行选民注册，只有通过考试、纳过赋税的公民才有资格选举。这些苛刻的选民注册条件，实际上剥夺了大多数非裔美国人的选举权。
5. “White Citizen’s Council”和“Ku Klux Klan”是两个非常极端的白人至上种族主义组织，在20世纪中期他们坚决支持种族隔离制度，残酷迫害了大批非裔美国人。但是在这封公开信里，他们并不是金的主要谴责对象。
6. 因篇幅关系省略了部分内容。省略部分主要是强调民权运动不仅是非裔美国人的事，也是每个美国公民的事。金表达自己对前面提到的白人牧师和大多数沉默的美国白人很失望，因为“There can be no deep disappointment where there is not deep love”。

思考题：

1. According to King, why is it necessary to take nonviolent direct action in the streets instead of negotiating within the legal procedure in the courts?
2. From this letter, what major social conflicts can you assess within African American society, within White American society, and between African Americans and White Americans?
3. King said, “One has not only a legal but a moral responsibility to obey just laws. Conversely, one has a moral responsibility to disobey unjust laws.” Do you agree or disagree with King, considering one of the basic American spirits is founded on law-obeying?

34. I Have a Dream (1963)①

Martin Luther King, Jr.

导读：

1955年到1968年美国的民权运动在马丁·路德·金的领导下如火如荼地展开，无数激进主义者（Civil Rights activists）投身废除种族隔离、争取平等权利的斗争。1955年，亚拉巴马州蒙哥马利“巴士抵制运动”正式拉开了民权运动的序幕。1963年4月16日，金发表了《来自伯明翰监狱的公开信》，控诉种族隔离制度，号召非裔美国人用“非暴力抵抗”的方式反抗现有的种族歧视法律。1963年6月11日，针对愈演愈烈的民权运动，肯尼迪总统在对全国人民的讲话中承认眼前的种族问题是美国道德危机的体现。这个道德危机既破坏了美国的国际形象，也威胁到美国的立国之本。6月19日，肯尼迪政府向国会提交了修改民权制度的法案，期望国会通过废除种族隔离、保障选举权利的法律。但是，这项提案在国会遭到种族主义者的大力阻挠。

当时的社会主要矛盾表现为，一方面种族主义者谴责激进主义者破坏社会稳定，另一方面激进主义者没有有效的法律渠道消除种族歧视和种族隔离。非裔美国人过着提心吊胆、捉襟见肘的生活，几乎享受不到第二次世界大战后经济发展给公民带来的福利。1963年8月28日，迫于经济和工作上的压力，25万民众涌向华盛顿，在林肯纪念堂前举行了美国历史上最具影响力的示威游行，期望政府制定相应的法律，确保非裔美国人能享有宪法规定的自由和平等的权利②。本文是金在这次游行中发表的演讲，它被誉为20世纪最著名的演讲。演讲内容承接了先前《来自伯明翰的公开信》中提出的民权运动主张，呼吁美国人以非暴力抵抗的方式来反抗种族歧视。金把一百年前林肯颁布的《解放奴隶宣言》比喻为一张支票，而今天，美国政府兑现这张支票势在必行。在充满种族

① Martin Luther King, Jr., “I Have a Dream”, http://kr. usembassy.gov/education-culture/infopedia-usa/living-documents-american-history-democracy/martin-luther-king-jr-dream-speech-1963/ (accessed Oct. 7, 2021).

② 这次游行最初的关注点是非裔美国人经济和工作上的权利，后升华为民权。

歧视的社会中，非裔美国人举步维艰，美国社会的道德根基岌岌可危。非裔美国人经济上的窘境源自社会制度的不平等，而社会制度不平等则来源于道德观念的退化。在这个社会中，只要还有人因肤色而受到不公正的待遇，民权运动就永远不会结束。金坚信，争取平等权利是每个美国公民的责任，因为“直到司法公正出现的那天之前，抵抗的旋风都会不断动摇我们国家的根基”。

I am happy to join with you today in what will go down in history as the greatest demonstration for freedom in the history of our nation.

Five score years ago, a great American, in whose symbolic shadow we stand today, signed the Emancipation Proclamation. This momentous decree came as a great beacon of hope to millions of slaves, who had been seared in the flames of whithering injustice. It came as a joyous daybreak to end the long night of their captivity. But one hundred years later, the colored America is still not free. One hundred years later, the life of the colored American is still sadly crippled by the manacle of segregation and the chains of discrimination.

One hundred years later, the colored American lives on a lonely island of poverty in the midst of a vast ocean of material prosperity. One hundred years later, the colored American is still languishing in the corners of American society and finds himself an exile in his own land So we have come here today to dramatize a shameful condition.

In a sense we have come to our Nation's Capital to cash a check. When the architects of our great republic wrote the magnificent words of the Constitution and the Declaration of Independence, they were signing a promissory note to which every American was to fall heir.

This note was a promise that all men, yes, black men as well as white men, would be guaranteed the inalienable rights of life liberty and the pursuit of happiness.

It is obvious today that America has defaulted on this promissory note insofar as her citizens of color are concerned. Instead of honoring this sacred obligation, America has given its colored people a bad check, a check that has come back marked "insufficient funds."

But we refuse to believe that the bank of justice is bankrupt. We refuse to believe that there are insufficient funds in the great vaults of opportunity of this nation. So we have come to cash this check, a check that will give us upon demand the riches of freedom and security of justice.

We have also come to his hallowed spot to remind America of the fierce urgency of Now. This is not time to engage in the luxury of cooling off or to take the tranquilizing drug of gradualism.

Now is the time to make real the promise of democracy.

Now it the time to rise from the dark and desolate valley of segregation to the sunlit path of racial justice.

Now it the time to lift our nation from the quicksand of racial injustice to the solid rock of brotherhood.

Now is the time to make justice a reality to all of God's children.

I would be fatal for the nation to overlook the urgency of the moment and to underestimate the determination of it's colored citizens. This sweltering summer of the colored people's legitimate discontent will not pass until there is an invigorating autumn of freedom and equality. Nineteen sixty-three is not an end but a beginning. Those who hope that the colored Americans needed to blow off steam and will now be content will have a rude awakening if the nation returns to business as usual.

There will be neither rest nor tranquility in America until the colored citizen is granted his citizenship rights. The whirlwinds of revolt will continue to shake the foundations of our nation until the bright day of justice emerges.

We can never be satisfied as long as our bodies, heavy with the fatigue of travel, cannot gain lodging in the motels of the highways and the hotels of the cities.

We cannot be satisfied as long as the colored person's basic mobility is from a smaller ghetto to a larger one.

We can never be satisfied as long as our children are stripped of their selfhood and robbed of their dignity by signs stating "for white only."

We cannot be satisfied as long as a colored person in Mississippi cannot vote and a colored person in New York believes he has nothing for which to vote.

No, no we are not satisfied and we will not be satisfied until justice rolls down like waters and righteousness like a mighty stream.

I am not unmindful that some of you have come here out of your trials and tribulations. Some of you have come from areas where your quest for freedom left you battered by storms of persecutions and staggered by the winds of police brutality.

You have been the veterans of creative suffering. Continue to work with the faith that unearned suffering is redemptive.

Go back to Mississippi, go back to Alabama, go back to South Carolina go back to Georgia, go back to Louisiana, go back to the slums and ghettos of our modern cities, knowing that somehow this situation can and will be changed.

Let us not wallow in the valley of despair. I say to you, my friends, we have the difficulties of today and tomorrow.

I still have a dream. It is a dream deeply rooted in the American dream.[1]

I have a dream that one day this nation will rise up and live out the true meaning of its creed. We hold these truths to be self-evident that all men are created equal.

I have a dream that one day out in the red hills of Georgia the sons of former slaves and the sons of former slaveowners will be able to sit down together at the table of brotherhood.

I have a dream that one day even the state of Mississippi, a state sweltering with the heat of oppression, will be transformed into an oasis of freedom and justice.

I have a dream that my four little children will one day live in a nation where they will not be judged by the color of their skin but by their character.

I have a dream today.

I have a dream that one day down in Alabama, with its vicious racists, with its governor having his lips dripping with the words of interposition and nullification; that one day right down in Alabama little black boys and black girls will be able to join hands with little white boys and white girls as sisters and brothers.

I have a dream today.

I have a dream that one day every valley shall be engulfed, every hill shall be exalted and every mountain shall be made low, the rough places will be made plains and the crooked places will be made straight and the glory of the Lord shall be revealed and all flesh shall see it together.

This is our hope. This is the faith that I will go back to the South with. With this faith we will be able to hew out of the mountain of despair a stone of hope.

With this faith we will be able to transform the jangling discords of our nation into a beautiful symphony of brotherhood.

With this faith we will be able to work together, to pray together, to struggle together, to go to jail together, to climb up for freedom together, knowing that we will be free one day.

This will be the day when all of God's children will be able to sing with new meaning "My country 'tis of thee, sweet land of liberty, of thee I sing. Land where my father's died, land of the Pilgrim's pride, from every mountainside, let freedom ring!"

And if America is to be a great nation, this must become true. So let freedom ring from the hilltops of New Hampshire. Let freedom ring from the mighty mountains of New York.

Let freedom ring from the heightening Alleghenies of Pennsylvania.

Let freedom ring from the snow-capped Rockies of Colorado.

Let freedom ring from the curvaceous slopes of California.

But not only that, let freedom, ring from Stone Mountain of Georgia.

Let freedom ring from every hill and molehill of Mississippi and every mountainside.

When we let freedom ring, when we let it ring from every tenement and every hamlet, from every state and every city, we will be able to speed up that day when all of God's children, black men and white men, Jews and Gentiles, Protestants and Catholics, will be able to join hands and sing in the words of the old spiritual, "Free at last, free at last. Thank God Almighty, we are free at last."

注释：

1. 以"I have a dream"开头的排比段是本篇演讲最著名的部分。演讲时，金面对25万听众，临时决定在准备好的演讲稿之外，添加如此气势磅礴的排比段，以表达非裔美国人对平等权利的渴望。这段感情充沛的演说激起了在场听众的强烈共鸣。

思考题：

1. How does King relate the destiny of African Americans to that of the nation?
2. What rhetorical devices can you identify from this text, and how do those rhetorical devices affect the deliverance and acceptance of the speech?

参考文献

Adams, James Truslow. *The Epic of America*. Toronto: Little, Brown, and Company, 1931.

Allen, Gay Wilson, Roger Asselineau. *St. John de Crèvecoeur: The Life of an American Farmer*. New York: Viking Press, 1987.

Armstrong, Jennifer. *The True Story behind Lincoln's Gettysburg Address*. New York: Aladdin, 2013.

Asukile, Thabiti. "The All-Embracing Black Nationalist Theories of David Walker's Appeal." *Black Scholar*, Vol. 29, No. 4 (1999): 16−24.

Bannister, Robert C. *Sociology and Scientism: The American Quest for Objectivity, 1880—1940*. Chapel Hill, NC: University of North Carolina Press, 1987.

Bergquist, James M. *Daily Life in Immigrant America, 1820—1870*. Westport: Greenwood Prees, 2008.

Blight, David W. *Frederick Douglass' Civil War: Keeping Faith in Jubilee*. Baton Rouge: Louisiana State University Press, 1989.

Bloom, Allan. *The Closing of the American Mind*. New York: Simon & Schuster Inc., 1987.

Boyer, Paul S., ed. *The Oxford Companion to United States History*. New York: Oxford University Press, 2001.

Braden, Waldo W. *Abraham Lincoln: Public Speaker*. Baton Rouge: Louisiana State University Press, 1993.

Brezina, Corona. *Sojourner Truth's "Ain't I a Woman?" Speech: A Primary Source Investigation*. New York: The Rosen Publishing Group, 2005.

Brookhiser, Richard. *Founding Father: Rediscovering George Washington*. New York: The Free Press, 1996.

Bush, George W. "Letter to Congressional Leaders Reporting on the Deployment of Forces in Response to the Terrorist Attacks of September 11," September 24, 2001. http://www.presidency.ucsb.edu/documents/letter-congressional-leaders-reporting-the-deployment-forces-response-the-terroist (accessed Oct. 10, 2021).

Carnegie, Andrew. *The Autobiography of Andrew Carnegie and the Gospel of Wealth*. New York: Signet Classics, 2006.

Carpenter, Frederic I. *Ralph Waldo Emerson: Representative Selections, with Introduction, Bibliography, and Notes*. New York: American Book Company, 1934.

Carton, Evan. "The Price of Privilege: 'Civil Disobedience' at 150." *The American Scholar*, Vol. 67, No. 4 (1998): 105−112.

Carwardine, Richard. *Lincoln: A Life of Purpose and Power*. New York: Alfred A. Knopf, 2006.

Cave, Alfred A. "Abuse of Power: Andrew Jackson and the Indian Removal Act of 1830." *Historian*, Vol. 65, No. 6 (2003): 1330−1353.

Chesebrough, David B. *Frederick Douglass: Oratory from Slavery*. Westport: Greenwood Press, 1998.

Clinton, Catherine, Christine A. Lunardini. *The Columbia Guide to American Women in the Nineteenth Century*. New York: Columbia University Press, 2005.

Curtis, Bruce. *William Graham Sumner*. Boston: Twayne, 1981.

Daley, James, ed. *Great Speeches by African Americans: Frederick Douglass, Sojourner Truth, Dr. Martin Luther King, Jr., Barack Obama, and Others*. Mineola, New York: Dover Publications, Inc., 2006.

Deloria, Philip J., Neal Salisbury. *A Companion to American Indian History*. Malden: Blackwell Publishers Ltd., 2002.

DeRosier, Arthur H. Jr. "Andrew Jackson and Negotiations for the Removal of the Choctaw Indians." *Historian*, Vol. 29, No. 3 (1967): 343−362.

Deusen, Glyndon G. Van. *The Jacksonian Era, 1828—1848*. New York: Harper & Row, Publishers, 1963.

Dougherty, Steve. *Hopes and Dreams: The Story of Barack Obama*. New York: Black Dog & Leventhal Publishers, 2007.

Douglass, Frederick. *The Life and Times of Frederick Douglass*. Mineola, New York: Dover Publications, 2003.

—. *My Bondage and My Freedom*. New York: Washington Square Press, 2003.

—. *Narrative of the Life of Frederick Douglass, an American Slave, Written by Himself*. New York: Signet Classics, 2005.

Du Bois, W. E. B. *Souls of Black Folk*. New York: Penguin Books, 1989.

—. "The Talented Tenth." In *The Negro Problem: A Series of Articles by Representative Negroes of Today*. Booker T. Washington, ed. New York: James Pott Company, 1903.

Dudziak, Mary L. *Cold War Civil Rights: Race and the Image of American Democracy*. Princeton: Princeton University Press, 2000.

Ellis, Richard E. *Andrew Jackson*. Washington, D. C.: CQ Press, a division of Congressional Quarterly Inc., 2003.

Emerson, Ralph Waldo. *Selected Works of Ralph Waldo Emerson*. Shanghai: World Publishing Corporation, 2010.

Evans, Sara M. *Born for Liberty: A History of Women in America*. New York: Free Press, 1997.

Finseth, Ian. "David Walker, Nature's Nation, and Early African-American Separatism." *Mississippi Quarterly*, Vol. 54, No. 3 (2001): 337−362.

Fleming, Alice Mulcahey. *Frederick Douglass: From Slave to Statesman*. New York: The Rosen Publishing Group, 2004.

Fuller, Margaret. *Women in the Nineteenth Century*. New York: Dover Publications, Inc., 1999.

Gilderhus, Mark T. "The Monroe Doctrine: Meanings and Implications." *Presidential Studies Quarterly*, Vol. 36, No. 1 (2006): 5−16.

Gilman, Charlotte Perkins. *Women and Economics*. New York: Dover Publications Inc., 1998.

Gitlin, Marty. *Brown v. the Board of Education*. Minnesota: ABDO Publishing Co., 2008.

Guelzo, Allen C. *Abraham Lincoln: Redeemer President*. Michigan: William B. Eerdmans Publishing, 1999.

Harlan, Louis R., ed. *The Booker T. Washington Papers*, Vol. 3. Urbana: University of Illinois Press, 1974.

Henderson, Simon. *Aspects of American History*. New York: Routledge, 2009.

Henriksen, Margot A. "Duck and Cover: Civil Defense and Existential Anxiety in America." Chapter 3 of Henriksen's *Dr. Strangelove's America: Society and Culture in the Atomic Age*. Berkeley: University of California Press, 1997.

Hinks, Peter P., ed. *David Walker's Appeal to the Coloured Citizens of the World*. University Park: The Pennsylvania State University Press, 2000.

Hoffman, Elizabeth Cobbs, ed. *Major Problems in American History*. New York: Houghton Mifflin Company, 2007.

Hofstadter, Richard. *Social Darwinism in American Thought, 1860—1915*. Philadelphia: University of Pennsylvania Press, 1944.

Holzer, Harold, and Sara Vaughn Gabbard, eds. *Lincoln and Freedom: Slavery, Emancipation, and the Thirteenth Amendment*. Carbondale: Southern Illinois University Press, 2007.

Hoover, Herbert. *American Individualism*. Charleston: BiblioBazaar, LLC, 2010.

—. "Principles and Ideals of the United States Government," 1928. http://www.speeches-usa.com/Transcripts/herbert_hoover-campaign.html (accessed Oct. 5, 2021).

Jefferson, Thomas. *Notes on the State of Virginia*. Frank C. Shuffelton, ed. New York: Penguin Group Inc., 1999.

Jo, Mari, and Paul Buhle, eds. *The Concise History of Woman Suffrage*. Urbana: University of Illinois Press, 1978: 94−97.

John F. Kennedy Presidential Library and Museum. "Life of John F. Kennedy," http://www.jfklibrary.

org/JFK/Life-of-John-F-Kennedy.aspx?p=1 (accessed Oct. 10, 2021).

Journal of the Senate of the United States of America, Being the First Session of the Eighteenth Congress. Washington: Gales and Seaton, 1823: 12, 21–22.

Karl, Lehmann. *Thomas Jefferson, American Humanist*. Charlottesville: University of Virginia Press, 1985.

Kateb, George. *Emerson and Self-Reliance*. London: Sage Publications, 1995.

Keegan, John. *The American Civil War*. London: Vintage, 2010.

Keller, Albert Galloway. *Reminiscences (Mainly Personal) of William Graham Sumner*. New Haven: Yale University Press, 1933.

Kennedy, David M. *Freedom from Fear: The American People in Depression and War, 1929—1945*. Oxford: Oxford University Press, 1999.

Ketcham, Ralph, ed. *The Anti-Federalist Papers and the Constitutional Convention Debates*. New York: Signet Classics, 2003.

King, Martin Luther, Jr. "Letter from Birmingham Jail." http://www.africa.upenn.edu/Articles_Gen/Letter_Birmingham.html (accessed Oct. 7, 2021).

Kissinger, Henry. *On China*. New York: Penguin Books, 2012.

—. *White House Years*. New York: Simon & Schuster, 2011.

—. "Strengthening the World Economic Structure." *The Department of State Bulletin*, Volume LXXII, No. 1875 (1975): 713–719.

Lekan, Todd. "Appreciating the Impersonal in Emerson (That's What Friends Are For)." *Journal of Speculative Philosophy*, Vol. 21, No. 2 (2007): 91–105.

Lerner, Gerda. "The Meaning of Seneca Falls: 1848—1998." *Dissent*, Vol. 45, No. 4 (1998): 35–41.

Lincoln, Abraham. *Abraham Lincoln: Selected Speeches and Writings*. New York: Library of America, 2009.

Maddox, Lucy. *Removals: Nineteenth-Century American Literature and the Politics of Indian Affairs*. New York: Oxford University Press, 1991.

Masur, Louis P. *Lincoln's Hundred Days: The Emancipation Proclamation and the War for the Union*. Cambridge: The Belknap Press of Harvard University Press, 2012.

Matthews, Glenna. *The Rise of Public Woman: Woman's Power and Woman's Place in the United States, 1630—1970*. New York: Oxford University Press, 1992.

May, Elaine Tyler. *Homeward Bound: American Families in the Cold War Era*. Revised edition. New York: Basic Books, 2008.

McKissack, Patricia C., Fredrick McKissack. *Sojourner Truth: Ain't I a Woman*? New York: Scholastic Inc., 1992.

Mead, Walter Russell. *Special Providence: American Foreign Policy and How It Changed the World*. New York: Routledge, 2002.

Meyers, Jason. "No Idle Past: Uses of History in the 1830 Indian Removal Debates." *Historian*, Vol. 63, No. 1. (2000): 53–65.

Myerson, Joel, ed. *Emerson and Thoreau: The Contemporary Reviews*. New York: Cambridge University Press, 1992.

Nathan, Schachner. *Thomas Jefferson: A Biography*. New York: Appleton Century Crofts, Inc., 1951.

Nossel, Suzanne. "Smart Power." *Foreign Affairs*, Vol. 83, No. 2 (2004): 131–142.

Parry-Giles, Shawn J. "Dwight Eisenhower, 'Atoms for Peace'," Last modified July 2006. http://archive.vod.umd.edu/internat/deafpcon.htm (accessed Sept 3, 2013).

Parsons, Lynn Hudson. *The Birth of Modern Politics: Andrew Jackson, John Quincy Adams, and the Election of 1828*. New York: Oxford University Press, 2009.

Phelps, A. Glenn. *George Washington and American Constitutionalism*. Lawrence: University Press of Kansas, 1993.

Porte, Joel, Saundra Morris. *The Cambridge Companion to Ralph Waldo Emerson*. Shanghai: Shanghai Foreign Language Education Press, 2004.

Regis, Pamela. *Describing Early America: Bartram, Jefferson, Crèvecoeur, and the Influence of Natural History*. Philadelphia: University of Pennsylvania Press, 1999.

Remini, Robert V. "Andrew Jackson versus the Cherokee Nation." *American History*, Vol. 36, No. 3. (2001): 48–56.

Renehan, Edward J. Jr. *The Monroe Doctrine: The Cornerstone of American Foreign Policy*. New York: Chelsea House Publishers, 2007.

Schurz, Carl. *Speeches of Carl Schurz*. Philadelphia: J. B. Lippincott & Co., 1865.

Sexton, Jay. *The Monroe Doctrine: Empire and Nation in Nineteenth-Century America*. New York: Hill and Wang, 2011.

Sloan, Gary. "Emerson's Self-reliance." *Explicator*, Vol. 55, No. 96 (1996): 19–22.

Smith, Jean Edward. FDR. New York: Random House, 2007.

Spanier, John, Eric M. Uslaner. *American Foreign Policy Making and the Democratic Dilemmas*. 4th ed. New York: Holt, Rinehart and Winston, 1985.

Spirling, Arthur. "U.S. Treaty Making with American Indians: Institutional Change and Relative Power, 1784—1911." *American Journal of Political Science*, Vol. 56, No. 1 (2012): 84–97.

Stowe, Harriet Beecher. "Sojourner Truth, the Libyan Sibyl." *The Atlantic Monthly* 11.66 (Apr. 1863): 473–481.

Sumner, William Graham. *What Social Classes Owe to Each Other?* New York and London: Harper &

Brothers Publishers, 1911.

The American Presidency Project. "Address of Senator John F. Kennedy Accepting the Democratic Party Nomination for the Presidency of the United States." http://www.presidency.ucsb.edu/documents/address-accepting-the-democratic-nomination-for-president-the-memorial-coliseum-los (accessed Oct. 10, 2021).

The American Presidency Project. "Radio and Television Report to the American People on Civil Rights." http://www.presidency.ucsb.edu/documents/raido-and-television-report-the-american-people-civil-rights (accessed Oct. 10, 2021).

The White House. "John F. Kennedy." http://www.whitehouse.gov/about-the-white-house/presidents/john-f-kennedy/ (accessed Oct. 10, 2021).

Thomas, Benjamin P. *Abraham Lincoln: A Biography*. Carbondale: Southern Illinois University Press, 2008.

Thoreau, Henry David. *Walden and "Civil Disobedience*". New York: New American Library, 1999.

Tocqueville, Alexis de. *Democracy in America*. Harvey C. Mansfield and Delba Winthrop, trans. and eds. Chicago: University of Chicago Press, 2000.

Trefousse, Hans Louis. *Carl Schurz: A Biography*. New York: Fordham University Press, 1998.

Trommler, Frank, Elliott Shore, eds. *The German-American Encounter: Conflict and Cooperation between Two Cultures, 1800—2000*. New York: Berghahn Books, 2001.

Truth, Sojourner, Oliver Gilbert. *The Narrative of Sojourner Truth*. New York: Dover Publication, 1997.

Turner, Frederick Jackson. *Rereading Jackson Turner*, with commentary by John Mack Faragher. New Haven: Yale University Press, 1998.

—. *The Frontier in American History*. New York: H. Holt and Company, 1921.

USC US-China Institute. "Getting to Beijing: Henry Kissinger's Secret 1971 Trip." Released July 21, 2011. http://china.usc.edu/getting-beijing-henry-kissingers-secret-1971-trip (accessed Oct. 10, 2021).

Walker, David. *David Walker's Appeal to the Coloured Citizens of the World*. New York: Hall and Wang, Inc., 1965.

Warren, Harris Gaylord. *Herbert Hoover and the Great Depression*. New York: W. W. Norton & Co., 1967.

Washington, Booker T. *Up from Slavery: An Autobiography*. New York: Penguin Books, 1986.

Washington, George, et al. *The Inaugural Address of the U.S. Presidents*. Beijing: Central Compilation & Translation Press, 2009.

Watson, Martha. *Lives of Their Own: Rhetorical Dimensions in Autobiographies of Women Activists*.

Columbia: University of South Carolina Press, 1999.

Wee, Herman Van der. *Prosperity and Upheaval: The World Economy, 1945—1980*. New York: Penguin Books, 1991.

Wheeler, Richard. *Witness to Gettysburg: Inside the Battle That Changed the Course of the Civil War*. Pennsylvania: Stackpole Books, 2006.

"White Clergymen Urge Local Negroes to Withdraw from Demonstrations." *Birmingham News*, April 13, 1963.

Whittier, John Greenleaf. *In War Time: And Other Poems*. Boston: Ticknor and Fields, 1864.

Wilson, Woodrow. *The New Freedom: A Call for the Emancipation of the Generous Energies of a People*. New York: General Books, 2009.

Wittke, Carl Frederick. *Refugees of Revolution: The German Forty-Eighters in America*. Philadelphia: University of Pennsylvania Press, 1952.

Woodard, J. David. *The America that Reagan Built*. Westport: Praeger Publishers, 2006.

Wright, Gavin. *Old South, New South: Revolutions in the Southern Economy since the Civil War*. Baton Rouge: Louisiana State University Press, 1987.

爱默生. 爱默生随笔. 蒲隆，译. 上海：上海译文出版社，2010.

奥巴马，巴拉克. 我父亲的梦想：奥巴马回忆录. 王辉耀，石冠兰，译. 南京：译林出版社，2009.

奥巴马，巴拉克. 无畏的希望：重申美国梦. 罗选民，王璟，尹音，译. 北京：法律出版社，2008.

贝克尔，卡尔. 论《独立宣言》——政治思想史研究. 彭刚，译. 南京：江苏教育出版社，2005.

布尔斯廷，丹尼尔. 美国人：殖民地的经历. 时殷弘，译. 上海：上海译文出版社，1989.

布莱福特. "五月花公约" 签订始末. 王军伟，译. 上海：华东师范大学出版社，2006.

布什，乔治·沃克. 抉择时刻. 东西网，译. 北京：中信出版社，2011.

曾尔恕. 试论《独立宣言》的思想渊源及理论创新. 比较法研究，2004（6）：1-15.

储昭根. 美国人为何怀念里根. http://news.sina.com.cn/w/sd/2011-02-16/114621963472.shtml（accessed Oct. 10, 2021）.

褚乐平.《联邦党人文集》思想探源. 江西社会科学，2003（2）：169-171.

戴维，巴尔塔扎，瓦伊斯. 美国对外政策：基础、主体与形成. 钟震宇，译. 北京：社会科学文献出版社，2011.

德沃金，罗纳德. 自由的法：美国宪法的道德解读. 刘丽君，译. 华东政法学院学报，2001（1）：55-64.

丁见民. 安德鲁·杰克逊政府迁移印第安人的动因分析. 世界历史，2012（3）：29-40.

丁则民. 美国内战与镀金时代：1861—19世纪末//美国通史：第3卷. 刘绪贻，杨生茂，总主编.

北京：人民出版社，2002.
弗兰克林，约翰·霍普. 评《解放黑奴宣言》//美国黑人斗争史. 乔安妮·格兰特，编，郭瀛，伍江，杨德，等译. 北京：中国社会科学出版社，1987：137-142.
格兰特，乔安妮. 美国黑人斗争史——1619年至今的历史、文献与分析. 郭瀛，伍江，杨德，等译. 北京：中国社会科学出版社，1987.
龚淑林. 美国第二次工业革命及其影响. 江西大学学报：哲学社会科学版，1988（1）：67-74，101.
何顺果. 美国史通论. 上海：学林出版社，2001.
何顺果. 美利坚文明论——美国文明与历史研究. 北京：北京大学出版社，2008.
何顺果. 鲜为人知的《五月花号公约》. 读书，2008（10）：118-123.
华盛顿，乔治. 华盛顿选集. 聂崇信，吕德本，熊希龄，译. 北京：商务印书馆，2012.
黄颂康. 美国对布克·华盛顿的再评价. 世界历史，1981（4）：68-74.
黄亚红. 试析美国女权运动的起源. 美国研究，1995（3）：127-132.
霍夫施塔特，理查德. 美国政治传统及其缔造者. 崔永禄，王忠和，译. 北京：商务印书馆，2010.
贯芳，张潇潇. 通过菲茨杰拉德看美国"爵士乐时代". 作家，2013（4）：63-64.
杰斐逊，托马斯. 杰斐逊选集. 朱曾汶，译. 北京：商务印书馆，1999.
杰弗逊，托马斯. 杰弗逊自传. 王秀莉，朱慧斯，译. 北京：中国长安出版社，2011.
金莉. 美国女权运动·女性文学·女权批评. 美国研究，2009（1）：62-79.
考克斯，托马斯. 美国宪法创制史观的演变. 张庆熠，译. 南京大学学报，2011（4）：32-42.
孔华润. 剑桥美国对外关系史. 王琛，等译. 北京：新华出版社，2004.
黎作恒. 美国宪法成文形式的历史渊源. 现代法学，2004（1）：178-186.
李剑鸣. 美国土著部落地位的演变与印第安人的公民权问题. 美国研究，1994（2）：30-51.
李剑鸣. 美国宪法何以成为"活着的宪法". 美国研究，2001（2）：124-134.
李剑鸣. 文化接触与美国印第安人社会文化的变迁. 中国社会科学，1994（3）：157-175.
李秀红. 论乔治·华盛顿在《1787年宪法》制定过程中的作用. 燕山大学学报：哲学社会科学版，2012（2）：71-76.
李秀红. 乔治·华盛顿与美国总统制的初步实践. 吉林：东北师范大学，2010.
李征戎. 爱默生的超验主义艺术观. 外国文学研究，2002（2）：159-160+176.
梁茂信. 美国移民政策研究. 长春：东北师范大学出版社，1996.
梁敏，吕文江. 稳定的宪法与妥协的宪法——以美国宪法为例. 山东社会科学，2006（2）：102-106.
刘畅.《一位美国农夫的来信》：美国重农主义的典范之作. 名作欣赏，2011（12）：55-57.
刘晨光. 美国共和制：形式与目的的统一. 政法论坛，2011（29）：145-154.

刘芳. 论伊丽莎白·卡迪·斯坦顿的女权思想. 文学爱好者：教育教学版，2010（8）：4-5.
刘玉安. 西方社会学史. 济南：山东大学出版社，1993.
刘祚昌. 杰斐逊传. 北京：中国社会科学出版社，1990.
洛克，约翰. 政府论（下篇）——论政府的真正起源、范围和目的. 叶启芳，瞿菊农，译. 北京：商务印书馆，1964.
马丽范. 克雷夫科尔作品中的人物描写. 西安外国语学院学报，2006（3）：78-80.
麦迪逊，詹姆斯. 辩论：美国制宪会议记录. 尹宣，译. 沈阳：辽宁教育出版社，2003.
美国驻华大使馆新闻文化处. 美国历史文献选集. 北京：美国驻华大使馆新闻文化处，1985.
珀杜，W. D.，等. 西方社会学——人物·学派·思想. 贾春增，李强，等译. 石家庄：河北人民出版社，1992.
邱惠林. 论美国印第安民族的衰落. 四川大学学报：哲学社会科学版，1995（4）：78-85.
邱惠林. 美国印第安悲剧的悖论分析. 西南师范大学学报：哲学社会科学版，1999（2）：122-128.
赛耶，威廉·罗斯科. 乔治·华盛顿传：美国宪法与国家的缔造者. 杨义强，译. 南昌：江西教育出版社，2012.
桑塔亚那，乔治. 美国的民族性格与信念. 史津海，徐琳，译. 北京：中国社会科学出版社，2008.
莎士比亚，威廉. 莎士比亚全集 28：罗密欧与朱丽叶. 梁实秋，译. 台湾：远东图书公司，1967.
尚新建. 论爱默生的“自立”概念. 云南大学学报：社会科学版，2009（5）：3-10.
施莱辛格，小阿瑟. 美国共和党史. 复旦大学国际政治系，编译. 上海：上海人民出版社，1977.
施瓦茨，伯纳德. 美国法律史. 王军，洪德，杨静辉，译. 北京：法律出版社，2011.
史晓鹏. “门罗主义”产生的背景及其对美国外交的影响. 南北桥：人文社会科学学刊，2010（10）：4-5.
孙建党. 浅论美国外交传统中的非殖民化思想. 历史教学，2003（11）：27-33.
梭罗，亨利·戴维. 瓦尔登湖. 修订版. 仲泽，译. 成都：四川文艺出版社，2011.
涂纪亮. 美国哲学史. 北京：社会科学文献出版社，2007.
托马斯，本杰明·普. 林肯传. 周颖如，魏孟淇，周熙安，译. 北京：商务印书馆，1995.
王波. 美国重要历史文献导读（从殖民地时期到19世纪）. 北京：北京大学出版社，2002.
王恩铭. 论B. T.华盛顿的妥协主义思想. 史学月刊，1998（3）：49-57.
王恩铭. 美国黑人领袖及其政治思想研究. 上海：上海外语教育出版社，2006.
王希. 原则与妥协：美国宪法的精神与实践. 北京：北京大学出版社，2000.
王政. 女性的崛起——当代美国的女权运动. 北京：当代中国出版社，1995.
韦伯，马克斯. 新教伦理与资本主义精神（罗克斯伯里第三版）. 苏国勋，覃方明，赵立玮，等译. 北京：社会科学文献出版社，2010.
沃什伯恩，威尔科姆. 美国印第安人. 陆毅，译. 北京：商务印书馆，1997.
吴金平. 自由之路——弗·道格拉斯与美国黑人解放运动. 北京：中国社会科学出版社，2000.
吴群. 1900年前美国政府对印第安人政策的演变. 云南师范大学学报：哲学社会科学学版，1992（4）：48-52.
吴晓春，汪世林. 门罗主义——美国拉美政策的基石. 当代世界，2006（7）：37-40.
徐世澄. 美国和拉丁美洲关系史. 北京：社会科学文献出版社，1995.
许爱军.《五月花号公约》和美国精神. 国际关系学院学报，2012（1）：112-117.
杨军. 美国对拉美外交政策的指导思想——门罗主义. 大观周刊，2010（48）：52-53.
杨生茂. 美国历史学家特纳及其学派. 北京：商务印书馆，1984.
姚亚芝. 论爱默生超验主义对"自我"的探索. 语文学刊，2009（11）：13-15.
叶英. 杜波伊斯的教育理论和理念评述. 河北师范大学学报：教育科学版，2011（1）：41-45.
叶英. 理想与现实、共性与个性的结合——析杜波依斯"有天赋的十分之一"理论. 西南民族大学学报：人文社会科学版，2012（1）：181-188.
叶英. 美国内战前和内战期间黑人在教育中的主动性. 成都：四川大学出版社，2007.
袁明. 美国文化与社会十五讲. 北京：北京大学出版社，2003.
岳西宽，张卫星. 美国历届总统就职演说. 北京：中央编译出版社，2001.
张成豪. 从软实力到巧实力——试析约瑟夫·奈实力思想的新发展. 华中师范大学研究生学报，2012（1）：27-30.
张澜. 伍德罗·威尔逊社会思想研究. 上海：复旦大学，2004.
张淑华. 19世纪末20世纪初美国妇女社会改革活动述论. 泰山学院学报，2008（2）：68-71.
张烨. "性别角度"和"妇女与发展". 美国研究，1995（3）：133-136.
张友伦. 美国的独立和初步繁荣 1775—1860//美国通史（第2卷），刘绪贻，杨生茂，总主编. 北京：人民出版社，2002.
钟龙彪. "巧实力"战略与奥巴马新外交. 现代国际关系，2009（5）：7-12+43.
周海波. 美国总统和国会的战争权之争——从《战争权力决议案》到《授权对伊拉克使用武力决议案》的历史分析. 安庆师范学院学报：社会科学版，2008（2）：66-70.
朱小琳. 重读梭罗：公民为何不服从？北京第二外语学院学报，2003（6）：96-99.